F

Information Sources for the

Press and Broadcast Media

Second Edition

Editor

Sarah Adair

Consultant Editor

Selwyn Eagle

BOWKER
SAUR

London • Melbourne • Munich • New Providence, NJ

© 1999 Bowker-Saur, a division of Reed Elsevier (UK) Ltd.

British Library Cataloguing in Publication Data
A catalogue record for this book is available from the British Library.

Library of Congress Cataloging-in-Publication Data
A catalog record for this book is available from the Library of Congress.

Published by Bowker-Saur, Windsor Court, East Grinstead House, East Grinstead, West Sussex RH19 1XA, UK
Tel: +44(0)1342 326972 Fax: +44(0)1342 336198
E-mail: lis@bowker-saur.com
Internet Website: http://www.bowker-saur.co.uk
Bowker-Saur is part of REED BUSINESS INFORMATION

ISBN 1–85739–261–2

Index compiled by Selwyn Eagle
Cover design by Pollett and Cole
Typeset by Florence Production Ltd, Stoodleigh, Devon
Printed on acid-free paper
Printed and bound in Great Britain by Anthony Rowe

Contents

Series editors' foreword

The second half of the 20th century has been characterized by the recognition that our style of life depends on acquiring and using information effectively. It has always been so, but only in the information society has the extent of the dependence been recognized and the development of technologies for handling information become a priority. Since the early 1990s the Internet and its adjunct the World Wide Web have transformed information retrieval. Online searching, which started in the late 60s and early 70s as a useful supplement for bibliographic retrieval, has become a means of finding directly current information of every conceivable kind. Networked computers enable us to track down, select, process and store more information more skilfully and transmit, via an intranet perhaps, more rapidly than we have dreamt possible even 20 years ago. Yet the irony still exists that, while we are able to do all this and are assailed from all sides by great masses of information, ensuring that one has what one needs just when one wants it is frequently just as difficult as ever. Knowledge may, as Johnson said in the well known quotation, be of two kinds, but information, in contrast, is of many kinds and most of it is, for each individual, knowable only after much patient searching.

The aim of each Guide in this series is simple. It is to reduce the time which needs to be spent on that patient searching; to recommend the best starting point and sources most likely to yield the desired information. Like all subject and sector guides, the sources discussed have had to be selected, and the criteria for selection will be given by the individual editors and will differ from subject to subject. However, the overall objective is constant; that of providing a way into a subject to those new to the field or to identify major new or possibly unexplored sources to those already familiar with it.

The Internet now gives access to many new sources and to an overwhelming mass of information, some well organized and easy to interrogate, much incoherent and unorganized. Further, the great output of new information from the media, advertising, meetings and conferences, letters, internal reports, office memoranda, magazines, junk mail, electronic mail, fax, bulletin boards etc. inevitably tend to make one reluctant to add to the load on the mind and memory by consulting books and journals. Yet they, and the other traditional types of printed material, remain for many purposes the most reliable sources of information. Despite all the information that is instantly accessible via the new technologies one still has to look things up in databooks, monographs, journals, patent specifications, standards, reports both official and commercial, and on maps and in atlases. Permanent recording of facts, theories and opinions is still carried out primarily by publishing in printed form. Musicians still work from printed scores even though they are helped by sound recordings. Sailors still use printed charts and tide tables even though they have satellite directed position fixing devices and radar and sonar equipment.

However, thanks to computerized indexes, online and CD-ROM, searching the huge bulk of technical literature to draw up a list of references can be undertaken reasonably quickly. The result, all too often, can still be a formidably long list, of which a knowledge of the nature and structure of information sources in that field can be used to put it in order of likely value.

It is rarely necessary to consult everything that has been published on the topic of a search. When attempting to prove that an invention is genuinely novel, a complete search may seem necessary, but even then it is common to search only obvious sources and leave it to anyone wishing to oppose the grant of a patent to bear the cost of hunting for a prior disclosure in some obscure journal. Usually, much proves to be irrelevant to the particular aspect of our interest and whatever is relevant may be unsound. Some publications are sadly lacking in important detail and present broad generalizations flimsily bridged with arches of waffle. In any academic field there is a 'pecking order' of journals so that articles in one journal may be assumed to be of a higher or lower calibre than those in another. Those experienced in the field know these things. The research scientist soon learns, as it is part of his training, the degree of reliance he can place on information from co-workers elsewhere, on reports of research by new and (to him) unknown researchers on data compilations and on manufacturers of equipment. The information worker, particularly when working in a field other than his own, faces very serious problems as he tries to compile, probably from several sources a report on which his client may base important actions. Even the librarian, faced only with recommending two or three books or journal articles, meets the same problem though less acutely.

In the Bowker-Saur Guides to Information Sources we aim to bring you the knowledge and experience of specialists in the field. Each author regularly uses the information sources and services described and any tricks of the trade that the author has learnt are passed on.

Nowadays, two major problems face those who are embarking upon research or who are in charge of collections of information of every kind. One is the increasingly specialized knowledge of the user and the concomitant ignorance of other potentially useful disciplines. The second problem is the trend towards cross-disciplinary studies. This has led to a great mixing of academic programmes – and a number of imprecisely defined fields of study. Courses are offered in Environmental Studies, Women's Studies, Communication Studies or Area Studies, and these are the forcing ground for research. The editors are only too aware of the difficulties raised by those requiring information from such hybrid subject fields and this approach, too, is being handled in the series alongside the traditional 'hard disciplines'.

Guides to the literature and other sources of information have a long and honoured history. Some of the old ones remain valuable for finding information still valid but not repeated in modern information sources. Where appropriate these are included in the updated Guides of this series along with the wealth of evaluated new sources which make new editions necessary.

Michael Hill
Ia McIlwaine
Nancy Williamson

This book is dedicated to Sally K. Hine, who died during the preparation of this book. Sally was an inspiration to the information profession and a rare and treasured friend to those that had the privilege of knowing her.

About the contributors

Sarah Adair received her Masters in Information Science from the University of Washington in Seattle, completing her degree with a term at the College of Librarianship Wales in Aberystwyth. After two years in school libraries in London, she moved to London Weekend Television where she worked for twelve years first as Reference Librarian and later as Head of Programme Rights and Services. She is a founding member of the Association of UK Media Librarians.

Debra K. Bade is currently Director of News Research for CNN. She has worked at CNN's Atlanta, Georgia headquarters for ten years, and in news research even longer, thriving on the variety and stimulation of this profession. Prior to CNN, she was a researcher with the *Star Tribune* newspaper in Minneapolis, Minnesota. She earned a Master's degree in Library and Information Studies from the University of Wisconsin. Experiences in a health education programme while serving in Peace Corps in the Gambia, West Africa continue to influence her interests in the world and desire to work in an environment with an international scope. She is currently chair-elect of the News Division of the Special Libraries Association where she previously helped create a special interest group for broadcast librarians and served as Director of Education.

Patricia M. Baird is Mirror Group Information Services Manager, responsible for information and library services to over 50 titles including seven Mirror Group and two Newspaper Publishing titles in Glasgow and Canary Wharf, the *News Letter* in Belfast, and Midland Independent Newspapers. Previously she was Senior Lecturer in the Department of Information Science at the University of Strathclyde and she was also Founding Editor of the international journal, *Hypermedia*.

Peter Cole is Professor of Journalism at the University of Central Lancashire, a post he took up in 1993 after 25 years in national newspaper journalism. Previously, he has been Deputy Editor of *The Guardian*,

Founder Editor of *The Sunday Correspondent*, and Editor of News Review at *The Sunday Times*. He writes on media affairs for various newspapers and periodicals and is a member of the editorial training committee of the Guild of Editors and is on the board of the National Council for the Training of Journalists. He delivers training courses for various regional newspapers, and has worked in Kenya and South Africa for the Commonwealth Press Union.

Annabel Colley is currently Chair of the Association of UK Media Librarians (AUKML) and has been Information Researcher at *Panorama*, the BBC's flagship current affairs programme since 1994 (since 1997 as a job-share). After completing her MLib at Aberystwyth she worked for both the BBC Film and VT library and the BBC Press cuttings library. She has run computer assisted journalism courses for BBC Journalist Training, the *Financial Times*, the British Library (SRIS) and Radio Netherlands Training Centre, Holland. She has lectured on Internet research to Aslib, Seagrams, at various UK Universities, and to the News Division of the American Special Libraries Association at their 1998 conference in the USA. She has run one-to-one Internet training for BBC multimedia training, and written *The trusty guide to the Internet* for the BBC Webwise Campaign Web site. She is currently developing a Computer Assisted research site on the BBC news intranet.

Selwyn Eagle edited the first edition of *Information sources for the press and broadcast media*. Since 1990 he has undertaken freelance work in the British Library Newspaper Library. He was Chief Librarian, BBC Data, 1983–89, responsible for the print-based library and news information services provided for the TV, Radio and World Services as well as the Pronunciation Unit. He had previously served on the library staffs of two Government departments and two Polytechnics, and had worked in a public library service.

Gertrud Erbach is Information Services Manager at News International Newspapers. She has an MPhil in Information Science from City University. Before joining News International in 1994 she was Chief Librarian at *The Independent* and *Independent on Sunday*. Between 1985 and 1986 she worked as a researcher on a British Library funded research project investigating the use of online databases by journalists and end-users in higher education and the business sector. Previously she has been Chairperson of the Association of UK Media Librarians (AUKML) as well as editor of *Deadline*, the AUKML newsletter.

Sally K. Hine began her career with Marylebone Public Libraries before joining the BBC Reference Library in 1966. With the exception of four years at Stoke City Libraries, the rest of her career was at the BBC. In 1987 she was appointed Librarian, Sound Archives and Effects and, in 1994, Sound Archivist and then Manager, Sound Archive and Gramophone

Library. In 1997 she was appointed Research Centre Manager, BBC Broadcasting House, with the challenge of bringing together all BH research services. This she was well on her way to achieving when her final illness rapidly took her life in January 1999. During her career, she regularly represented the BBC at the International Association of Sound Archives (IASA) giving papers and hosting visits to the BBC by many sound archivists from around the world.

Lynda Iley is the Electronic Information Manager at News International Newspapers. One of the primary functions of the role is the development of the News International Intranet. She joined *Today* Reference Library in 1989 and moved to the News International Reference Library in April 1992 due to the merger of the two libraries. Between 1986 and 1989 she worked for Industrial Market Research Ltd.

Jacqueline Kavanagh has been in charge of the BBC Written Archives Centre since 1974. She qualified as an archivist at University College, London and worked in local government archives in Worcester before joining the BBC. She has been involved in the development of the archives as a major research resource and preparation for the introduction of EDMS for the management of the BBC's records. She is an Associate Editor for the *New dictionary of national biography* as well as the author of various articles and chapters on the BBC archives.

Adam Lee is the Projects Manager for BBC Information and Archives, the London-based libraries of the BBC. He is responsible for the implementation of IT and broadcast technology developments in the libraries and archives. After working at the Bodleian Library, he completed a degree at the College of Librarianship, Wales followed by a Masters Degree in History. Since joining the BBC in 1983 as an Assistant Librarian he has worked as the Television Archivist and the BBC's Head of Records Management before taking on his present post.

Barrie MacDonald has been Librarian of the Independent Television Commission and its predecessor the Independent Broadcasting Authority since 1979, working previously with the BBC Reference Library from 1966 to 1979. He is the author of *Broadcasting in the United Kingdom: a guide to information sources* (2nd edition, 1994), co-author of *Keyguide to information sources in media ethics* (1998), and has published various articles and bibliographies on the literature and information sources on broadcasting.

Sue Malden qualified professionally from the Polytechnic of North London and has since held several posts on the staff of the BBC Film and Video Tape Library at Brentford, Middlesex and with the wider library grouping of BBC Information and Archives. In her current role as Corporate Affairs Manager, she has responsibility for upholding the BBC's professional standard within the BBC and in the wider Archive and Library world. The role involves the development of appropriate policies to ensure that the archives meet the requirements of the BBC both now and in the future. She is on the executive board of the Federation of Commercial Audio Visual Archives (FOCAL International) and Vice-President of the International Federation of Television Archives (FIAT/IFTA).

Helen Martin has been Information Manager at *The Guardian/Observer* since 1976. She is a founder member of the Association of UK Media Librarians and has been involved in several studies examining journalists' information seeking needs, the latest of which was a British Library funded study by City University looking into journalists and the Internet. She is a member of the Internet Studies Research Group and is on the editorial board of *Aslib Proceedings*.

Nora Paul is Library Director and Institute Associate of the Poynter Institute for Media Studies in St. Petersburg, FL, responsible for holding seminars in the areas of news research and news library management, computer assisted reporting, and leadership in new media newsrooms. She came to the Poynter in 1991 after 12 years at the *Miami Herald*, where she was the Library Director then Editor, Information Services. She earned her Master's in Library Science from Texas Women's University. Prior to this she was a partner in one of the USA's first information brokerage services, Freelance Research Service, Houston. She is the author of *Computer assisted research: a guide to tapping online information*, and contributes to the National Institute for Computer Assisted Reporting's *Uplink* newsletter and *Searcher*. She is a frequent speaker at journalism conferences and conducts newsroom workshops on the use of computer-accessed information. She has held Internet training courses in Russia, South Africa, the Netherlands, Denmark and England and also consults with news organizations on improving their research services and information management.

Barbara P. Semonche is the Library Director for the University of North Carolina at Chapel Hill School of Journalism and Mass Communication. She has taught courses in Computer Assisted Research and written over a dozen articles on special librarianship and a book *News media libraries; a management handbook* was published (1993). She is the list owner for NewsLib, an international mailing list for over 1000 news librarians and researchers, educators and journalists. She is a frequent presenter on news library technology in the US, Canada and Europe. She is a Fellow of the SLA, a Freedom Forum International Library Fellow, and the recipient of several news librarian awards and honours.

Richard Withey is Head of Independent Digital UK Ltd. He was previously Director of New Media, for News International Plc. He joined this company in 1987 to create databases derived from newspapers and sell them. His new media portfolio includes ventures producing CD-ROMs,

online services and Internet activity. During the last five years he has been
co-ordinating the strategy for new media development at News
International, through joint ventures, company start-ups and collaboration. He is a director of a number of digital publishing companies in
which News International has an interest, and he has written and lectured
extensively on new media and digital information. Prior to joining News
International, he was Head of Information Services for the British Institute
of Management.

Introduction

Sarah Adair

Information revolution, the new information age, the information explosion – all of these terms are so familiar to us now that many would say it seems it has always been here. In fact, it has only just begun; we are still in only the earliest stages of the new information age and making only educated guesses at where or how far we go from here.

This second edition of *Information sources for the press and broadcast media* strives to demonstrate the radical leap taken in virtually every area of information provision over the past eight years. In considering scope, Selwyn Eagle stated in his introduction to the first edition, 'the world and all its works' are of interest to this profession and it is therefore impossible for a book of this kind to present a comprehensive coverage of sources for the field. In agreement with this I have made an effort to expand the topic as much as possible rather than just to expand the list of sources. As a second edition therefore it does not mean to replace, but to enhance the first and to be used in conjunction with it. This edition is similar to the first in that it contrasts with other volumes in the series. Rather than being a Guide to the literature of a recognized subject field, it attempts to show 'how the press and broadcast media make use of information from various sources and how they organize their library and information departments to this end' (Eagle, 1991, p.1). From the first edition, only two chapters, film and video, and sound archives have been updated and included.

The scope has been expanded to include the unexplored issues of media ethics, the underused resources of television written archives, and the innovations in the digitization of stills, film and video, and written archives. For a view of our future Richard Withey has gazed into the 21st century newsroom. Several authors have provided the reader with an insight into the current media information world, particularly Debra Bade's descriptive chapter of life at CNN International, Annabel Colley's experiences on the BBC *Panorama* programme team and Helen Martin's introduction of the Internet at the *Guardian/Observer*. Experience being the best teacher and people the greatest resources, authors have in many cases been encouraged to personalise their contributions, to share their experiences as a means of lending a helping hand, alerting others to a multitude of pitfalls, thus hopefully saving time and frustration.

The coming of the Internet naturally figures largely in this second edition. As you will see, nearly every chapter focuses on the Internet demonstrating the radical changes it is bringing about. Nora Paul devotes her chapter to its impact in the newsroom; Barbara Semonche applauds the Internet, but reminds us of its dangers; Gertrud Erbach corrals its forces through the newly created intranet at News International; Annabel Colley describes how the existence of the Internet has completely changed her career. Peter Cole, journalist of wide experience, describes how he has made the greatest use of the Internet not on the newspapers he has worked on, but within the context of his new profession as an academic training new journalists, and he describes the gulf between the two spheres.

The interconnected nature of media operations makes it imperative as well as inevitable that we follow the leaders and keep up with innovation. Whereas many, either information specialists/librarians, journalists, or their managers, might have resisted change in the 1980s, the explosion of resources and vastly improved access to them of the 90s makes change irrepressible. Progress in electronic information sources has been so rapid and so widespread that any library without electronic connections may well find itself relegated to the position 'morgue' as Nora Paul describes the earliest newspaper libraries. Journalists are increasingly obtaining direct access to the Internet whether at work or at home. Unbelievably in this day and age, there are still librarians in media organizations denied sufficient, and in some cases any, computer equipment; while their journalists, higher up the hierarchy, are handed the most up to date technology as a matter of course.

One major change brought about by the Internet is that now when a particular institution is behind the times, the individual need not be. Armed with a PC and modem, and this clearly assumes personal financial capability, he/she need not necessarily be constrained by what the employer is willing or able to provide, but instead can plug in directly. Here lies the difficulty for librarians: the status and income, rather than the particular skills or job responsibility of the journalist compared to that of the librarian, could in some cases determine who is able to take advantage of the new opportunities. A library thus unable to stay with the game will be bypassed. Management must be made aware that there is potentially a tremendous waste of professional expertise here; librarians as information professionals have the precise skills and training required to take optimum advantage of the electronic information explosion. For their part, librarians must be aware that to be successful they must now take the initiative and be even more ahead of their time than has ever been demanded in the past.

Peter Cole describes the training which journalists receive with state of the art technology and free access to the Internet, and the expectations this creates of the work place. These new recruits arrive at their first job to find only the most basic computer facilities accompanied by a newspaper or television management blissfully unaware of the revolution. I know from experience that this can hold true for the training of information professionals as well. Management cannot ignore much longer the impetus these young recruits are providing. Peter Cole has had a long and varied career in journalism experiencing it from all angles as journalist, editor, newspaper founder, and academic. We benefit from his views on the developments in both journalism and information provision evolved during his unique career.

Bade describes the 'chaos and teamwork' that go into dealing with breaking news stories at CNN International, and the vital link the research centre plays in the process. Bade not only describes in detail the demands of this work – strong research skills across the spectrum from print to picture, great flexibility, stress tolerance, quick thinking and confidence in emergencies – but also offers comprehensive guidance to others involved in news research and in the archiving of stills, video and film, complete with evaluative lists of sources and the means to search them efficiently.

Annabel Colley carries on this theme from the perspective of a librarian evolved into television programme information researcher. As part of the programme team, her experiences have shown that the skills of the information professional make him or her the perfect partner to the journalist. All researchers will find her 'webliography' an invaluable resource, always bearing in mind the constant changes taking place in the content and address of Web sites.

Richard Withey shows us the future, first affording us a perspective with a comparison of the journalists' experience 'Times Past' (the sixties) vs 'Times Present' (the nineties). Tracing development from past to present, he demonstrates convincingly that the future, and not too distant future, is digital. Perhaps this does not come as a surprise when one reads the chapters presenting the digitization of one medium after another in this book. However, envisage as Withey does, complete and entire digitization and we have a seemly limitless new world, open to the imagination.

Nora Paul argues that news librarians must change with the resources now available, specifically the Internet. The Internet has given news reporting the ability to reach a new dimension, and it is the responsibility of the news librarian to facilitate this change, indeed to spur the expansion. She offers us a summary of the growth and change currently taking place in news libraries and techniques for staying ahead of the game. Paul echoes other contributors in her insistence that a librarian's training in understanding, evaluating, cataloguing and compiling information make him or her 'the key partner in helping reporters form and master the material at hand'.

Helen Martin has always kept the *Guardian/Observer* Research & Information Library at the forefront of change in the newspaper libraries in the UK. She describes the successes and the frustrations inherent in encouraging progress within a large organization, in this case the introduction of the Internet, and the problems of often being more advanced and yet less recognized than one's colleagues in the information specialist/journalist partnership. Her honest portrayal of behind the scenes operations is an eye-opener to anyone interested in this industry. Martin also incorporates into her chapter the findings of the City University/British Library survey of print and television journalists' use of the Internet adding a valuable perspective to our study of the impact of this new resource.

Intranets are internal and private networks that operate on the same open protocol as the Internet, using Internet-related tools and standards (Web browsers, search engines, and HTML), allowing staff to share information in-house and at remote sites. The information specialist is again precisely qualified to create and maintain this operation. Erbach and Iley's case study of the News International project describes the process of involving all relevant personnel from drawing board through to on-going improvement to ensure that the new system truly reflects the needs of the users. Beginning as an access for journalists to the archive of the four News International titles, the intranet has grown to include further in-house databases created by the library such as celebrity births and deaths, and a subject index to major news events. Links are added to relevant Web sites thus expanding the information source as far as the user wishes to go. Erbach discusses how journalists' tight schedules and *ad hoc* use dictate that the system be simple and the training schedule flexible and provides a guide. Kathy Foley, contributor to the first edition and now Information Editor at the San Antonia Express-News, is a pioneer in intranet development. Foley maintains a Web site dedicated to intranet issues, linking to excellent examples of news research intranets as well as to further information covering the topic at: http://www.metalab.unc.edu/slanews/intranets/.

In this age of information proliferation, epitomized by the Internet, it is the responsibility of the information professional to provide the message of caution along with the guidance journalists and programme makers require to navigate this maze. Barbara Semonche opens her chapter with a quote from Joel Achenbach of the *Washington Post*, 'The Information Age has one nagging problem: much of the information is not true. We live in a time besotted with bad information'. Semonche makes it clear that the Internet is not a news service and there is no means of judging the quality of what it offers. This very daunting job is down to the information professional; as Semonche so elegantly points out 'such is their professional heritage and responsibility'. Her chapter with its extensive list of further resources including Web sites to amplify her subject, is an invaluable guide to meet this challenge.

I am especially pleased at the inclusion of archival management in this edition. Jacqueline Kavanagh introduces us to a relatively little used resource. Though repeat television transmissions are familiar to us all, it is relatively recently that the reuse of programmes, either in part or in whole, for compilation programmes, repeat broadcasting, terrestrially and via satellite and for overseas sales, has been recognized as a huge financial resource. As these sales depend upon access to original paperwork such as contracts and programme documentation, there is now a massive and insatiable demand for these archival resources.

As a result, a revolution is taking place in this area as well. In the past, archives have often been underused due to the difficulty of access. Increasing demand is now causing the digitization of paper archives to be introduced. The sheer volume of paperwork involved, and the BBC is a perfect example, will of course require time and money to convert. Adam Lee, in his chapter on the future, discusses how the BBC intends to proceed. Access difficulties are becoming a thing of the past with electronic document management.

Sally Hine expands and updates two of the chapters from the first edition to present a more comprehensive picture of the sound element in broadcasting, from oral history to mood music. This covers not only the BBC holdings, but also the National Sound archive now housed at the new British Library as well as lesser-known collections. She incorporates, as we have attempted to do in all other areas, the expansion of the new technologies now in use in the field.

Sue Malden's chapter on film and video sources in the UK updates her chapter in the first edition. Malden demonstrates that the plans laid out in the first edition are now coming to fruition. As does Pat Baird in a later chapter on stills, Malden describes the massive job of converting her collection to the required digital format.

Adam Lee's chapter outlines the BBC's future plans for all BBC resources, including the three collections covered in this volume, evolving into the final (is anything final?) stage of desktop access to all BBC research facilities from press cuttings to music. Lee points out that the catalogue, once the library is digitized, is no longer just a catalogue, but the collection itself. Search for an item and it is before you, not just the reference, but the still, the contract, the video sequence and, one day, the music. The BBC is currently establishing standards which will allow one search to investigate all existing systems and resources within the BBC simultaneously.

This is the dream. However, Adam Lee looks into the costs. The challenge to broadcasting is unique. Whereas other industries employing electronic document management systems can make use of off the shelf software with some customization, broadcasting is such a specialized industry and involves such a wide variety of elements, that custom designed software would be necessary to meet the requirements of the diverse systems. Both Bade and Withey touch on this problem as well. As Lee states 'no broadcasting organization can afford to invest in a closed proprietary software application'. The costs are prohibitive and it can be imagined that due to its specialized nature, there is little chance of recouping losses by marketing the final product.

He shows that the Internet has raised the user's expectations of search facilities and availability of sources and yet this is particularly difficult to fulfill in the area of film and video. Whereas the BBC stills system already delivers both the catalogue and transmission quality photographs directly to users, it is not yet possible to provide the same for the moving image. These images certainly exist on the Internet, but of a standard unsuitable for broadcasting as the storage capacity required thus far makes this impossible.

In the first edition, Roger Wemyss Brooks covered the use of still pictures in the press and in broadcasting. In this edition we turn to Pat Baird for a description and guide to the conversion of a stills archives into digital format, now the industry standard for stills management. Still picture technology is now an integral part of the electronic newspaper production process and therefore archiving must now be done on an electronic platform. Baird covers in detail every question that must be asked before embarking upon such a project, and each step that must be taken along the way. The process requires a complete rethinking of all traditional methods not only of receipt and delivery, but of cataloguing, storage, and retrieval, and the author argues convincingly for the enhanced role of the librarian/cataloguer as both the collection and new opportunities for searching and exploitation increase. Finally, Baird brings us back to the Internet once again in stating that this is destined to be the marketplace for digital transmission of still and moving images in the new millennium.

Underlying all of the above is Barrie MacDonald's chapter on media ethics which establishes the basis upon which we as information professionals and journalists are to proceed. For all the Internet's positive attributes, it also presents a threat to our existing code of honour. As Macdonald states 'the basic right of freedom of expression is well served by the Internet – but it is sorely tested by the flood of poor quality, inaccurate, biased, obscene, racist, sexist, and often libelous material'. Macdonald echoes Semonche as he describes the ever widening body of resources from which information professionals are now meeting the needs of their clients, and the moral ethical and legal issues that flow from it. As it grows 'our knowledge and understanding of the legal and moral issues of accessing and disseminating information must increase ... (We) need to exercise even more judgement on the quality, integrity and accuracy ... a librarian's expertise is now more valuable to the user than the collections they manage'.

The age of electronic information has created new pressures, new challenges. Librarians and information personnel willing to tackle the challenges need not be in fear of losing their position. Indeed, as most of our contributors have pointed out in one way or another, this new age of information is by definition an age of new opportunities for the information specialist.

Finally, my thanks to all the contributors for their constancy and advice, and to Simon Rooks of the BBC for his assistance after the death of Sally Hine. I also thank Catherine Lain at Bowker Saur for her calm, patience and guidance. To Judith Steele, longtime friend and colleague, I add my gratitude for her steadfastness as sounding board, advisor, shoulder and punching bag. I would that everyone had such a friend.

REFERENCE

Eagle, S. (1991) (ed) *Information sources for the press and broadcast media*. London: Bowker-Saur

A journalist's view of the changes in information access for newspapers over the years

Peter Cole

The career of a journalist aged 53 in 1999 will inevitably have spanned change of a serious order. Change in the nature of newspapers: their appearance, content, market success and means of production. Changes in the market place: electronic rivals, from radio to Internet. Changes in ownership: from newspaper barons to international media conglomerates, and to venture capitalist firms. Changes in distribution: from train to truck and to screen. Change in the place of the journalist in society: from reporter to sometimes celebrity. Change in the sophistication of those dealing with the media: from innocent victims or friendly co-operators to titans of spin. Changes in the methods of gathering and researching information, and consequently in the nature of those non-journalist service functions carried out within media organizations by information professionals. It was all very quiet and constant for 100 years. The last 20 years have witnessed the electronic revolution, affecting almost every area of life. One of these areas is journalism, and it is on this that this chapter concentrates.

One piece of basic research undertaken before setting about writing this piece was to read, on paper, an earlier version of this book and within it an earlier version of this article. It was written by a former colleague of mine on *The Guardian*, Harold Jackson, vividly remembered as a reporter of great repute in both Northern Ireland, at the onset of the present era of 'troubles', and Washington. I also recall clearly his role in the office in the early days of the 'transformation'. Not necessarily predictably, he took an early and intense interest in the possibilities for journalism of the electronic revolution, and while the luddites were still gathering around *The Guardian*, as around so many newspapers, Harry, with just one or two others, saw the future almost before it had threatened to happen. He was 'wired' at a time when other journalists, some of them much younger, had yet to recognize, and would be a long time in doing so, the possibilities, challenges and difficulties of what lay around the corner.

His piece was thus ahead of its time and ahead of reality then. In some ways it is even ahead of reality today, for while the possibilities now are infinitely greater than then, there remain wide sections of the media – in management and journalism – where they have either failed to be recognized or failed to be exploited. Therefore, work in progress in 1999 is not so very different from work in progress when Harry Jackson was writing. A gulf remains between those at the cutting edge and those with varying enthusiasm, or lack of it, who are trying to catch up. That will inevitably be a theme of this piece.

But first, some context needs to be set. As every journalist knows, in order to evaluate the information and opinions the reader needs to know their provenance. If the writer of this article specialized in the supply of lead to newspaper companies, he would be a tainted source, as indeed he would be if he owned online newspapers. Where there are microchips there also lives hyperbole, just as where there is lack of imagination luddism thrives.

Any journalist of my age will have spent much of his or her career trying to keep abreast of change, or digging in the sand for somewhere to put his head. The latter is not an option, although some try to treat it as such. When I started in journalism, as a reporter on the *London Evening News* (now dead), it was 1968 with hot metal and a wonderful library full of cuttings. There were library staff who regarded the vagueness of your inquiry as a challenge, and, although the concept was meaningless in those days, were human search engines.

Working later for the same newspaper in the United States underlined the dependency on cuttings. The situation was exacerbated by the time difference, particularly when one was working for an evening newspaper. The typical pattern was an editorial conference in London at 8.00 am, an idea for a feature from one of those people whose opening words in any telephone conversation were 'What time do you have?' a brief to the half asleep correspondent at 9.00 am London time, which was 3.00 or 4.00 am in New York and a need to file copy by 1.30 pm in London, which was 7.30 or 8.30 am for New York insomniacs.

The trick was to be on top of the material because few potential sources welcomed a pre-dawn telephone call, even if you did have the home number. So before you went to bed you went out to buy the first editions of the *New York Times* and *Daily News*, read them and cut them, while at the same time trying to predict London's feature request. Each week you would cut the fat Sunday papers (long before they were fat in the UK), the news magazines from *Time* and *Newsweek* to *US News* and *World Report*, the general women's and gossip magazines – anything which might get you out of a 4.30 am information blockage. You could, and did, phone the library in London from time to time, but it was of limited use because you could not 'see' the cuttings. No, there was no fax then, and even as I write those words it seems extraordinary that this was only 30 years ago.

'When you ain't got nothing, you've got nothing to lose', a singer popular at the time, called Dylan, used to sing, only if you were the sole New York correspondent for your newspaper, and the last thing you wanted was to be recalled to London, then you had to find ways of overcoming the information famine. That meant reading and cutting and filing in such a way that you could find it fast when the need arose. Reporters could then better understand the skills and value of library staff.

Visiting the US later I watched the process getting easier for the correspondents. They called it monitoring, which meant watching the everalive television in the office, the CNN, the live feed from Congress, accessing the various archived material, receiving the transcripts from every press conference on Capitol Hill and, *in extremis*, ordering the fax or e-mail from the London office if the information could not be acquired by any other means.

But we leap ahead, from the *Evening News* to *The Guardian* as a reporter, still with paper cuttings from the library, and messengers dropping relevant pieces of Press Association copy on your desk, and to the House of Commons with none of the electronic facilities available today. It was like being a foreign correspondent. You could not access copy filed within the office by a specialist writer, could only access cuttings from the library via a messenger who took hours to arrive, and you could only see Press Association copy through the grace and favour mechanism of being provided with their raw copy as filed to the office, but before it was put out on the wire.

We progress further, to the *London Evening Standard* and another paper cuttings library, then back to *The Guardian* as news editor. The news desk is the fulcrum of any newspaper, where editors go to find out what is happening, where agency copy and post and telexes drop, where informants of many descriptions telephone, where the expectation is that you will know everything about everything and, if not, know where to get it. During that time leading up to the early/mid-eighties a new expression has entered the vocabulary – New Technology. The world is about to change, the lead and the chases and the Linotype machines, and of course the typewriters, are living on borrowed time. Working parties are planning. There are missions to Spain to see ATEX in action. Life is dominated by print unions fighting for survival. Eddie Shah and Rupert Murdoch are doing the dirty work for those who prefer to take things stage by stage, but know deep down that this will not deliver.

Yet for the journalist and the library, life carries on much as before. The library, because they move in these circles and are excited by information technology, know what is possible and what is going to happen. The journalists are too busy to contemplate the future, or so they say, except the Harry Jacksons. But the big bang is happening, and of course in amongst the excitement and the technological progress many things are confused. Try these. New technology puts the journalists in control. No more printers to slow the process, to obstruct, strike or resist. Deadlines will be later, page changes will happen as and when they are needed. Costs will drop, more staff will be employed. Only nothing works out that way. Deadlines are earlier. Edition changes are fewer. Staff numbers are smaller. Bottom line: costs are cut and profits increased. But that is about power and politics and the market, not about technology.

Let us pause here, interrupt the flow of history and technology, and take stock of the world we left behind, the world of libraries and cuttings and, first mention, books.

Good journalists are inquisitive, sceptical, tenacious. Good journalists make connections where others might not. Good journalists know how to go about getting information, about asking the right questions. They have instincts and techniques; they have skills and cunning. They tend to know a little about a lot rather than a lot about a little, although the balance will be tipped in the case of the specialist journalist. Journalists research but tend not to use the word. They are wary of library professionals because they do not see themselves as professionals. They are more wary of information scientists because they do not see themselves as scientists. Good journalists know they are only as good as their contacts, because their contacts are people who will help them out of a corner, who will provide the information they are looking for, or another place to go to find it, quickly, because they are usually in a hurry.

Journalists, almost up to the present generation, like newspaper cuttings for a number of reasons. The cutting allows them to 'weigh' a story. It tells them, because they are instinctively aware of typography and design, where the original story was published, and with what prominence. Their memories are often for the position of a story – 'a right hand page of *The Telegraph*, early in the paper' - and they will search cuttings folders with a memory of how that cutting 'looked' on the page. Online text looks 'all the same' to them, is devoid of editorial feel. Cuttings folders allow the journalist to extract clippings, to form the small pile of those they will be drawing from in their research, and to ignore the fact that they could print off selected cuttings from the online database – because they will.

Cuttings are also attractive to the reporter in that some selection will have been done already. The famous person will have a range of files dealing with different aspects of their lives, personal and professional. Politicians will have a separate file for speeches. Essentially the first selection will have been carried out by the librarian. And perhaps this encourages a more personal link between reporter and librarian. Journalists are notoriously egocentric, but when they want something, especially information, they can be thoroughly ingratiating. The good journalist will value the relationship with the library staff, knowing how useful it can be. I well remember the occasions when the search did not yield what I was looking for yet hours later the librarian would turn up with another wallet of cuttings, perhaps with a label I would never ever have thought of, and it contained vital information.

The downside of the cuttings as a research tool – I put to one side any considerations of costs and staffing – is that cuttings get lost (sometimes in the reporter's bottom draw!), or are returned in out of date order. Nevertheless, they remain popular among those who have used them. The Press Association, as 'new tech' an organization as you will find with its own sophisticated Web site, still maintains a cuttings library. Part of this is to do with the difficulty of archiving electronically the amount of material they produce further back than the few years this has been happening automatically.

To me, cuttings libraries have always induced ideas of body disposal. Those huge metal shelves, requiring such strength to move in order to reveal further shelves of cuttings, have always seemed a likely place to be trapped for eternity or to bury a body!

You appreciate a cuttings library when you do not have one. More than that, you appreciate a library of any description when you do not have one. We resume the account of this author's experience of libraries with the birth and short life of *The Sunday Correspondent*. In 1988 I was a member of a small team which went out to raise money from the venture capital community for a new Sunday newspaper in the quality broadsheet sector of the market. I was also the editor designate. We raised the money, and from early 1989 until launch in September of that year we set about not only creating a new newspaper, but putting together the infrastructure to support it.

That meant hiring a complete staff, finding and equipping a building, arranging printing and distribution and much, much more. You take so much for granted if you work for a newspaper that is there, and has been for some time. Starting from scratch is complicated. Along the way somebody said 'library'. So what do you do? You cannot acquire the backnumbers of everything and hire 1000 people to cut them. If you are a relatively small budget start-up you do not have the space to house a cuttings library or the money to hire an adequate staff. And even by this point online was very much around. We bought the vital books – a few of them. We did a deal with the Press Association, then still in Fleet Street and only about half a mile away from our Clerkenwell offices, to use their cuttings library on occasion. We made a similar arrangement with *The Guardian*, only 150 yards away, to use their library, and the staff there were understanding and helpful. We did not take a subscription out to FT PROFILE, though I forget why not.

There we were, a new quality national newspaper without the library support all of us were used to (most of us had come from well-resourced national newspapers). Journalists felt very exposed without their cuttings, on paper or online. In rain and shine the traffic to *The Guardian* and Press Association was extensive and frequent. Our staff learned how vital the library support system is.

When the *Correspondent* closed 15 months after launch, I found myself in Wapping, at *The Sunday Times*. There an impressive library served a range of newspapers, and the library staff were ever helpful. It was still, in 1990, a basically cuttings-driven operation. From the point of view of the editorial staff the editorial computer system made this inevitable. We had one of the most primitive forms of ATEX. We could cut and paste and divide our screens, but even if they wanted to give us an online library our screens would not allow it.

So I left newspapers never having had much opportunity to move beyond cuttings and reference books. The more modern systems of gathering information came with the move to higher education.

The real culture change was from Wapping to academe. On *The Sunday Times* they referred to the office as the plant. In higher education they refer to the university as the institution. Both terms have their element of accuracy. In the university, of course, the Internet is long established and much used, whereas on most newspapers – all of them when I left the national press – you have to leave your desk to access the Internet elsewhere, in academe every computer will connect with the Internet. It is the only perk in higher education. You leave behind the company car and the expense account, the lunches and the trips (there are fewer of these lunches and trips, in journalism than legend indicates), but you can spend as much time as you like on the World Wide Web, free – and you need a lot of time because, being part of a university network, the Web grinds slowly.

In the university you enter a different information culture. Books, journals, and research papers are more important than newspapers and periodicals. Immediacy is less important than authority and comprehensiveness. So the newspapers are there, stored on CD-ROM, on the university network, but nobody worries if the most recent copies are two months old. When an article for a refereed research journal takes months to place, more months to referee and more again to be published, then urgency is not the watchword. Research resources are good; library staff are committed and capable and academic staff's capacity to locate information from elsewhere in the academic community all over the world is highly developed. But there is always time – time to wait, time to read, time to think. If you have spent 25 years on newspapers these are forms of time you do not recognize.

The situation is complicated if you remain a journalist, still writing for newspapers, still talking to journalists, reflecting (a word not used in journalism) on newspapers and journalists. It is complicated further if the reason you are employed in higher education is to teach journalism, to train young people to work in journalism, print, broadcast and now online. It is your job to impart the core skills of journalism – writing, researching, ordering and structuring information, and interviewing. It is also your job to draw out the creative side of the potential journalist, so that he or she will produce the ideas every editor demands all the time. It is the job, too, to consider standards and ethics, so that the next generation of journalists realizes that these considerations assume greater importance to the audiences which journalists serve.

So you end up as a hybrid, unable and unwilling to shed all those personal qualities that made you a journalist and made you care about journalism, charged with producing a new generation of journalists better than your own, and yet operating in a world which is both dismissive of journalism and impressed by journalists. Ideally the two cultures should be bound together by common themes: the spirit of inquiry, the desire to test assertions and hypotheses, the need to collect, distil, order and present information. And yet there are other dividing themes: one culture often driven by a political agenda, the other by a political correctness agenda, one susceptible to fashion and conventional wisdom, the other dismissive of intellectual ephemera, one contemptuous of the imperfections of working at speed, the other contemptuous of the ability to take so long over so little, and so on.

Journalism as a university discipline still sits uneasily with the more traditional subjects. This is not true in the United States or much of Europe, but in the UK the culture of craft, training, and apprenticeship remains too ingrained, particularly in areas of the regional press. When so many senior journalists on national newspapers have been through little formal training, and only relatively recently has journalism become a graduate career, then too often you hear the opinion that journalism cannot be taught. The school-leavers do not believe this, and queue up for university places to study media related subjects. The universities, mindful of the need to recruit students, support, indeed spawn, such courses.

The fact is, however, that journalism education today is provided almost exclusively by higher education institutions, which saves on the newspaper proprietors' training budgets. And most newspapers and broadcast organizations hire young reporters from university courses.

Students today receive their education, whether in journalism or any other subject, from institutions where IT is a major priority. Through the UK's Joint Academic Network (JANET) lecturers have been online for years, Net-wise when the world was just beginning to hear about it, and certainly before newspapers and broadcasters gave it any attention at all. While schools remain frequently very light on IT – there are exceptions, but provision in the maintained schools sector is usually inadequate – young people at university are inducted in the use of IT as soon as they arrive. Government inspectors take account of IT provision when assessing subject areas in universities. Students are shown how to search on the Internet.

There are pockets of resistance – there is a lecturer in my own department (of journalism) who refuses to use a computer – but these are very rare. So increasingly journalism students, who have never seen a library of cuttings, are learning to research electronically while at college.

At my institution they go to the library to access FT PROFILE, they receive Press Association copy online in their student newsrooms, they have Internet access on every computer in the university, and they can search CD-ROMs with back numbers of the major newspapers from the same computers. They vary in interest and skill, but they are taught in an electronic environment, to the extent that we weep about their lack of interest in books, and wish they would spend as much time on the shelves as they do on screen.

Then they leave, and the problems start. They are employed on regional or local newspapers as trainee reporters, or they go to small radio stations, and in one or two cases they may work as television researchers. They are amazed at the lack of facilities they find. Local newspapers usually have no libraries, just back numbers of their own newspapers. They have no Internet access. They have no online service like FT PROFILE. Radio stations, particularly commercial radio stations, are often in much the same state. BBC facilities all over the country are much better because of their networked computerized system which allows them to access all manner of material.

I have recently been part of a research team, led by Dr David Nicholas of City University, examining journalists' use of the Internet (Nicholas *et al*, 1998). The project, funded by the British Library, painted a far from encouraging picture of modern research facilities available to working journalists.

The group of student journalists interviewed were overwhelmingly Internet users, 80 per cent of the sample using it frequently. But when we came to regional and local newspaper use it was a very different picture. Even on one of the biggest regional evenings, the *Yorkshire Evening Post*, Internet access for reporters was provided on just two terminals but 'most reporters don't use the Net at all'. It was much the same at the *Lancashire Evening Post*, where there was just one Internet terminal in the newsroom, 'used by just one or two people'. When you came to the smaller weekly papers this resource was simply non-existent. Of a group of trainee journalists on such papers just 17 per cent ever took advantage of the Internet, or had the opportunity to do so.

You would expect the situation to be different on the national newspapers, with their better resources and supposedly more sophisticated attitude to information gathering. But here again the picture was patchy at best. An interview survey of 50 randomly selected journalists on *The Times* showed that over two thirds of them did not use the Internet. And only around 10 per cent of journalists on *The Guardian* searched the Internet.

There are reasons for this, partly human, partly technological. The technological one is easily dealt with. Most current newsroom computer systems were brought in with the first wave of new technology in the eighties. They tended to be mainframe word processing systems, networked among reporters, sub-editors and news desks. They allowed copy to be moved around, edited, formatted and type-set. Information was stored on a large central computer and there was basically no access to the outside world, apart from news agency copy brought in through some exchange programme which allowed it to be stored on the main computer and distributed to journalists' terminals. The system was big but it was not beautiful.

More modern systems are PC-based, and these are only now coming into newspaper offices. Proprietors more interested in getting the last squeak out of what were at the time expensive systems, and which still, in their terms, do the job, did not rush to keep up with technological advance. These first generation systems did not allow the Internet to be distributed to every desk, and journalists were disinclined to find the single terminal in the newsroom (not always provided) where they could access the Internet. This is beginning to change as replacement systems are installed in an increasing number of newspapers.

This brings us to the human component. Journalists are not alone in their resistance to change, and technologically-driven change – often meaning very different working practices and reductions in staffing levels in the name of productivity – but they are, perhaps, rather particular kinds of people in that they go out of their way to mystify the work they do, are by nature secretive and are often insecure. Since nobody, least of all the journalists themselves, can easily define precisely the nature of what they do and what qualifies them to do it, they often prefer not to share skills, techniques, methods – still less sources or contacts – because they fear losing the mystique that surrounds them and their trade.

Part of this self-image involves a need to be dismissive of technology, and therefore a resistance to changes in technology. The reporter only needs a notebook and pencil by way of equipment; the rest comes from within – or so runs the myth. Journalists fear letting others into the information gathering process, for fear that others can do it as well as they can. Add to that the job insecurity of journalism, the tradition of summary firing, particularly on national newspapers, and the self-perception that the rejected journalist is unequipped to do anything else, and you begin to understand the inexplicable reluctance of journalists to take advantage of modern research sources.

Most of the above is easily dismissed. Good journalists do have unique qualities. The simple of task of finding things out and telling other people about them is not simple at all. The average non-journalist would not know where to start. The two most important qualities of the good journalist, having ideas and making connections, are not commonplace. And yet all these fears and paranoias make journalists resistant to taking advantage of what is now available to them.

Take two examples to illustrate the point. On *The Sunday Times* we had trainees, new graduates selected out of many hundreds of applicants to join the paper on a short contract. They were often used as researchers – leg people – for the reporters, who would send them off to find out basic information, from the library or other reference sources. Fresh from university and their dissertations, and with endless excitement about journalism, they were effective researchers. And who was to say they could not go further, and write the story. In fact the reporter would write the story, and at the bottom, in italic, would run the line 'additional research by . . .'. The strength of the reporter who wrote the story and briefed the researcher was that he or she understood the importance of the story, the context – in terms of the nature of the newspaper and the background to the story – and was able to structure and write the story in the way the paper demanded. But these reporters often regarded the work done by the researchers as ancillary or subordinate, rather than as central to the production of the story.

Second, the library. In the first example the researcher is removing the library one more notch away from the journalist, who does not have to contact the library but has an assistant to do the job. Thus a hierarchy is reinforced. It was often as bad in the cuttings days, in that it was not unusual for the library to have a counter which the journalist would approach with his or her query. That said a lot about perceived roles and status. Attitudes to the library, traditional attitudes, go a long way to explaining why, particularly in the UK, journalists have not adopted electronic research as readily as, say, their American counterparts.

Journalists, who tend to be left of centre and egalitarian in political attitude, seldom practise what they preach. Insecure they may be, perhaps for that very reason, but they have a sense of position. So too often they have treated the library as a service industry, and have been reluctant to credit it with the capacity to uncover some kinds of information just as well, or better, than the journalists in the newsroom. For their part, library staff have suffered from a lack of self-esteem; they have often portrayed themselves as dogsbodies, because they have accepted their position in the hierarchy below journalists.

This is much less true of television than of newspapers. The television researcher (the description is part of the culture in a way that it is not in newspapers) is held in high regard in programme teams, whether it be current affairs or lifestyle.

It is true the researcher will not necessarily be a person who has been through librarianship training – he or she may be a journalist by training who has entered television in a research capacity – but some of them are just such people. The important thing is that TV journalists, particularly those on current affairs programmes like *Panorama*, regard the researcher as a key player in the production team, without whom the programme would not happen. There is no sense of hierarchy.

Library staff have sought to increase their status by rebadging. I have to admit I smiled the first time I telephoned *The Guardian* library to be met with the answer 'Research and Information'. It is a perfectly accurate description of their activities, but it was the politics that lay behind the name change that amused me.

Electronic information has brought all these issues to a head, and they remain unresolved. There are more advanced skills to searching and retrieving information electronically. Information professionals such as library staff have these skills, and the range of knowledge of what is available and how it can be used. They know more about all this than most journalists, who are also information professionals of a different kind but would never use the description. Journalists fear handing over certain tasks to those better equipped to undertake them. There are exceptions, of course, that spattering of journalists who, like Harry Jackson, saw the possibilities early on and saw how they could exploit them to their own advantage.

There has to be a way out of this temporary impasse. Journalists and the library/research staff who support them have to realize that they are in the same business but make different contributions. They are not in competition, but together they can make for better journalism. It takes much more than technical skills to make a good journalist; it takes much more than understanding search engines to make a good member of the library staff. The latter, at least those in the more enlightened media organizations, are no longer dealing with queries about spellings, or *Who's Who* entries. They are constructing intranets so that routine information needed by journalists in their daily lives is available on their desktops. Journalists should be working with them to ensure that what is constructed is what is needed. And library staff are building a knowledge of the Internet, and identifying sites of relevance to journalists (including specialist sites for specialist journalists) which can only be of immense use to journalists. And yet they are often unreceptive.

Media organizations have been notoriously reluctant to train their journalists in the use of the new information technology (actually they are notoriously reluctant to train at all). Training journalists to exploit electronic information, to develop computer-aided journalism, should be high on the agenda of any such organization. Library/research staffs have the knowledge and skills to undertake this training. Management is slow because training costs. But it costs very little. And if the result is better journalism, information sources in small local newspaper offices where now there are none apart from the reporters and the telephones, then it is better for all. As in any major change, the enemy is fear, and that is understandable.

The electronic sources remain very new. We are still at that stage where the complexities which allowed exclusivity to the faithful few who could manage are being removed to make the new technologies user friendly. Transition is always difficult. The democratization of the new order is well under way. Library researchers will have more interesting jobs. Journalists will still require all the core skills that make for good journalists. They will still have to apply judgment to sources, still have to order and structure, and prioritize and present information. And they may have to be more prepared to take advantage of other expertise available in their own offices.

But potentially it could produce better journalism, with journalists explaining a complex world to a public increasingly cut off from those who have the power, which is what it is all about.

▶ REFERENCE

Nicholas, D. et al (1998) *The media and the Internet.* London: Aslib

2 I'm watching you CNN: real-time research in a global news environment

Debra K. Bade

▶ THIS IS CNN: BREAKING NEWS

While news anchors and reporters are certainly the most visible of CNN staff members, they represent only one piece of the journalistic puzzle at CNN. Hundreds of creative people working behind the scenes to create CNN's final product constantly support those reporters and anchors. Researching and writing stories, co-ordinating satellite feeds, script editing, retrieving the best images to illustrate a story, editing those images, and combining the images and words, hopefully in a moving and intelligent way, are all crucial elements in creating our news product.

To understand CNN one must look at the chaos and teamwork accompanying breaking news stories. Crisis calls upon all of the individual strengths, skills, creativity and knowledge people have in responding to the situation at hand. Reporters, researchers, archivists, writers, producers, editors and camera crews are united in the desire to get a grip on the facts and present them in the best way possible.

The American Embassy bombings

Let us take one example of CNN in action. News of the bombings at American Embassy buildings in Kenya and Tanzania broke early in the morning on August 7, 1998. This was unexpected news of course, and the kind of news that brings corresponding adrenaline level spikes in everyone around my office as we shift into 'breaking story' mode. What happens? For a moment we are the man or woman on the street – hearing the first news, seeing the first pictures we feel the same shock and horror felt by countless others watching this grim story. There is no time to hesitate however, or be overwhelmed by the horror, since it is our job to tell the story. We spring into action.

Questions began to fly. How many people have been killed or injured in the blasts? Who did this? Why have Americans in Kenya and Tanzania been targeted? Telephone lines light up next to the researcher on my team who is on duty at the time. Our Central Bookings staff (responsible for booking guests who will appear on CNN air) are among the first to call looking for help. They need to locate experts on terrorism, people with special knowledge of Kenya and Tanzania, names of Americans stationed in the Embassies, names and addresses of family members or friends here in the United States. Good background research on guests is critical in determining their appropriateness for use as an 'expert', identifying their special areas of knowledge – things they may or may not be able to address – this background helps us conduct a better interview. As potential guests are identified pre-interviews are done to flesh out directions in which the interview may go and questions which may come up with a guest on the air. We also scramble to find video images of guests for promotional bumps and lead-ins and seek out footage that will help viewers to understand better Kenya and Tanzania and the tragic story unfolding.

Throughout CNN Center and in many of our remote bureaux tension builds. People live and breathe the Embassy bombing story. State Department reporters pursue the question of possible Libyan, Iranian or Iraqi connections to people or terrorist groups in Kenya and Tanzania. Relying primarily on database sources such as LEXIS-NEXIS, Dialog and DOW JONES INTERACTIVE, along with Internet sources, the research staff quickly track down background on counter-terrorism experts and look into the history of relations between the United States and Kenya and Tanzania.

A NEWSEDGE profile is created and saved, enabling us instantly to view incoming wire stories from Associated Press and Reuters on the bombing. Country data, street maps of Dar es Salaam, State Department updates and travel advisories are pulled from the Internet and other sources. General reference information on Africa, Kenya and Tanzania is readily available on the desktops of newsroom staff via BRITANNICA ONLINE, an *Encyclopaedia Britannica* Web-based product.

Previous terrorist acts against Americans are investigated, a chronology develops and we explore retaliation for previous attacks and the past US record for bringing international terrorists to trial. The name Osama bin Laden comes up early on August 7 because of his high profile links to terrorist activities and terrorist training programmes along with his strong anti-American sentiment. Peter Arnett's interview with bin Laden from the previous summer is in demand. CNN Business News staffers in our New York bureau begin to pursue business angles on the story and we conduct research on US investments in Africa, and the economic situations in Kenya and Tanzania. Instant research files are created at the Research Desk to organize the growing volume of data. The level of concentration, the effort to do it well, do it right, is audible.

The United States strikes back in Afghanistan and Sudan

For the next few days the Embassy bombing story was in competition with coverage of the scandal encompassing President Clinton and dominating news coverage for most of the summer of 1998. President Clinton had arrived in Martha's Vineyard on vacation when a briefing was called suddenly on Thursday, August 20. We learned that at 1:30pm Eastern Standard Time US military strikes took place against Sudan and Afghanistan. CNN was instantly in Breaking News mode again. In Sudan, the El Shifa pharmaceutical facility, believed to produce chemical precursors in the production of nerve gas, had been hit. And in Afghanistan a group of camps and buildings making up a terrorist training facility near Khost had been targeted.

The *Periscope* Web site and *Jane's* military sources were consulted for graphics and data on Tomahawk cruise missiles which had been used in the strike. Within minutes of the announcement, through the wonders of satellite technology and a major push from our satellite gurus, CNN was taking in a live feed from Sudanese television and CNN viewers listened to Sudanese news anchors relaying details of the US strikes from their perspective. We pushed to learn as much as possible about the sites targeted and about bin Laden's connections to those sites. The archivist on duty searched for footage to supplement breaking news reports – pictures of Khost, Khartoum, terrorist camps, previous military strikes following terrorist attacks.

The Clinton scandal seemed to intermingle quickly with this story as *Wag the Dog* questions surfaced. (The movie, *Wag the Dog*, starring Dustin Hoffman and Robert De Niro, involves a president in the midst of a personal scandal who finds a Hollywood producer to 'invent' a war as a distraction.) President Clinton and his military advisors were almost immediately questioned about the timing and motivation of this military action. Constant questions poured into the Research Desk about the bombing suspects and their families, the reaction of other countries to the strikes, the possibility of retaliation, vulnerable targets in the United States and security measures being taken.

Gradually, the heat of breaking news dissipates and the entertainment, business, medical, and travel segments which may have been moved to make room for live reports begin to return. Things return to business as usual around CNN.

► THE 24-HOUR NEWS LIBRARY

Researchers on my staff are among the many talented people who play an important role in creating our product and maintaining quality during a breaking news event like the African Embassy bombings. Every day, research librarians work closely with bookings staff, writers, reporters, editors and producers in the development of CNN programming.

A breaking news event enhances that relationship. A researcher may be locating information via a quick database search while a reporter or writer holds on the telephone, or the reporter may sit alongside the researcher discussing results while scrolling through citations on the computer screen. Dashing down to the Archive to retrieve the perfect footage for a news package, an editor or producer may be part of the discovery process as the archivist conducts video research.

CNN's Library is perhaps an unusual one in the television world in that the Archive and the News Research functions are merged. It is similar in many ways to newspaper libraries that maintain photograph collections or digital photo archives inside their research centres, except of course that in television, our image collections are made up of film or video or – as we rapidly move toward the implementation of newer technologies – digitized video collections. At CNN, one physical space provides a home for both the videotape archive and the more traditional reference collection with the now indispensable bank of research computers for heavy online database research. One staff handles the demands of both research and archiving, requiring a high degree of versatility from people but rewarding them with tremendous variety in the range of research work they might do on any given day.

News does not always happen at the most convenient hour. A late night breaking story – the sad death of The Princess of Wales for example – can mean a long night or even an overnight shift in the office. For CNN, somewhere in the world it is always primetime, and because of that global nature of our business we are always open, always on call. Librarians cover the 24-hour Reference Desk seven days a week, working a variety of schedules to make this possible. A librarian is typically assigned to cover the Reference Desk for a four or five hour shift and during those hours could be providing non-stop video archive research or online database research along with traditional reference services. The Reference Desk, as is true of most news research centres, demands a lot from our news junkies. Staff must have strong research skills, a high degree of flexibility, stress tolerance, the ability to think on their feet and the confidence to deal with emergencies.

During hours when librarians are not scheduled to work on the Reference Desk they are working on short-term projects as assigned or indexing video records for the Library's internal database. Large-scale projects tackled in addition to primary duties include circulation system maintenance, book cataloguing, tracking periodical orders and also more advanced projects such as Computer Assisted Reporting work. Building an event and video chronology to meet research and video needs for millennium programming has been another large project.

Documentation assistants (loggers) are paraprofessional workers who view CNN footage to be archived in the collection and write an abstract or description of the action taking place on the footage. An eye for good visual images, current events knowledge and the ability to identify people and events are essential in this database building position. Clerical assistants are responsible for office filing, checking in and re-shelving periodicals and video. Two managers who handle daily operations supervise librarians, documentation assistants, and clerical assistants and all report to the Director of News Archives, the Director of News Research and the Vice-President.

► THE NEWS ARCHIVE OPERATON

This section touches briefly on elements of two Archive systems: the current system, already rather a hybrid of the old and new methods, and the digital system towards which CNN is quickly moving. Presently, the Archive holds footage going back to the launch of CNN in 1980. In addition, the Archive contains older footage acquired by CNN to enhance the collection – World War II era footage for example. A number of different videotape formats exist in the Archive stacks including 1-inch reel, ¾-inch cassette and the currently used Betacam SP format. A small Betacam SP would typically hold a two- or three-minute package or piece of raw footage (a *package* is the finished edited product with voiceover suitable for broadcasting while *raw* footage is the footage shot by a field crew before any editing has been done). Large 60-minute or 90-minute Betas hold multiple stories that have been transferred or bumped up to that archival tape. This process is a mixed blessing – the transfer process means that small Beta tapes can be recycled and it helps the Archive live within its physical space – but the downside is the loss of a generation in terms of quality.

Video enters the Archive through a selection process. Newsroom system (currently BASYS but we are migrating to an Avid News system) files with text logs for footage generated on a given day are examined and relevant material is flagged to come to the Archive. All packages produced by CNN are archived, as is most of the raw footage used in producing those packages since that raw footage can be used in future work and is the most historically valuable in any archive collection of current events. This raw footage represents the true wealth of our Archive.

At the point of selection a computer record is generated within the Archive database and preliminary information is added to that record: the title or slug of the piece, the format, the reporter's name, a dateline locator, and perhaps some basic keywords depending on what else can be gleaned from the title and the newsroom log files. Those basic terms assure that footage is retrievable in the database immediately – one can not do very fancy searching at this point but one can definitely track it down. Tapes then physically move out of the newsroom system and into the Archive system, generally about five days after air. They acquire bar codes for use with the Archive circulation system and become available to reporters, editors and producers for future work. Approximately 1500 pieces of footage come into the Archive each week.

In the next phase of the archival process a documentation assistant or logger views the footage. After queuing up a package or piece of raw footage, the logger locates the corresponding record in the Archive database and creates an abstract of the story being told in the video. This description goes into an active text field in the database record and is searchable, allowing power searchers in the system to fine-tune searches as one can look for a more subtle term that may be mentioned in the abstract but not used as a keyword. After a description is generated the final part of the process is for additional keywords to be added to each record as needed. A librarian reviews each record and adds final keywords, making the record fully retrievable in the Archive system. Searches can be performed either in the native database or through the Intranet Web site interface.

Other unit and bureau archive collections

In addition to the main Archive collection there are smaller collections (subsets of the main collection if you will) located in the Features unit, Sports group (CNN-Sports Illustrated), and the CNN NewsStand unit. CNN maintains bureaux in many domestic and international locations and those in Washington DC, New York, Los Angeles and London have small satellite libraries, extending the reach of Library services. Each bureau reflects a very distinctive personality in its archive collection. Washington, of course, is skewed toward the political and government arenas, New York is heavy with glitzy entertainment and Wall Street business news; Los Angeles also leans toward the entertainment industry but has special pools of O.J. Simpson footage and powerful California earthquake images. In London one can find a wealth of European news footage of all kinds. All CNN packages produced in bureau cities are archived in the headquarter's collection but the bureau might archive additional raw footage or field tape shot locally, adding to an incredible bank of image resources upon which to draw.

The future for preservation and a digital archive

Life expectancy for videotape is seven to ten years and much of our footage on 1-inch reel has passed that age. Video is transferred from

1-inch reel to Beta on an as-needed basis in the absence of a full-scale preservation programme. This is a temporary fix. Saving this video hinges on the implementation of wide-scale digital technologies. As digital archiving becomes a reality older tapes will be converted to digital format, first as a general conversion of the Archive collection is launched and more than 70 000 hours of archived material are digitized.

CNN has been a beta test site for a Sony/EDS digital asset management system which is defined as 'an open framework or platform that supports the acquisition, creation, manipulation, storage, archival, retrieval, transmission, and display of digital assets' (*Information Today*, 1 June 1998); or, in other words, a system that can bring together many of the processes which have developed in isolation over the years (incoming feeds and the archiving done in the Library for example). CNN is working closely with Sony and IBM to design a digital archive system that can work for us – no off-the-shelf product available addresses completely the kind of 24-hour volume of news footage we deal with or provides full capability of accessing to a specific image in a package or raw footage segment. Merging digital images with corresponding words or transcripts and being able to jump to a precise spot in a video package has long been a goal. That goal will come to fruition over the next year as a working central system is created to deal with incoming video images, cataloguing the video, storing, and later retrieving those images.

Currently, our Media Operations unit still rolls on tape and it is that tape which comes physically to the Archive. But, at the same instant we roll on tape, a low-resolution digital version is also encoded and loaded onto a server. From there it can be viewed on computer desktops in our newsroom. Ultimately, a high-resolution version of footage will be encoded as feeds come into CNN and those images will exist digitally as datatape. Datatapes will be stored in a server where high-speed robotic arms will load specific pieces of footage as requested by searchers. Users will browse and make video selections from low-resolution footage at their desktops and then go on to edit from a high-resolution version of the footage as needed.

▶ CNN IMAGESOURCE AND OTHER RESOURCES FOR CNN VIDEO AND TRANSCRIPTS

The ever-growing bank of image resources is used to good effect by CNN ImageSource, the division of the Library responsible for the licensing and sale of CNN footage to outside clients such as educational organizations, large corporations, non-profit groups, motion picture production companies, and other news organizations. Because of the primary source nature of our news materials, and the powerful images to be found in the Archive,

CNN footage is frequently a desirable element in the production efforts of many different kinds of corporations.

ImageSource staff members dig through the Archive database to locate images, soundbites, packages, or programmes needed by clients. Video might be used in a film, for research projects, in corporate presentations, in the production of a video game or in educational programmes. Depending on how a client wishes to use CNN footage ImageSource may decide against licensing our footage, or place restrictions on how the footage may be used. ImageSource provides a wonderful repurposing of CNN products. This ability to generate future income and new products is increasingly valuable, and illustrates the philosophy of paying for something once (i.e. shooting great raw footage) and using it many times (in CNN programming, Web site development, for sales to outside clients, in CD-ROM products, etc.). The development of this revenue-producing unit within the Library has reinforced the message that the archive and research work carried out is of great value to CNN and promises a continued return on investment.

A selection of video clips is available at our external Web site (http://www.cnn.com) and many more can be found on Footage.net (http://www.footage.net) – a subset of some of the best CNN video is loaded there and can be searched and licensed for use.

Several outside companies also license limited CNN footage to viewers, handling more routine types of requests. Federal Documents Clearinghouse (FDCH) is the primary resource. FDCH is also the company which does actual transcription of CNN programming, a task previously handled by Journal Graphics. Transcripts come back to us from FDCH for inclusion on our external Web site and are also exclusively available on the LEXIS-NEXIS service. In addition, FDCH makes copies of transcripts available directly to viewers.

▶ THE VIRTUAL WORLD OF NEWS RESEARCH

Historically, CNN has centralized research services in the Library, realizing the benefit and cost-effectiveness of having expert researchers conduct online database research. Library researchers in Atlanta provide research services to all domestic and international bureau staff. Researchers in the New York and Washington bureau libraries assist by taking on some of the local demands for research during prime daytime hours. While very entrenched in the virtual library world, most research questions with urgent deadlines still tend to come in as telephone or walk-in requests because they need immediate attention. Requests with more long-term deadlines are typically handled via e-mail correspondence directly with the researcher on the project.

Frequently we hear requests like 'I need you to search these keywords' or 'I need everything you can find on abortion', or 'I need any stories on this person'. Such statements do not reveal a great deal about the true information need and a reference interview begins. 'Tell me more about what you are doing with this story?' 'Are you looking for information about a particular case or person?' 'Do you need general news stories – or are you looking for court records or for financial reports?' 'Are you looking for information about abortion in a particular area of the United States or part of the world?' 'Is there a particular abortion case you are tracking?' 'Is this for an investigative piece or do you just need fairly recent information for background purposes?' 'What do you know about this person – where does he/she work?' 'Is there a particular issue or topic this person might have spoken or written about in which you are interested?'

Anne Mintz, Director of Information Services at Forbes Inc., has spoken of the essential neuroticism and other qualities of good online searchers:

> 'a really great searcher is both detail-oriented enough to be a cataloguer part-time, but also spunky enough to be a great reference librarian. That's why the best online searchers come from special libraries, especially smaller special libraries, where they have to do more than one thing in their jobs.' (Basch, 1993)

CNN gives researchers a buffet table of job responsibilities – it is the creative, resourceful, detail-oriented ones who survive at this party.

A partnership often develops between reporter and researcher as ideas generate a team energy and enhance the quality of the story and the direction in which it proceeds. Uncovering a bit of trivia or a potentially questionable activity from a person's past can be a red flag to the researcher – perhaps prompting a reporter to avoid the person as an on-air guest, ask different questions during the interview or take the story itself on a different tangent.

Navigating the world of online research resources

Following the reference interview the research librarian must weigh all the information just gathered and make a decision on the best way to fulfil the information need. A number of factors go into choosing which database to search when – factors familiar to any information specialist:

(i)   *Content and Comprehensiveness* – which services provide access to the specific publication or most comprehensive type of data being sought? Exclusive content deals between vendors and information providers may mean there is only one choice in terms of where to search, the *Wall Street Journal* and its exclusivity with DOW JONES INTERACTIVE for example.

(ii) *Ease of searching* – which online service provides the best search features to get to the desired information easily?

(iii) *Cost* – always a factor at CNN; if the same data is available in two different online services but one offers a better deal in terms of pricing that is a strong reason to use that service.

(iv) *Delivery options* – with so many staff members working out of remote locations delivery options must always be weighed, e.g. 'How can I get this to Brent Sadler in our Baghdad bureau?' Fax and express or regular mail delivery of research information, while still used, have been largely replaced by delivery via dedicated printers in remote locations or e-mail delivery to individual users.

(v) *Speed* – this actually is one of the most critical factors at CNN because there is so little lead-time with deadlines on the Research Desk. Breaking story mode forces the researcher to consider where the search can be run and results printed or delivered most quickly.

Power searching at CNN means being able to search across thousands of publications (what information professionals refer to as a multifile or group file) in one swift blow, a tactic which can be used with a variety of online database providers. Full-text source files are chosen for those 'needle in the haystack' questions. Some favourite and frequently searched group files in the LEXIS-NEXIS news library system include: *wires* (a group file of wire stories from around the world), *papers* (a group file of newspaper sources from around the world), *mags* (a group file of magazine sources), *script* (a group file of radio and television transcripts), and *majpap* (a group file containing major newspaper sources both domestic and international). Along with the News Library, the Business and Finance (BUSFIN), Bloomberg (BLMBRG), Company (COMPNY), Docket (DOCKET), Entertainment (ENTERT), Markets and Industry (MARKET), People (PEOPLE) and State Public Records (ALLREC) libraries are popular choices when searching LEXIS-NEXIS.

We often need to locate an individual who is connected to a breaking news story or is perhaps an expert on a topic in the news. Checking the Phonedisc CD-ROM, Who's Who sources, and other print or Web-based directories would be initial stops. Then sources like Autotrack would be consulted, or the Locator Library (FINDER) in LEXIS-NEXIS which provides access to P-TRAK and P-FIND people locator files along with military locators, death records and business and professional locators.

Another common way to use the power of searching a group file is with research on a particular geographic region: major database vendors make it possible to search publications from a particular region of the world or area of the United States. End-users, as well as information specialists, are finding group file searching to be a great feature. Often less familiar with publications in a given area than an information specialist would be, reporters working on regional stories love being able to select a preferred geographic area from a list (of group files) and run a search in the publications most likely to have reported on their topic or person of interest. For example, a reporter using DOW JONES INTERACTIVE can easily select all publications from Africa or the Middle East or the state of New York and search across all those sources swiftly. As more end-users gain direct experience with some of the frustrations of searching on the Internet this appreciation for group file search capability grows.

Some of the most highly prized database search features at CNN are listed below.

- The *Focus* command on LEXIS-NEXIS allows a researcher to combine different elements in a search strategy and then, when the retrieval exceeds 1000 stories, use the Focus command to search for a word not included in the original strategy or look specifically at one element at a time. A great money-saving feature for researchers, Focus creates a new subset without loss of the original strategy.

- The *atleast* feature on LEXIS-NEXIS and DOW JONES INTERACTIVE provides a quick way to request that a search term or name is mentioned in the text or segment fields at least a certain number of times. So, for example, *atleast7(space shuttle)* or *atl7(space shuttle)* would search for news stories which mention 'space shuttle' seven or more times.

- *Truncation* features make it easy to cover more distance with search terms and save time while constructing a search strategy. *Merg?* (DIALOG), *merg!* (LEXIS-NEXIS), or *merg$3* (DOW JONES INTERACTIVE) will each retrieve merge, merged, merging or merger in their respective database systems.

- *Proximity* searching is routinely used in online research to search for words physically close to each other within the text of an article or within a field. It is a critical search technique within the full-text databases we prefer. One could search *econom! w/15 (France or French)* in LEXIS-NEXIS to find the word economy (or economic) within 15 words of France or French. Or, one could search *hlead(econom! w/15 France or French)* to limit results of the search to stories with the word economy (or economic) within 15 words of France or French in the headline or lead segments of the article. In DOW JONES INTERACTIVE, a search of *econom$3 same (France or*

> *French)* would locate stories containing the words economy (or economic) and France or French within the same paragraph of a document.

- *Segment* searching or *field* searching is a favourite of searchers here, making it possible to search for terms in the headline or lead paragraph of a news story, for a byline, a publication title, a section or a company name perhaps.
- *Length* limitations (*length* > 1000 in LEXIS-NEXIS, or *wc* > 1000 in DOW JONES INTERACTIVE for example) help researchers narrow in on longer, more substantial news stories when the mission is to locate comprehensive background or biographical material.

Good researchers flow from one task to the next, often juggling several things at a time and keeping a close eye on deadlines as they go. Research results are delivered in hard-copy form locally or to a remote printer (CNN has dedicated printers for LEXIS-NEXIS research in our largest bureaux so that Atlanta researchers can send research instantly to those locations), by fax, express mail or e-mail. Results are generally full-text documents, but with more lead-time, or when a story is more investigative in nature, a reporter may want to see how much has been reported on a particular topic or person. Under those circumstances a citation list may be more appropriate, allowing the reporter to work with the librarian in selecting full-text documents.

While this sounds strange, there are times when a low retrieval during a search can actually be a desirable thing. Some things of course can sabotage your search – a bad spelling, searching with the wrong time frame or choosing the wrong database/files in which to search. But barring those problems, limited results can be good because they tell us the research topic has not been written about by every news organization under the sun. So, while an investigative reporter wants to see what other news groups have done, they may sometimes hope they have not done anything yet because this will mean a unique story or angle for CNN, a *scoop* in the news world.

Corporate research

In addition to research for CNN, the headquarter's Library also provides research services to corporate segments of the Turner Broadcasting System family such as Turner International, Strategic Planning, Turner Entertainment Network and Marketing. Typical research might involve looking at the Hispanic television market in the United States, cable television markets in Asia or Internet content providers in Europe. Some useful resources in the LEXIS-NEXIS system with these examples in mind would be the MARKET library, the Asia-Pacific library (ALLASI), or the Europe library (ALLEUR.)

Favourite research tools

Collection development issues are changing along with the arrival of new technologies. As news publications and research tools become available on the Internet and the sophistication of search engines increases a shift is happening with the format of some products. Print subscriptions of magazines and newspapers and those stocked in CD-ROM format on a networked server will migrate to Web-based subscriptions. Reference books will take on new life, becoming available to more people via Web-based versions.

Lists of some of the online services, reference books and periodicals used regularly at CNN which offer truly vital content are appended. Many of these are referred to in this text and there is also additional contact information. (Internet research tools and suggestions are being covered in a separate chapter so will not be addressed here.)

▶ RESEARCH ON THE DESKTOP

Charles S. Clark has written about his 'new vision of an up-to-the-minute, speed-of-light, electronic information nexus' (Clark, 1997, pp.460–461), and that seems an appropriate way to look at movement towards a virtual library. At CNN several factors play a part in this virtual surge. First and foremost, there are better desktop technologies. As CNN's newsroom has moved away from the dumb-terminal structure of the BASYS system and towards a PC-based newsroom system great strides are being made towards providing desktop access to Library systems and products. On the Archive side end-users are empowered to conduct their own searches for video images using a Netscape browser. Without needing to know any special search language reporters can visit the Library's Web site on the company intranet, fill out a search form with data such as keyword, reporter's name or date, and search across the full Archive database.

News research has used and tested many end-user research tools in the newsroom, some of them with only a handful of users, others with large groups of users. Products have included NEWSEDGE, LEXIS-NEXIS Universe (formerly LEXIS-NEXIS for Business), DOW JONES INTERACTIVE, LEXIS-NEXIS Statistical Universe, LEXIS-NEXIS InfoTailor, and LEXIS-NEXIS News Quickcheck. Native command-based searching with LEXIS-NEXIS has also been tested but did not prove a good option with novice or occasional users who were unable consistently to retrieve desired research data independently. Controlling search costs was also difficult. The most successful of these products have been NEWSEDGE – providing local area network access to real-time wire stories, internal news and other data – and the Web-based DOW JONES INTERACTIVE and LEXIS-NEXIS Universe products. With any type of end-user research tool we have seen a wide range of interest and skill among the targeted groups of users. Some quickly become proficient and self-sufficient. Others need considerably more guidance or simply do not have the time or interest in conducting their own research.

Desktop access creates the option for reporters to perform a quick search to verify a fact, identify a person, or pull together preliminary background information, freeing Library researchers from those ready reference questions and allowing them to concentrate on more complex questions and research projects.

One danger with end-user research is that a reporter may incorrectly assume no information is available on their topic, or believe all the bases have been covered when that is probably not true. A desirable result of more end-user searching is a corresponding increase in the sophistication of questions coming to the Research Desk as reporters and producers now might perform some preliminary research before beginning to dig into the topic and calling for deep research.

Moving away from products that require installing and maintaining client software on end-user workstations has opened up huge possibilities for both reporters and information specialists. The availability and ease of using new Web-based research tools means that information specialists can now dedicate time to training staff and functioning as research consultants. 'The challenge facing librarians and information professionals is how to package knowledge to make it usable by individual knowledge workers and communities of practice' (Chase, 1998, pp.20–21). The News Research Web site strives to live up to this challenge. The fast-paced news environment of CNN demands that information be packaged in a streamlined bundle guiding users easily to the best places to find the information they need and providing options for help when they have to go beyond the basics. Recommendations for top-notch Internet research Web sites, links to Web-based subscriptions like LEXIS-NEXIS Universe, DOW JONES INTERACTIVE, HOOVER'S, BRITANNICA ONLINE, GALE.NET etc. and help information for those products come together in a one-stop search environment. Training opportunities, again drawing on the teaching skills of librarians, start here also, for classes on news research, database searching and more.

▶ HEART AND PASSION

Another big news day at CNN: October 29, 1998. We are reporting live from Cape Canaveral to cover STS-95, the launch of Space Shuttle

Discovery, which will carry John Glenn into space a second time. Journalism icon Walter Cronkite has joined CNN as co-anchor for the event and there is the anticipated action and excitement of covering launch preparations. We have interviewed NASA officials and many who played roles during Glenn's historic 1962 space flight aboard Friendship 7 making him the first American to orbit the Earth. The Discovery launch is picture-perfect.

Yet on this day filled with thoughts of heroes and science and discovery, many of us around CNN find our thoughts drifting to one who is not with us today, one who would have most loved this story, our friend and colleague John Holliman. Only 49 years old when he died in a car crash on September 12, 1998, John joined CNN's original reporting team back in 1980. He became known to many around the world as one of CNN's 'boys in Baghdad' during the Persian Gulf War and of course more recently, for his splendid work on the space programme. John embodied the spirit, the passion, the dedication and willingness to go the extra mile that is such a part of CNN, qualities almost certainly as important as the information and video technologies upon which we rely. We will remember him always, and hopefully some small spark, some remnant, of John's passion and spirit will remain in our hearts.

This is CNN. Signing off.

▶ REFERENCES

Basch, R. (1993) *Secrets of the Super Searchers*. Wilton, CT: Eight Bit Books

Chase, R. (1998) Knowledge Navigators. *Information Outlook*, **2**(9), 17–26

Clark, C. (1997) The Future of Libraries. *CQ Researcher*, **7**(20), 459–479

CNN becomes first U.S. beta test site for Sony/EDS digital asset management system (1998) *Information Today*, 1 June, 39

Further reading

Basch, R. (1994) The 24-hour library. *Searcher*, **2**(7), 34–39

Chepesiuk, R. (1992) The CNN Library: Growing Up with Ted Turner. *Library Journal*, **117**(15), 31–33

Foley, J. (1997) Video Indexing Via Speech Recognition – Software will automate archiving. *Information Week*, 29 September, 104

Semonche, B. (1993) (ed.) *News Media Libraries: a management handbook*. Westport, CT: Greenwood Press

Recommended sources and publisher information

Periodicals

Atlanta Journal-Constitution. http://www.accessatlanta.com/ajc/

Business Week. http://www.businessweek.com

Fortune. http://www.cgi.pathfinder.com/fortune/

Financial Times. http://www.ft.com

Los Angeles Times. http://www.lat.com

New York Times. http://www.nyt.com

Newsweek. http://www.newsweek.com

Time. http://www.time.com

U.S. News and World Report. http://www.usnews.com

Washington Post. http://www.washingtonpost.com

Reference works and publisher information

Almanac of Famous People (1997) 6th edition. Detroit, MI: Gale Research Inc.
Gale Group (formerly Gale Research Inc.), 835 Penobscot Building, 645 Griswold
    Street, Detroit, MI 48226, USA. Tel: +1 313 961 2242.
    http://www.galegroup.com

Bartlett, J. (1992) *Bartlett's Familiar Quotations*. Boston, MA: Little Brown
Little, Brown Publishers, 1271 Avenue of the Americas, New York, NY 10020, USA.
    http://www.pathfinder.com/twep/little_brown/

Broadcasting & Cable Yearbook (1997) 2 vols. New Providence, NJ: R.R. Bowker.
R.R. Bowker, 121 Chanlon Road, New Providence, NJ 07974, USA. Tel: +1 888 269
    5372. http://www.bowker.com

CQ Researcher (1994). Washington, DC: Congressional Quarterly Inc.
Congressional Quarterly Inc., 1414 22nd Street, Washington, DC 20037, USA.
    http://www.cq.com

Current Biography Yearbook (1995). New York, NY: H.W. Wilson Co.
H.W. Wilson Co., 950 University Avenue, New York, NY 10452, USA. Tel: +1 718
    588 8400. http://www.hwwilson.com

Encyclopaedia Britannica (1998). Chicago, IL: Encyclopaedia Britannica.
Encyclopaedia Britannica, 310 S. Michigan Avenue, Chicago, IL 60604, USA. Tel: +1
    312 244 2112. http://www.eb.com

Facts on File publications. New York, NY: Facts on File.

Facts on File, 11 Penn Plaza, New York, NY 10001 USA. Tel: +1 800 322 8755. http://www.factsonfile.com

Guide to the Presidency (1996). Washington, DC: Congressional Quarterly Inc.

Hoover's Handbook of American Business (1998). 2 vols. Austin, TX: Reference Press. (Also their other publications.)

Jane's publications (e.g. *All the World's Aircraft, Armour and Artillery, Fighting Ships, Infantry Weapons, Naval Weapon Systems, Space Directory, Weapons Systems* etc.).
Jane's Information Group, 1340 Braddock Place, Suite 300, Alexandria, VA 22314, USA. Tel: +1 707 683 3700. http://www.janes.com

Permanent Missions to the United Nations (New York, NY: United States Mission to the United Nations.)

Politics in America, 1998: the 105th congress (1998). Washington, DC: Congressional Quarterly Inc.

Statistical Abstract of the United States (1997). Washington, DC: United States Department of Commerce, Economics and Statistics Administration, Bureau of the Census.

Washington Information Directory 1996–1997 (1997). Washington, DC: Congressional Quarterly Inc.

Who's Who in America, 1998 (1998) (and other Who's Who publications). Wilmette, IL: Marquis

Marquis Who's Who Inc., 121 Chanlon Road, New Providence, NJ 07924,USA. http://www.marquiswhoswho.com/default.htm

World Almanac & Book of Facts, 1998 (1998). Mahwah, NJ: World Almanac Books.
World Almanac Books, One International Boulevard, Suite 444, Mahwah, NJ 07495, USA.

Online database services and products

Autotrack (dialup and Web-based access to public records information). Database Technologies Inc.,
4530 Blue Lake Drive, Boca Raton, FL 33431, USA. Tel: +1 561 982 5000. http://www.dbtonline.com

Baseline (Web access to entertainment industry data and information). 838 Broadway, Fourth Floor, New York, NY 10003, USA. Tel: +1 212 254 8235. http://www.pkbaseline.com

CNN Interactive. http://www.cnn.com

Dialog (Web and dialup access). Dialog Corporation, 2440 W. El Camino Real, Mountain View, CA 94040, USA. Tel: +1 650 254 8800 or in Europe: Dialog

Corporation, 48 Leicester Square, London, WC2H 7DB UK. Tel: +44 171 930 6900. http://www.dialog.com

Disclosure Inc., 5161 River Road, Bethesda, MD 20816, USA. Tel: +1 301 951 1300. http://www.disclosure.com

Dow Jones Interactive (Web and software versions. Note that Dow Jones Interactive is focusing on Web product development, software versions will most likely not be enhanced after 1999). Dow Jones Inc., 200 Liberty Street, New York, NY 10281, USA. Tel: +1 212 416 2000. Coporate Web site: http://www.dj.com. Dow Jones Interactive Web site: http://www.djintereactive.com

Footage Net. http://www.footage.net

Hoover's Online (Web access to public and private company information, financial data, capsule summaries). Hoover's Inc., 1033 La Posada Drive, Suite 250, Austin, TX 78752, USA. Tel: +1 512 374 4500. http://www.hoovers.com

Hotline (Web access to political information and reference sources such as the Almanac of American Politics). National Journal, 1501 M Street, Washington, D.C. 20005, USA. Tel: +1 202 739 8531. http://nationaljournal.com/abouthotline.htm

LEXIS-NEXIS (software versions 4.0, 7.0; InfoTailor; News Quickcheck; LN Universe; LN Statistical Universe). 9443 Springboro Pike, P.O. Box 933, Dayton, OH 45401, USA. Tel: +1 937 859 5398. http://www.lexis-nexis.com

NewsEDGE (real-time delivery of newswires and other sources). 80 Blanchard Road, Burlington, MA 01803, USA. Tel: +1 781 229 3000. http://www.newsedge.com

Periscope (Web-based product which contains USNI Military database and special reports on military and defense issues). Periscope/United Communications Group, 11300 Rockville Pike, Suite 1100, Rockville, MD 20852, USA. Tel: +1 301 287 2700. http://www.usni.com

Westlaw/Information America (software version, Web product also available for legal and public records information). West Group 610 Opperman Drive, St. Paul, MN 55123, USA. Tel: +1 612 687 8000. http://www.westlaw.com

3 From Gopher to Guru: the changing role of a BBC Television programme information researcher

Annabel Colley

▶ INTRODUCTION

This chapter will illustrate how the nature of my job as an information researcher for the BBC's flagship current affairs programme, *Panorama*, has changed. This is as a direct result of the rise of the Internet and the increased use of online databases for journalistic research. The chapter is in four main sections. Section one will explain the different roles librarians and journalists play in putting together a programme. There are many different job titles in broadcasting and the variations between the roles of researcher, information researcher, assistant producer and producer will be explained as they apply to *Panorama*. The order of production tasks will also be discussed to aid understanding of the time scales involved in the making of an investigative weekly current affairs programme. The second section will cover the research tasks required and the gradual impact the Internet has had on both the investigative journalist and the information researcher. The third section features particular examples of Computer Assisted research from *Panorama* programmes, and will explain how the Internet is used for journalistic research in general. Finally, conclusions will be drawn regarding the changing future roles of librarians and journalists in television programme research in the light of new technology.

▶ DEFINITION OF ROLES AND THE PRODUCTION STAGES OF A *PANORAMA* PROGRAMME

Definition of roles

The way in which teams of producers, reporters and assistant producers work together on a weekly investigative current affairs programme differs from that of a daily BBC news bulletin. Throughout this chapter, the term 'journalist' will refer to producers, reporters and assistant producers and 'librarian' will be used as a broad term for information or programme information researchers. These definitions are based on personal experience at the BBC although job descriptions may differ slightly across the UK media in independent television, newspapers and magazines.

BBC information researchers

This chapter will refer to the BBC information researchers who work with text or printed material: books; newspaper cuttings; online databases; and the Internet. The librarians who are employed at the Information Research Centres are known as information researchers and do not necessarily hold professional library qualifications. These text-based librarians work at large Information Research Centres at Television Centre, and Broadcasting House, Bush House in London, and at smaller locations in the BBC regions. They serve production teams across the whole range of BBC output, as well as management, and are not allocated to any particular programme. The BBC also has film, videotape, sound and stills libraries (see chapter 12 in this volume) and there is a pronunciation unit and a written archives centre (see chapter 10) which employ librarians.

BBC programme information researchers

During the 1980s librarians from one press cuttings library began working on secondment to individual television programmes, e.g. *Panorama*, *On the record*, *The money programme* and *Newsnight*. They became known as programme information researchers. Today all programme information researchers work permanently for their respective programmes. They act as a link between the BBC libraries, external information sources and the programmes. Programme information researchers differ from their colleagues in the main BBC Information Research Centres in the depth of research they can provide.

In the 1990s, the BBC has operated an internal market policy known as Producer Choice. The programme information researchers have moved from working in the Information Research Centres that provide a service to programme makers, to becoming customers of these services. Programme information researchers are thus valuable contacts for the Information and Archives directorate when it comes to trying out new services, because they have seen programme making from both sides.

On an average day I might research up to ten subjects, from the history of Britain's relationship with Saudi Arabia to the implications of a clause of the latest Education Bill, or alternatively, a whole day can be taken to check that an on-screen graphic is expressing a statistic correctly. This may entail going through newspaper cuttings, or telephoning research centres such as the Institute for Fiscal Studies for expert analysis.

In a typical day, as the *Panorama* information researcher, I obtain secondary sources of information, i.e. those published, either in print or electronic form. On a daily basis, press cuttings obtained from national newspapers, magazines, and local papers and original newspapers from agencies are retained so that montages of headlines can be used on screen. Literature searches of the specialist and academic press are carried out and I use commercial online databases and CD-ROMs extensively. Particularly valuable sources are:

- LEXIS-NEXIS, a database with thousands of full text international news sources;
- JUSTIS: *Hansard* House of Commons proceedings online;
- Celex, a European parliamentary information database;
- Medline, a database of references to medical research.

Some of these services are available via the programme information researcher's own office PC or personal connection to commercial data-bases. The BBC Libraries and the excellent BBC Political Research Unit are both frequently used and an inter-loan service of publications from the British Library is also available through the BBC Information Research Library.

Another task of the *Panorama* information researcher is forward planning. I keep a diary of future events through liaison with outside organizations such as quangos, pressure groups, think tanks, government press offices, and parliamentary committees. This is supplemented by information from approximately 50 press releases that flood into the office daily: legislative timetables, upcoming major court cases and anything that may be predicted as newsworthy. These serve to spark off ideas for programmes.

Researchers

Researchers in broadcasting deal with primary sources of information, those obtained at source, or from the press officers of public figures and by private interviews over the telephone. This information may never have been printed, published or transmitted before. A researcher also writes briefs and submits programme ideas. Most television and radio researchers working in production teams are journalists on the first rung of the career ladder. Researchers sift through vast amounts of material in order to pinpoint exactly what is needed.

The special qualities required of an information researcher on an investigative programme like *Panorama* are very strong powers of persuasion, and an absolute belief in the story. Further essential qualities for any television researcher is an ability to think laterally and to come up with an unending supply of fresh ideas and treatments for single programmes, items or programme strands to jaded editors who have heard it all before. Researchers have to think creatively how an idea will transfer to screen in the form of a programme treatment.

Assistant producers

The assistant producers on *Panorama* carry out most of the research, writing briefs, and submitting programme ideas and treatments. They deal directly with the public to find case studies to illustrate the programme's topic and spend a lot of time on the telephone searching for political and academic pundits who are excellent communicators and who will look or sound good on screen. When approaching a topic from scratch they have to digest all the secondary material, especially press cuttings and journal articles, to become a mini expert or at least a good bluffer on, for example, the latest sentencing laws or educational theory. Whereas all assistant producers set up filming locations and organize shoots, the more experienced ones will also be directing short sequences or conducting interviews. All assistant producers are involved at each stage of the programme including the editing.

Producers

Producers on *Panorama* carry out some of the same tasks as assistant producers, but they have ultimate responsibility for their programme. They direct most of the sequences, work closely with the reporter on the script and have the difficult task of juggling all the elements including negotiating the budget. They also work closely with the programme editor and the videotape editors to decide on the overall look and feel of the programme. This demonstrates that journalists and librarians in broadcasting have a number of different job titles and responsibilities. Yet, how is all the research material put together into a coherent programme, and on Panorama, how long does it take?

The Production stages of a *Panorama* programme

Research and filming

Once the material has been collated, briefs are written and lists of contacts made, leads are followed up and locations found. This all falls under the umbrella of research. The producer writes the basic structure of a programme, setting out the main issues to be covered with the relevant sequences and interviews to be filmed. The budget is then set with the unit manager. Film crews are booked and despatched and together with the producer, assistant producers and reporter, they film all the sequences. An assistant producer working in a research capacity sometimes goes ahead of the crew, and may stay in locations for a period of anything up to a month making local contacts and building up relationships.

Post-production: editing, dubbing, and legal checks

Once the material has been filmed, it is logged, edited and assembled. The reporter usually writes the words to the pictures, although this is not always the case. Voice-overs and music are dubbed on to the pictures. Graphics are inserted, library footage added and copyright cleared. Once the content has been checked by lawyers, the programme is transmitted.

▶ THE DIFFERENT TYPES OF *PANORAMA* AND TIME SCALES

Our core team of producers, reporters and assistant producers will all be working simultaneously on many different programmes, as well as constantly developing ideas. A standard *Panorama* (although there really is no such thing) may take around seven or eight weeks from idea to screen – three weeks of research, two weeks filming and two weeks editing. In-depth investigations like Jane Corbin's investigation on Bosnian war crimes (War Crime, 1996) take months to make. Programmes that depend on exclusive access to people or institutions also take a long time. Particular programmes, such as that on the case of the British nurses in Saudi Arabia charged with killing Yvonne Gilford (The Nurses' Story, 1998) for example, depend on a skilled reporter building up an exclusive relationship with the contributor or their family. Other programmes which are a reaction to an unexpected news event such as the death of Diana Princess of Wales, or an IRA bombing, mean that almost the entire team is involved and a programme will be turned around in three or four days (and nights). Sometimes these reactive programmes are conducted as a studio debate, such as that on the subject of boxing which followed the death of James Murray (Boxing Debate, 1995). As the BBC flagship current affairs programme, *Panorama* has a duty to put out the right programme at the right time and also to be aware of the sensitivity of transmitting the wrong programme at a time of national disaster. These are the sort of editorial decisions are made every day. More recently the *Panorama* production team has created specials originating in the current affairs department such as a studio debate on drugs, a series on The Gulf War (1996) and *Provos* (1997), a series reported by Peter Taylor on the history of the provisional IRA.

▶ INVESTIGATIVE JOURNALISTS AND THE IMPACT OF THE INTERNET

The research needs of investigative journalists

The huge difference between investigative and straight journalism is the sheer amount of time, energy and resources allowed at the research stage. Research for investigative journalism never stops and because of this, demands for information are consistently high. As with all information in a news environment, books, cuttings, and government publications, etc are needed almost instantly, despite the fact that a programme such as *Panorama* takes weeks or months to make. This is because the information gathering stage at the beginning is to enable the producer to make a programme idea 'stand up'. The more time this stage takes, the more is at stake, and the less the idea can afford to be dropped. Also, lines of inquiry must be pursued and negative checks made in order to dismiss information, 'feed' the investigation and ensure that broadcast material is accurate.

When a subject is being investigated at Panorama, every angle and every piece of literature is studied, and every contact is spoken to initially. All research notes must be documented and kept as the team of experienced lawyers may need to call on them if a legal case follows or a complaint from a member of the public is upheld by the Broadcasting Standards Commission.

With regard to programme ideas, a '*Panorama* treatment' must be fresh, have something new to say, or present a topic in a different way by employing particular filming techniques. To prepare for an ideas meeting one must have done the groundwork to turn an abstract idea into a creative treatment – made telephone calls, developed a hook or special angle. A reporter with a reputation of some years standing may have obtained an influential interview, or have a leaked document. An assistant producer or researcher may have found some interesting case studies that illustrate the issue, or gained access to unpublished research. *Panorama* has a history of taking on untouchables. The producers and reporters need skill, experience and sheer courage to run the risk of potential libel actions. Their ability to see the wider picture may take the initial idea for a programme on to expose an injustice, jog the national conscience or prompt the courts and governments into action.

The impact of the Internet

Traditionally, information researchers dealt with secondary sources such as books or cuttings, and journalists dealt with primary ones, personal accounts, interviews, etc. Now, a great deal is available on the Internet, as hearsay, gossip, personal accounts, official and unofficial sources. News Librarian Nancy Garman makes the following observation:

> 'Isn't it great these days to go to a social event and have people actually understand what you do for a living? Usually they are anxious to tell you that they too search the Internet, America Online or Compuserve for information. Why, in just a few short hours online they've become online experts dipping into the wealth of information on the Internet . . . just when you thought you were about to get some respect as an online professional, it turns out that everyone thinks they can do your job themselves – better, faster, and more easily'. (Garman, 1996)

'Surfing' is not the same as properly conducted information research on the Internet. It is possible for everyone to now find some information, but is it the right information? Is it timely, accurate and from a quality source? Is it not only retrieved but also interpreted correctly? Proper electronic research takes training and experience, particularly when dealing with online databases or the Internet.

The role starts to change

Back in 1996, several of my colleagues found me searching the Internet for information previously obtained from the press cuttings files. Gradually, interest within the *Panorama* team grew and a number of members began to want to search for themselves. I started to circulate tips by e-mail about new sites where they could get ideas for stories, plan their location filming or obtain briefings from pressure groups. In the early days many programme makers did not know how to use e-mail, let alone feel it was their job to search the Internet when working in such a pressurized environment. At that time, not many national newspapers had online editions as they do today. Much of the press coverage about the World Wide Web and, in particular newsgroups, focused on its use by paedophiles and terrorists.

Despite this bad publicity about the Internet, with the search engine, DejaNews (http://www.deja.com), it became possible to find some interesting contributors as well as feedback on *Panorama* programmes from newsgroups which could be passed on to producers. The more contributors or comments that were found, the more the respect for both the Internet as a research tool, and for the researcher's ability to find the information gradually increased.

At the same time, American news librarians started to write about 'Computer Assisted Research and Reporting' (CAR). This new label, for what news librarians had been doing all along, seemed to be furthering the reputation and professionalism of librarians simply by offering the concept a new name. Many of the Americans writing about CAR were from a daily newspaper environment, and discussed transforming straight news stories into features by backing them up with hard evidence or data. What they were advocating, appeared to constitute part of an investigative researcher's normal work. One aspect of CAR is that American reporters, under more liberal Freedom of Information laws, can obtain and interpret public records electronically. This can transform journalism. UK laws are more limiting. However, CAR, and its potential use for streamlining the research process appealed to me.

In 1996 I ran a seminar entitled 'The Wired Journalist'. The hunger among production staff when it came to how to use the Internet was palpable. Almost two hundred people turned up from top level management and foreign correspondents to researchers. It appeared that suddenly news librarianship at the BBC was sexy. Interest took off after this seminar and people from all over the BBC began to call me for Internet research tips, and they continue to do so. In spring 1998, a 'Webwatcher' project was set up by News and Current Affairs to look at the most efficient ways of using the Internet for programme research, and the findings from this project continue to be assessed across the BBC News and Current Affairs Directorate.

The new *Panorama* editor Peter Horrocks who began in 1998 was particularly encouraging. He carried a respect and vision for the use of information technology in journalism. I instigated one-to-one training in Internet research techniques for the *Panorama* team. In addition to the main dialup service to NEXIS-LEXIS news database, I took out a subscription to LEXIS-NEXIS ReQuester (http://www.lexis-nexis.com/requester) an end user Internet version than enabled the *Panorama* team to search for over 5000 full text news sources themselves. This freed me to facilitate the services, train the staff to use electronic sources, and to really think about accessing all the information that is available in commercial databases and on the Internet. *Panorama*'s current editor is keen to enable journalists to search databases for themselves and with NEON (BBC News Information Online), the new Information and Archives internal database of 80 full text newspaper and magazines now on the BBC intranet, it is an unstoppable development. The more that journalists can be taught to carry out routine searching of the Internet and online databases for themselves, the more time I can spend on in-depth research and additional journalistic input into the programme itself. The more journalistic the input, the more one is expected to present and develop ideas for programme content, write up ideas and to find potential interviewees and locations.

In four years, my role of information researcher at *Panorama* has changed from being someone who ran up and down the road to the cuttings library in the next building, to becoming the first point of contact for all aspects associated with CAR and something of an Internet Guru. Today, I maintain a CAR site on the BBC intranet and work with BBC multimedia training in developing and delivering some of their Internet research courses.

► COMPUTER ASSISTED RESEARCH AND REPORTING AT *PANORAMA*

Turning a hunch into an investigation

Since 1995, more and more research has been carried out using the Internet. The potential of the Internet was particularly visible in an environment where commercial databases had been used heavily. Databases such as LEXIS-NEXIS offer a thoroughness that is particularly suited to investigative journalism, and a database search can turn a hunch into an investigation.

Case study 1: The Men Who Kill Children, transmitted 18 September 1995

This programme focused on paedophiles, the central issue being that because of a loophole in the Mental Health Act, dangerous psychopathic child killers are dealt with by the penal system. In prison, they may receive no effective treatment for their condition and are then released back into the community to re-offend. A number of very good case studies existed to illustrate this problem, but the team needed to prove that these were not just a few unfortunate examples which had slipped through the net. It was suspected that many paedophiles who kill children had a history of offences against children but evidence was needed to prove this. I was set the task of documenting every child murdered in the UK in the last twenty years and answering a number of criteria. A list was required containing the names of the murderers, the relationship of the murderer to the victim (they had to be a stranger), and whether the murderer had a history of sexual offences against children. A week of telephoning round all the police press offices in the UK and ploughing through all the press cuttings did not produce a really definitive list and many of the police forces just did not keep a comprehensive list of all the types of sensitive information needed.

Searching on LEXIS-NEXIS brought to light the name of a unique internal database held by one of the UK police forces, detailing every child murder in the UK. A prompt telephone call and a lot of persuasion later, we negotiated for one of the assistant producers to interrogate, under police supervision, the CATCHEM (Central Analytical Team Collating Homicide Expertise and Management) database at Derbyshire Police. It was then possible to ask the sort of questions that only computerized sources can answer when there are a number of different variables. From information on the CATCHEM database of child homicide it was deduced that out of 38 people convicted of child murders in the past decade, 24 or almost 2/3rds, had previous records of sexual and/or violent offences. Thus, using computers had made the journalism more definitive as the figures could be backed up with a police source. This underpinned the central point of the programme.

Case study 2: Greenhouse Wars, transmitted 1 December 1997

A programme was produced in the lead up to the Kyoto climate conference, on the politics of cutting carbon dioxide emissions. Early research started by looking at the carbon lobby – oil companies and car manufacturers who deny the seriousness of global warming. What were the effects of the lobby on the international negotiations to cut global carbon dioxide emissions? There was a hunch that US research projects denying global warming had some interesting backers but it was important to get to the bottom of who was funding which scientists to deny the existence of global warming. It would have taken many days to establish these facts by telephone. Various searches on the World Wide Web ('carbon lobby', 'global warming' etc.) came up with the CLEAR site (Clearing House on Environmental Advocacy and Research: http://www.ewg.org/pub/home/clear/clear.html) and this linked to the environmentally friendly sounding Global Climate Coalition. The CLEAR site had a fantastic chart (now so large that it has become a database on the site) of all the individuals that the respective oil and motor companies were funding to deny the seriousness of global warming. It gave names, addresses and phone numbers of all the companies, and all the individuals – an investigative journalist's dream right there in the public domain. *Panorama* went to the USA and interviewed someone from CLEAR and one of the scientists found on the site. It transpired that the Global Climate Coalition is running a very effective lobby of TV meteorologists and this in turn helps to influence many Americans to deny the existence of global warming.

Databases can provide an international angle on a national story or indeed a local angle on a national story, featuring case studies or contributors from small local newspapers. A database search is also an excellent way of finding potential filming locations. A simple search can discover whether a story has been over- or under-covered internationally. By adding the power of the Internet to commercial databases, very powerful research methods exist indeed. For every story on *Panorama*, electronic sources will be searched at some stage. If used efficiently, electronic research can be done in a fraction of the time taken by conventional methods and often discovers information which would never have been found otherwise.

Finding programme contributors

Some *Panorama* contributors, both academics and members of the public, have been found via bulletin boards on the World Wide Web, newsgroups mailing lists, and e-mail. In May 1998, a programme was broadcast on the 'Diana industry' and the running of the Princess of Wales Memorial Fund (The Diana Dividend). An American woman who had been found via an Internet bulletin board was featured on the programme because she owned fifteen Princess of Wales dolls. It is very unlikely that she would have been discovered through other means, certainly given the same short space of time. The programme also featured another key interviewee, Alishia Munday from the US magazine *Adweek*. She was discovered on a CNN transcript on LEXIS-NEXIS.

Newsgroups are the area on the Internet where the public discusses topics and exchange ideas and tips. Potential case studies or programme contributors can be found by searching communities of newsgroups by subject. It is also possible to search them for comments and feedback on programmes. For example, reactions from British teachers to comments that the Chief Inspector of Schools had made were obtained in an interview about school standards. Newsgroups quite often give quirky information that is simply not available anywhere else. They are particularly useful for grass roots discussions on, for example, a new disease or drug, and hearsay and informal networks of information on any topic. Potential contributors for a variety of programmes have been found, from

Kawasaki disease, a rare heart disease in children, to the effects of rail privatization on the consumer.

Tapping into informal networks of professionals for ideas and support

Mailing lists on the Internet tend to be used by professionals and academics and are often more controlled, and on the whole more serious than newsgroups. Subscribing to a mailing list is therefore a useful means of monitoring any subject, tracking story ideas and finding new angles. Carefully chosen mailing lists can be found by searching one of the mailing list search engines such as: http://www.Liszt.com. Journalists can use mailing lists as a form of informal networking to tap into the latest trends and developments in their profession and they can also support one another by asking international colleagues for information. The major benefit of mailing lists is that they free the individual from surfing, but at the same time, pertinent information is being pushed directly to a mailbox. For example, when the growth of antibiotic resistance to disease was being researched for a programme, I took out a subscription to PROMED   (http://www.healthnet.org/programs/promed.html#sub)   an emerging infectious diseases mailing list. This is run by the World Health Organization. Subscribing to a number of lists enables me to keep up to date with new Web sites, in particular Newslib, an international mailing list for news librarians to exchange ideas. This is a very speedy process. Within hours of posting a request onto Newslib for a particular article or database to search on, someone will have shown the right direction.

Finding experts

If journalists do not wish to commit themselves to a regular mailing list subscription, then they need only use their e-mail on an *ad hoc* basis to call for expertise or ongoing research by using the Expertnet (http://www.cvcp.ac.uk/expertnet.html) service for journalists. One e-mail message sent to the Expertnet service will go to every UK university. The press office of the Committee of Vice Chancellors and Principals of the UK universities then forwards the e-mail and replies take from two to 24 hours. Experts have been found on football finance and sponsorship, the potential effects of the computer millennium bug on UK banks, future research into childhood obesity in the UK, and agricultural consultants for a programme on farming, to name just a few. By sending a similar request for expertise to Profnet on the Internet (http://www.profnet.com), it is possible to find international experts. Profnet offers the choice of sending a request for

expertise to think tanks, national laboratories and professional associations as well as up to 700 universities.

Obtaining briefings and overviews

The World Wide Web is very useful starting point as a beginner's guide
to a topic. It is possible to find the salient issues and an overview or a
chronology on any subject from ecology to formula one motor racing.
The Internet is particularly strong in the areas of the environment, medi-
cine and US political information. *Panorama* producers and researchers
have to come to new subjects frequently and absorb vast amounts of
information quickly. This usually entails reading and condensing press
cuttings into briefings, but quite often a quality source on the Internet
will offer a readily compiled briefing. Sites such as that of the Department
of Education and Employment (http://www.dfee.gov.uk) feature briefings
on policy issues and all Government sites provide the ability to search
archived press releases, a useful source for ministerial quotes. Other useful
sites are run by US journalists or journalism educators, such as: the Poynter
Institute (http://www.poynter.org/research/reshotres.htm) in the USA; the
United States Embassy Information Service (http://www.usia.gov); and
most of the quality international newspapers. The *Washington Post*
(http://www.washingtonpost.com) has special report pages on running
stories, the House of Commons Library have a useful site of briefings
written for MPs (http://www.parliament.uk/commons/lib/research/rp98/
rp98.htm) and BBC News Online (http://www.bbcnews.co.uk) has a search
facility that enables one to view BBC briefings and special reports on any
news topic going back to November 1997.

Obtaining full-text source documents

The time and expense of sending despatch bikes all over London are slowly
being reduced by using the Internet to retrieve an increasing number of full
text primary source documents. Hard copy is gradually being replaced for
those who want rapid access to documents with the use of Adobe Acrobat.
This piece of software enables documents to be downloaded in exactly the
same layout and format as the hard copy, complete with charts and
pictures. OFSTED (Office for Standards in Education: http://www.ofsted.
gov.uk/ofsted.htm) has all its reports on its Web site. It also possible to
download the full text of a large number of Parliamentary Acts and Bills
and HM Prisons inspection reports. Downloading foreign source documents on the Web is especially cost-effective. The range of American
Governmental publications is enormous and it may be in the future that
official publications become only available in electronic form.

Real-time news

The Internet is a superb place for obtaining real-time news in the form of news wires. Most of the newspapers and news sites like CNN, MSNBC and the BBC feature live news. The BBC News site has a news ticker that can be downloaded to remain on a desktop whilst other applications are being used, and which alerts the user to live news as it happens. Historically, in the event of a major incident, journalists have relied upon exclusive access to wire services run by the major news agencies like Reuters and Press Association (PA). The BBC continues to have access to all the international wire services, but this is now supplemented by Internet sources. The Internet also means an end to journalists' privileged access to information since the public can now view some news agency copy. The public also has more power in choosing what type of news it wants, and is able to more interactively contribute to discussions and bulletin boards on news Web sites. Recently, when a major aircrash happened in the USA, Radio 5 Live was the first to break the story because they were listening to an account of it by an eyewitness on the local American radio station on the Internet. For monitoring live coverage of court cases like the trials of British nanny Louise Woodward, or O.J. Simpson, the Internet has become the first port of call.

Forward planning and finding story ideas

Predicting the news is a constant concern in investigative journalism. An increasing number of electronic forward planning services allowing keyword search, is making predicting as well as compiling and distributing ideas an easier task. Many of the services are Internet versions of printed ones. News Ahead (http://www.newsahead.com), Foresight (http://www.fifi.co.uk), Amiplan (http://www.amiplan.com), and Future Events News Service (http://www.hubcom.com/fens) are all subscription services now available on the Internet. There are a growing number of public relations companies putting their press releases on to searchable archives on the Web and some company Web sites will deliver releases by e-mail. Pressure groups, charities and most major organizations' Web sites are beginning to replace the telephone and fax machine as a means to communicate basic information. A good example of this is on the Alcohol Concern Web site (http://www.alcoholconcern.org.uk). Previously, updating facts and statistics would have involved ringing a press officer, now one can access the information directly from their Web site. Although some press releases are passed on to producers, investigative journalists differ in their use of press releases to journalists on daily newspapers or news bulletins, as they look for long-term ideas rather than for straight coverage. Once information is in the public domain, particularly if it is news about a company or product, it is essentially old news for investigative journalism.

Keeping in touch with journalists on the road

For keeping in touch with journalists who are on location, the Internet is ideal. For example, when one of the senior reporters on *Panorama* was in Jerusalem researching a programme on the Middle East peace process, she was able to receive, via the Internet, a digest of the Hebrew press in translation. Admittedly, it had to be faxed but the service was found via the Internet. This saved on the time and cost of getting a foreign fixer to buy papers and translate the information.

Is it always appropriate to use the Internet?

One of the golden rules about using the Internet as a research tool is to realise that it *is* just another research tool. The Internet has certainly not (yet) replaced other traditional methods but it is useful to apply a list of criteria to assess when to use the Internet for research and when to go elsewhere. The criteria I use at *Panorama* are similar to the guidelines of information broker Mary Ellen Bates. She explains them in a speech given to the Internet '98 conference in Copenhagen, the transcript of which featured on her Web site (http://www.batesinfo.com/net-vs-fee.html). Further information on quality control is at: http://www.bbc.co.uk/education/webwise/know/quality_l.shtml.

Evaluating quality

Finding the right information that is accurate, timely, objective and from a reliable source is a governing factor for librarians and journalists alike. The Internet breaks all the rules because of its ability to carry self-publications. As with traditional methods of research, a range of sources from across the political spectrum should be consulted. The journalist's golden rule of not relying on one source is never more applicable than in the electronic age: it is important to always back up an Internet source with other methods. However, to a large extent the Web sites of recognized government bodies and organizations can be relied upon. As a result of the interactive nature of the Internet, it is often possible to e-mail the author of a page or site for verification. If genuine, they can become good contacts for other Web resources on their subject.

Saving time: using corporate intranets and push technology

One of the major (and valid) complaints from journalists who want to use the Internet for research is that is too slow, particularly in a daily news environment. The telecommunications infrastructure should improve with time but effective training also gives quicker and more accurate results. For professionals in high pressure work environments with little time to search the Web, filtered information, in the form of favourite sites or bookmarks, maintained via an internal company intranet should be exploited to the full. Ideally, this information should be compiled by the corporate library or by an individual information researcher. At the BBC, the corporate intranet, Gateway, began as a place to read the staff magazine, *Ariel*, to find out about jobs or read policy documents. Gradually, the realisation has spread that the BBC intranet can be used to share valuable programme research material. It is an ideal place for programme makers to access in-house research databases, and an efficient way for them to link to readily-compiled WWW sources. The Information and Archives Directorate and the BBC Political Research Unit are currently developing projects along these lines.

The real future for the Internet as a research tool in journalism is exploiting the increasing push services, known previously as SDI (http://www.journalismnet.com/services.htm). Time is thus not wasted surfing the Web and information is pushed to personal mailboxes in the form of tailored newspaper headlines and information from carefully chosen mailing lists.

▶ JOURNALISTS AND LIBRARIANS – THE FUTURE OF THE RELATIONSHIP

The chapter will conclude by looking at the differing approaches to information gathering of journalists and the librarians who work with them. Their ultimate aim is the same: to get the story broadcast or printed. Given this, how can they work together to the ultimate benefit of all?

The different approaches

If the ultimate aim of journalists and librarians is the same – the dissemination of information – how do they differ? Essentially, the answer is in their approaches to the gathering of information. Journalists, particularly investigative journalists, protect their sources whereas librarians share, co-operate, and advertize their sources to others. This is the ultimate dilemma of the librarian working in a journalistic environment, particularly an investigative one. An investigative journalist cannot always go to the most obvious source for information, since that source may then be alerted that they are being investigated. A librarian, not carrying the burden of secrecy, can head directly to the quickest source. The journalist likes to approach direct primary sources, feeling that they are getting to information first and that it is straight from the horse's mouth. A journalist will not share ideas with colleagues, the scoop must be their own. Many journalists, in particular those in daily news, see a library as a second-hand source; in the USA, newspaper press cuttings libraries were referred to for years as 'the morgue', carefully guarded by librarians. This attitude is less prevalent among investigative journalists where the depth and quality of research is paramount, and the authority and attention to detail that libraries can supply is an essential element.

In the USA there is a move, particularly among newspaper libraries, to call librarians 'news researchers'. They work closely with journalists teaching them Computer Assisted journalism techniques. In the UK, researchers in newspapers and broadcasting tend to be journalists at the beginning of their career, and librarians work separately from them.

How we can work together in the future information age

One of the key findings of a recent UK study on journalists' use of the Internet was that it has blurred the distinction between primary and secondary sources of information (http://www.soi.city.ac.uk/~pw/ji_home. html). My experience of searching commercial databases as a librarian enables me to do in-depth Internet searches. Many journalist colleagues do not have the time or inclination to do in-depth Internet and database research but they will carry out quick basic searches. Librarians are skilled at finding information while journalists are skilled at interpreting the information. It is likely that many journalists do not want to be overwhelmed with the huge range of information sources available. Librarians are good at editing the information overload, pushing only what is required towards the journalist. Good journalists have highly developed powers of persuasion when dealing with people, and an eye for a good story. Librarians can provide background to a straight news story. In the future, news will continue to be increasingly analytical as different media for broadcasting continue to be developed. News Online such as that found on the BBC's online site is deeper and provides more background analysis to a news story than can be found either in newspapers, or on television and radio news. Librarians are needed to provide that background, and to help to organize archive news Web sites.

Most broadcasters, and certainly those with their own Web sites have separate editorial guidelines for the provision of their online news services. How many of them also have guidelines for the evaluation of Internet research sources that they may use in compiling the news? Librarians with their experience of evaluating reference sources for quality accuracy and currency are ideally placed to help to develop these guidelines for Internet research.

The demise of the librarian? Further new roles

The hype about the Internet is that all the information possibly needed is out there on the Internet, and anyone can access it. Predicting the end of libraries and librarians is a fashionable pastime of the media, however, exactly the opposite is true. Librarians are needed more than ever to organize, index and catalogue the chaos of the Internet. A number of high quality subject gateways and indexes on the Internet are compiled by librarians. These include BizEd (http://www.BIZED.ac.uk), a business and economics gateway, and SOSIG, the Social Sciences Information Gateway (http://www.SOSIG.ac.uk).

Journalists are able to search *Global Books-in-Print* and find citations to journal articles on the Internet, rather than going through the Information Research Centre. They can be alerted when books are due out on a topic via e-mail and may even choose to bypass the library and use one of the document delivery services such as Uncover (http://www.uncWeb.carl.org) to get some of their journals delivered via the Internet. When a journalist comes to the library armed with full bibliographic details, a lot of the traditional librarianship tasks have been done. There are now many new roles for media librarians to replace these: information editor; intranet developer; Web site editor; and Internet trainer to name but a few.

Conclusion: is the information researcher a librarian or journalist?

This chapter has described the tasks carried out by the information researcher on *Panorama* and how at times this involves journalistic research. Therefore, the role runs across the two different professions of librarian and journalist. My job has moved away from traditional librarianship so that now the key skills of librarianship are applied to journalism. However, although working very closely with journalists, I am first and foremost an information professional.

Only two years ago most of my time was spent in the BBC press cuttings library ploughing through press cuttings files. Now because of the Internet, time spent at the Information Research Centre has been reduced by about half. Again because of the Internet, people value the skills of organizing the information overload better than ever before. As more information is delivered to the desktop, I am more visible, rather than being hidden in the bowels of the library going through cuttings files. The implementation of the BBC News Information Online (NEON) in 1999 now means even more work at my desktop and even more training and facilitating at *Panorama* and beyond.

▶ REFERENCES

Boxing Debate (1995) *BBC Panorama*. Presenter John Humphries, Producer Mike Robinson. 23 October 1995

Garman, N. (1996) Finding the Right Answer at the Right Cost. *Online*, **20**(2), 51. http://www.onlineinc.com/onlinemag/marOL/invert3.html

Provos (1997) *BBC1*. Reporter Peter Taylor, Producer Andrew Williams. 23 September–14 October 1997

The Gulf War (1996) *BBC1*. Producer Eammon Matthews. 7 January–16 January 1996

The Nurses' Story (1998) *BBC Panorama*. Reporter John Ware, Producer Nick London. 21 March 1998

The Diana Dividend (1998) *BBC Panorama*. Reporter Jane Corbin, Producer Mark Dowd. 21 May 1998.

War Crime (1996) *BBC Panorama*. Reporter Jane Corbin, Producer Andrew Williams. 11 March 1996

▶ APPENDIX: ANNOTATED 'WEBLIOGRAPHY' OF INTERNET SITES OF USE TO UK JOURNALISTS, AND INFORMATION PROFESSIONALS

Major starting points for news on the Internet

BBC News Online

Text, audio, video, stills and graphics are intertwined to tell stories in a unique way. Big set-piece issues are supplemented with background detail and expert analysis. Hot topics opened up for public debate in 'talking point'. Follow the instructions on the site for downloading a live news ticker that can be personalized and sits on the desktop. http://news.bbc.co.uk

Journalism Net

Web page of Canadian journalist Julian Sher has many useful Computer Assisted journalism links and sections on UK news. http://www.journalismnet.com

News Now

This claims to be the first news headline aggregator service just for the UK. There is a news feed updated every five minutes. UK sources include FT, BBC, ITN Sky and sporting news. The live feed box enables the user to run an updating window of headlines over other applications as they work. http://www.newsnow.co.uk/NewsFeed.htm

Online News Articles

A useful article on finding news on the Web. http://www.researchbn22.com/articles/420NewsArchives.html

UKPlus

Sites are reviewed and edited by a team of experienced journalists for relevance to UK Internet users. Especially useful for linking to all the UK regional papers. UKPlus has a mailing list to keep the user up to date on new information on the site. http://www.ukplus.com

Major UK subject gateways to Internet resources

These well-indexed and organized subsets of the Internet are useful starting points in particular subject areas. They are maintained by UK librarians or academics who apply quality criteria for inclusion into their site.

All subject areas – BUBL

Highly organized index to Web sites by librarians using Dewey subject (library) classification. Reliable. http://bubl.ac.uk

Business and economics – BizEd

This major subject gateway to quality UK business and economic information is maintained by University of Bath and aimed at the UK academic community. There is much of use to all. It has a chart with direct links to all FTSE 100 companies, a review of UK high street bank sites and a search facility. http://www.bized.ac.uk

Crime and home affairs – The Penal Lexicon

This is a subscription service but it is well worth it. An excellent starting place for research on prisons, penal affairs, crime and police. Links to all sorts of goodies, pressure groups, prisoners families, Government documents, digests of the press and police sites in the UK and abroad. http://www.penlex.org.uk

Medical – OMNI

The Online Medical Networked Information is the UK's gateway to high quality biomedical Internet resources (includes links to search *BMJ*, the *Lancet* etc. via Medline). http://www.omni.ac.uk

Social sciences-SOSIG

Social Sciences Information Gateway lists quality sites and is run by Plymouth University. Search facility. http://www.sosig.ac.uk

News only search engines

http://www.newsindex.com
http://nt.excite.com
http://www.totalnews.com

UK only search engines

Excite UK

Netscape teamed up with Excite to provide this UK-specific navigation service offering nine channels on business and investing, sport, technology, entertainment, lifestyle, news, travel, motoring and weather. The service features a top news headlines section. http://www.excite.co.uk

Search UK

A British company runs this service which claims to cover at least 95 per cent of all UK domains. http://www.searchuk.com

The UK Directory

This enables you to search for strictly UK only Web sites in all areas. It has a useful bi-monthly print edition too. http://www.ukdirectory.co.uk/full_search.htm

Yahoo UK

http://www.yahoo.co.uk

Yellow Web

An index type search engine from the *Yellow Pages* UK people. http://www.yell.co.uk

Reference information and UK guides

192 Telephone Number searches

Enables reverse telephone number and conventional searches of some European Countries including the UK. Small fee charged per search. http://www.192.com

BT UK Telephone Directory

http://www.bt.com/phonenetuk

CountyWeb

Local news, sport contacts and more by UK county. Click on interactive map or search by area or county name. http://www.countyweb.co.uk

Knowhere – a user guide to Britain

This is a bit different from the standard tourist guides as it has been compiled by locals. 500+ towns can be searched on the site which lists shops and restaurants but also street entertainers and other more unusual information. This site is useful when planning filming trips and it is necessary to find out where, for example, is the best place in a town for teenagers to hang out. It also has a nice feature: famous people who were born or lived in the town. http://www.knowhere.co.uk

Mulitmedia Mapping – interactive atlas of Great Britain

Enter the name of a British City, town, village or street name (London only) and it will show a map of the area which can be zoomed in on. What is good about this site compared to other mapping sites is that it also automatically links to local hotels, businesses and Web sites based in the areas chosen. http://uk.multimap.com/map/places.cgi

Scoot

A *Yellow Pages* style site to search for UK businesses and companies by name/type of business and location. However, it seems to be more thorough than the electronic *Yellow Pages*. http://www.scoot.co.uk

Up My Street

Award winning site set up initially for the use of estate agents. Enables you to plot house prices, crime clear-up rates and school performance against national UK average by UK postcode. It is also possible to find out local MPs' attendance rates and links to their *Hansard* speeches. By entering a UK postcode, everyone from plumbers to solicitors can be found in a given area. http://www.upmystreet.com

UK Hotels and Bed & Breakfasts

Search view and book by area and price range. http://www.theaa.co.uk/hotels/index.html

UK newspapers with full-text archives

Full text Internet archives of UK papers are growing but still somewhat limited. Most rely on commercial database services. The national daily with the best Internet Archive is *The Daily Telegraph* with issues going back to 1994. Searching the full text is free and it has good links but the user must register first. The other national dailies all have sites but with limited archives. Some choose to group previous articles into topics that can be searched. Listed here are four newspaper groups or individual papers with Internet archives.

Belfast Telegraph

The archive dates back to November 1995. Users can search the archive free of charge to identify if there are stories of interest before accessing the complete story. In order to access the full text of stories on the archive, users have to apply for a password. http://www.belfasttelegraph.co.uk/archive/search.html

Daily Telegraph

http://www.telegraph.co.uk

Newsquest Lancashire

This is the largest publisher of UK regional newspapers in England. Online versions of 11 newspapers in the Lancashire area are available on this site and there is also a searchable and browsable news archive. http://www.newsquest.co.uk/archive

Nottingham Evening Post archive

http://www.nottingham-online.co.uk

Sunderland Echo archive

http://www.sunderland.com/echo/index.html

Televisual

This site offers subscription services to fully indexed archives in a range of British newspapers. Includes the Mirror Group, the *Northern Echo*, the *Scotsman* and *Scottish Daily Record* groups, the *Western Daily Press* and *Bristol Evening Post*, and the *Newcastle Chronicle*. More to be added and all the archives go back to 1994. A free 24 hour trial to Isearch and CD Online which carry the service is also available. http://www.televisual. co.uk/access/televisualonline.html

UK press reviews/digests

For a summary of UK Press coverage try the following sites:

Anorak Press Review

This light-hearted look at the UK press breaks papers down into 'The Broads' and 'The Tabs'. http://www.anorak.co.uk

The British Media Review

Maintained by the Information Department of the British Embassy in New York, it takes a topical approach. There is a limited archive of running issues but no search engine. http://www.britain-info.org/bis/mediarev/ mediarev.htm

Current affairs TV programmes

Dispatches

The investigative weekly news programme forms part of the C4 site. There are edited transcripts of previous themes the TV team has tackled, as well as follow-up information since their transmission. Archived reports include programmes on the Louise Woodward case, cervical smears, tax avoidance and new drugs and their impact on resources. http://www.channel4. com and carry out an advanced search on 'dispatches'.

Business information sources

aRMadillo

This holds UK company information and trademark services. Order a UK company report and accounts for £14, or search the disqualified directors database. http://www.rmonline.com

Business information sources on the Internet

Comprizes a very comprehensive list of news and other sources compiled by the Department of Information Science, University of Strathclyde. Not only Web sites but mailing lists and push technology too are included – an excellent starting point. http://www.dis.strath.ac.uk/business/newsuk. html

Current Annual Reports Online

Gives access to UK Company Annual reports (not full accounts) online. http://www.carol.co.uk

UK Business Park

UK business news headlines are arranged by industry and company. The headlines can be browsed or there is an e-mail news service to subscribe to for 50p a week following the free trial. http://www.ukbusinesspark. co.uk/index

UK Government and politics

Citizens Online Democracy

Find UK political opinion from individuals. Read serious debate (some from MEPs) on topics like European integration http://www.democracy. org.uk. Another good source for finding public opinion on political and current affairs topics is on the BBC News Online 'talking points' area. http://news2.thls.bbc.co.uk/hi/english/talking-point/

House of Commons Information

A treasure trove of information on the Commons and the people who work there. The FAQ section is still being developed, but has a handy 'Who is my MP?' section as well as a teasing series of queries on the Gunpowder Plot. Elsewhere surfers can access basic information such as the state of the parties in the Commons, MPs and their responsibilities and details about the Cabinet and Opposition Front Bench. http://www. parliament.uk/commons/CMINFO.htm

House of Commons Library Research Papers

Contains briefings written by the House of Commons Librarians for political researchers and MPs on hot political topics. http://www.parliament.uk/ commons/lib/research/rp98/rp98.htm

Official Documents. HMSO the Stationery Office

Contains all current bills before parliament, all public Acts since 1996, some of which are in full text and all Parliamentary Papers. http://www. official-documents.co.uk/menu/uk.htm

Search Hansard proceedings of Parliament

Written and verbal questions, answers and speeches in the Commons and Lords by speaker or subject (last few years only). Search results are full text. http://www.parliament.uk/parliament/index.htm

Search UK Electoral Role with Cameo (fee based)

Search the UK electoral role via this substantial subscription service. http:// cameo.bvdep.com

UK education sources

Mailbase

Comprizes electronic discussion lists for the UK Higher Education community. Some lists are moderated or closed, but it is possible to browse archives to get ideas, search for people, or subjects, and generally use the 2057 mailing lists to find UK academics or research. http://www.mailbase.ac.uk

Search all UK Higher Education Establishments

If looking for a University or specific departments within universities in the UK, this is the place to start. Contains a search facility. http://acdc.hensa.ac.uk/

University of Wolverhampton UK sensitive map of academic institutions

This is one of the easiest and best ways of locating and linking to a British University. http://www.scit.wlv.ac.uk/ukinfo/uk.map.html

European news and information

Central Europe Online

This site offers a broad range of news, both international and local, plus demographic-geographic information on Hungary, Poland, the Czech Republic, Romania, Slovakia and Slovenia. As well as text, news is available in RealVideo. http://www.centraleurope.com

Euro Documentation Centre at Glasgow University

This is one of the allocated documentation repository libraries for all European Union official publications. The best feature of this site is the link to Useful European WWW sites. http://www.gla.ac.uk/Library/Depts/MOPS/EU/index.html

Europa – The European Parliament Site

Multiple-language site with mountains of background detail on the community. The news strand is actually a series of press releases. There is also a calendar of events, statistics, Euro rates, and an ABC guide to the EU. Follow the links to Rapid – the flexible database of European

Commission Press releases where current and archived press releases can be searched. http://europa.eu.int

Europages

Search for business and company information in Europe. http://www.europages.com

Radio Free Europe/Radio Liberty

Daily news from Eastern and Central Europe gathered by correspondents and regional specialists of Radio Free Europe/Radio Liberty. It claims to provide more immediate and accurate information about events in these countries than virtually any other source. Certainly many of the stories here would be hard to find in mainstream sources. It is possible to browse news headlines and archives or regular headlines can be received for free by joining the RFE Newsline mailing list. http://www.rferl.org

Magazines and Ezines

The Economist

This Web version enables key articles and to be browsed and a limited archive searched. The user must subscribe to download full articles and it is also possible to subscribe to free e-mail summaries 'politics this week' or 'business this week'. http://www.economist.co.uk

Foreign Wire

This is a good quality international news analysis Ezine. Journalists are ex-*Independent*, *New York Times*, Reuters, London *Times* etc. http://www.foreignwire.com/index.html

Press releases

Two Ten Press Releases

This long established PR agency Web site enables press releases to be searched by company or topic. It includes government press releases too. http://releases.twoten.press.net/

UK Government press releases

From the UK government home page, go via the organization index to the COI the Central Office of Information. Press releases are listed by department and archived press releases can be searched via the departments. They are often a good source for briefings http://www.open.gov.uk/

Information Professional Sites

AUKML

The Association of UK Media Librarians is an independent organization representing media librarians. Membership is largely in the UK National and Regional press and broadcasting, although there are some international members. Their new site carries membership information, past and current conferences, issues of *Deadline*, the regular journal of the AUKML, media links and information on how to join the AUKML listserv. http://www.aukml.org.uk

ASLIB – The Association for Information Management

This organization represents special librarians in the UK and abroad. It provides information on consultancy, professional development and training, conferences and recruitment. http://www.aslib.co.uk/index.html

Independent information consultants

The consultants below have useful information on their sites. They are all key speakers/consultants in Internet and online research.

Phil Bradley (UK)

http://www.philb.com

Mary Ellen Bates (USA)

http://www.batesinfo.com/speeches.html

Amelia Kassel (USA)

http://www.marketingbase.com/bio3.html#SPEECHES

Mailing lists for journalists and information professionals

These Web sites have instructions and background details on the lists. Dip into the archives of messages first to see if they interest prior to joining.

British

AUKML – Association of UK Media Librarians
http://www.aukml.org.uk
BOPCAS
British Official publications alerting e-mail service. Run by the University of Southampton and associated with ASLIB, this is soon to become a paid service for details go to the link below. http://www.soton.ac.uk/~bopcas/announce.htm#4e
LISLINK – UK Library and Information Science group for news and discussion
http://www.mailbase.ac.uk/lists/lis-link
UKOLUG – UK Online User Group list
http://www.mailbase.ac.uk/lists/lis-ukolug

American

NEWSLIB – US Special Libraries News Division
http://metalab.unc.edu/journalism/newslib.html

US Special Libraries News Division

This Web site has lists on everything from newspapers who are experimenting with online publishing to Computer Assisted journalism. http://metalab.unc.edu/slanews/internet/resource.html#mailing

News alerting services by e-mail

A list by American journalist Bill Dedman

http://powerreporting.com

Lizst

A search engine specifically for finding mailing lists on any topic. http://www.Lizst.com

Journalists looking for experts

ExpertNet

One e-mail sent to the e-mail address on this site will go to all the UK university press offices. Journalists can use this free service to call for ongoing research or find experts to consult or interview. http://www.cvcp.ac.uk/expertnet.html

Profnet

The main source for journalists seeking experts from abroad mainly USA and Canada. http://www.profnet.com

Think tanks/pressure groups

Institute for Fiscal Studies

With expert in-depth analysis on taxation, wages, pensions etc., the site has press releases, working papers, articles from their journals etc. Always ready and willing to help journalists. htp://www.ifs.org.uk

Institute for Public Policy Research

This independent organization specializing in social economic and political research is a useful source for ideas. http://www.ifs.org.uk/home.htm

London School of Economics

Not a pressure group but a College within the University of London. It has been included on the back of its international reputation for research across the full range of social, economic and political sciences. Its many experts are used regularly by the BBC. http://www.lse.ac.uk

Current awareness – how to keep up with new sites

BBC Web Guide

Sites are reviewed by BBC specialists and selected for Web users in Britain, although not all the sites are British. http://www.bbc.co.uk/Webguide/index.html

Free Pint

This free e-mail newsletter contains tips, tricks and articles in which UK information professionals share how to make the most of the Web and where to find quality and reliable information. http://www.freepint.co.uk

Internet Resources Newsletter

Produced monthly by Herriot Watt University Internet Resource Centre, it lists new Web sites alphabetically. There is an archive of all the previous editions of the newsletter. The newsletter tends to list serious research sites not trivial or hobby sites and there is also a UK bias. http://www. hw.ac.uk/libWWW/irn

The Official Netscape Guide to Internet Research

This American site is a good one and contains a related newsletter on tips for effective Internet research. It started in April 1998 as a companion site to *The Official Netscape Guide to Internet Research* (2nd edition). As the book is a year old the site has evolved to focus more on Internet research resources. http://www.researchbuzz.com

Forward planning news diaries

Amiplan

Covering at least a year ahead, there is month by month searching, and a good contact database with links from the event listed to the appropriate Web page/contact. Subscription charge. http://www.amiplan.com

Foresight

Foresight electronic news diary features everything from product launches to presidential visits. It is an electronic version of established a hard copy service. Subscription charge. http://www.fifi.co.uk

Future Events News Service

This is a subscriber-only service for which there is a fee. Non subscribers can apply for a temporary password to try it out first. FENS is a news service that contains a huge database of forthcoming information and events searchable by date, region of the world, organization and keyword. Subscribers can also receive e-mail alerts of events vital to their business. http://www.hubcom.com/fens/

News Ahead

There is a selection of forthcoming news events on the site arranged by region of the world and also a section on developing stories. For full access to the year ahead diary there is a charge to obtain a password. Subscription charge. http://www.newsahead.com

Story ideas for journalists/academic research in progress

ESRC Regard Database

This is the Economic and Social Research Council database of research both completed and current. Try using the concept search to search by dates to find forthcoming research. http://www.regard.ac.uk

Medical research in progress

This is the Medical Research Council (UK) database of current research. Search by keyword. The home site will also enable searching for US federally funded research. http://fundedresearch.cos.com/mrc/mrc-intro.html

4 The news information industry and the media library into the 21st century

Richard Withey

'Now that knowledge is taking the place of capital as the driving force in organizations worldwide, it is all too easy to confuse data with knowledge and information technology with information'. Peter Drucker

To try to understand some of the difficulties that face the media library of the future, it is instructive to imagine two scenarios. Both involve experienced, senior journalists familiar with using the information services available to them to prepare story background, but let us imagine they are separated by thirty years. One is writing his story at the end of the sixties, and the other is writing her story at the end of the nineties. (That gender change neatly encompasses another major development in those 30 years.) To aid comparison, let us make the subject areas compatible: our sixties journalist is writing a story on the impact of the Beeching cuts on the rail network, and our nineties journalist is writing about the effect of privatization on the railways. Both are writing about their subject at a distance of a handful of years, and both therefore have a body of documentation to explore.

The first and most noticeable physical difference, I would suggest, will be in the sheer volume of copy available to be reviewed. The volume of newspaper text now produced is huge compared with that in the late sixties. In November 1966 the *Daily Telegraph* stood at 24 pages, and *The Times* at a similar size. By 1998 both are running, typically, at a 48 page book during the week, and more than doubling that on Saturdays. Even taking into account the highly graphical layouts of all newspapers in the nineties, and therefore reduced textual copy, they all carry many more stories than in the sixties. One only has to run a visual check along the cuttings shelves of most major newspaper libraries to validate this by the sheer thickness of modern cuttings files compared with those formerly, and this despite the reduction in cuts taken by these libraries, for reasons to be explored below.

The second is the hybrid nature of the sources, and the mixed media from which they are drawn. In the sixties, broadcast media could certainly not be ignored in covering stories like this, but there was little or no recording of news channels, they were far fewer in number and their impact as a medium of record was negligible. Teletext and viewdata had not yet arrived, and online was a purely academic medium (and even when it arrived in the late sixties with the advent of Dialog, it remained a professional researcher's tool until very recently).

So our poor (or lucky, depending on your viewpoint) sixties hack would be reduced to cobbling a story together based on personal interviews with contacts – probably mostly conducted face-to-face rather than over the telephone as now – and through the cuttings library. Reliance on the front-of-house librarian to provide the right folders was almost total: although then, as now, the total grounding many experienced journalists had in their disciplines gave them an implicit understanding of whether they were being short-changed by the librarian. Hard to imagine, but it did and still does happen.

Our lucky, liberated nineties journalist is able to mine a veritable sea of riches in information sources compared with the tiny stream her predecessor enjoyed. Since the advent of the Web, the sources are truly a multimedia repository. We have already seen that the sixties provided multimedia, in a way, but that the recording of it was desultory or non-existent outside print journalism. The advent of broadcast media Web sites has changed that. Sites such as BBC online and BSkyB give us a semi-permanent record of breaking broadcast news stories and allow previously difficult functions such as searchability and archiving to be added.

To the traditional media sources such as press and broadcast, the Web is now adding a whole body of new ones that our 60's journalist may never have encountered (because most of them did not exist, or if they did, they would have had difficulty disseminating their information and opinions). In contrast, our 90's journalist is beginning to take these sources for granted. For example, a quick and dirty search on AltaVista under the term 'rail privatization' produced well over 400 Web pages, many of them very relevant, and many from diverse and interesting sources. Microsoft MSN coverage of a National Audit office report, mixed with a report of parliamentary statements covered by the UK Railways Online service, a response made by the Scottish Liberal Democrats to the subject and reports from the Institute of Transport services – all useful, and not a cutting in sight. Moreover, the search took less time than it would take for a fit young journalist to pop down to the cuttings library to pick up a folder of yellowing cuttings, and I could use the material from my screen while writing a new story.

That is the other significant change in this 30-year comparison: our 90's journalist did not use a conventional library to compile her background out of necessity, whereas the 60's man almost certainly had to.

That is not to say she did not use the services of a librarian, but the contact was hidden, discrete and automated. We will explore this concept further, but first, let us finish our comparison with Times Past and Times Present to tease out more fully the shape of Times Future. Let us put our sixties journalist in the early 70s, and have him reporting on Watergate and the threatened impeachment of Nixon, and let us have our present journalist writing about Monica Lewinsky and the possible impeachment of Clinton. A direct comparison in many ways: each story starting small, with new revelations creating an international story over time. Two Presidents are in trouble, and both are trying to minimize the damage caused by media coverage of their indiscretions.

The most instructive difference is in the way each story broke. Watergate was a case of the classic, traditional dogged journalists following a dimly lit lead, going on a hunch, using sources close to the culprits (remember 'Deep Throat'?) and finally getting national attention. They worked for a respected, traditional, establishment title, run by a no-nonsense tough proprietor and an even tougher, seasoned editor who was to back them all the way. The exciting film re-enactment of this starred Robert Redford and Dustin Hoffman as the intrepid reporters, but it would have made a gripping film even if the lead parts had been played by Norman Wisdom and Charlie Drake.

Shift to today, and where do we find the Lewinsky scandal breaking? On the Web, of course. And by whom? Matt Drudge, that aggressive, confident representative (even paradigm) of 90's Web reporting. This seems to have rattled a few old bones in the media world. The Drudge Report (http://www.drudgereport.com) for Tuesday 6 October 1998 is instructive, carrying the following, justifiably self-congratulatory report:

> WOODWARD: 'DRUDGE JUST GOT LUCKY'
> The *Washington Post*'s Bob Woodward declared on Wednesday that this reporter just 'got lucky' in the Monica Lewinsky story. While appearing on the *PBS Newshour* to discuss journalism standards in Lewinsky coverage, Woodward suddenly turned green on camera.
> Moderator Terrence Smith asked a panel, that included Jack Nelson of the *Los Angeles Times* and former White House special counsel Lanny Davis, if 'Matt Drudge was now the standard in news reporting?'
> Jack Nelson threw a hernia, and barked: 'Heavens No!'
> Watergate Woodward interrupted: 'Drudge just got lucky that something in the Lewinsky story turned out to be true'.
> Something?

One certainly hopes that Woodward's coverage of who reported what in the Lewinsky story does not represent his accuracy in other areas.

The Drudge Report was first with the story of the intern, after his sister publication *Newsweek* went for a walk around the block and put it all on hold ... First to report that Lewinsky had signed an affidavit denying a relationship with the President ... First to report that there were tapes ... First to report that Starr had moved in ... First to report the dirty dress ... First to report that the president had invoked executive privilege ... First to report the cigar, the sex before church on Sundays ... First with over 20 exclusive stories later confirmed in the Starr impeachment referral ... First to report that Bob Woodward looks great in green.

It is clear from this report that US journalism at least is in transition. Professional jealousies apart, there does seem to be a debate under way about the nature of journalism, and how this is affected both by how journalists gather material for stories and how they break them. In the UK last year, there was a well-publicized spat between James Naughtie of the *Today* Radio 4 programme, and senior journalists from the print media about who sets the news agenda in Britain. It was too early for the Web to figure much in that debate, but just a year later, the Web is also on the agenda in Britain for any discussion about news, the nature of reporting.

All of this is bound to have a huge impact on the information services provided to journalists in all forms of the media. Librarians can not have a meaningful discussion about services to clients without taking into account the wider nature of the digital revolution and the impact this will have both on how journalists gather data and how they disseminate stories. We should therefore have a close look at:

- the nature and speed of digital take-up generally;
- the growth and impact of Computer Assisted Reporting.

▶ DIGITAL GROWTH

The demographics of the Web so far are just what one would expect from an industry that has so far been PC-driven: in the US 77 per cent of users are aged between 18 and 49; they are still predominantly male (just), middle-class, educated and affluent. Some pundits have pointed to this fact to suggest that this indicates that the Web, and online in general, is probably the preserve of the affluent and educated. One significant factor, however, indicates changes to this view: Web growth as measured by new users has started to peak, in the US at least, and most interestingly could settle at the same level of penetration as PC penetration in terms of number of households online. At an SPS seminar in London, June 1998, Jupiter predicted that, by the year 2002, the number of US households online will almost match the number with PCs, and stabilize at around 55 per cent.

Another recent trend is also worth watching. In the early years of the graphical browser, aficionados, predicting the quick and painful death of all other forms of media, were trying to develop the Web as an entertainment medium. Following the (so far) failure of the industry to deliver the bandwidth, access speeds and ease-of-use that were all predicted at the time, these efforts are now being moderated. Most are now concentrating on the Web as an information and commercial medium, and newspapers and television are claiming that rumours of their death were greatly exaggerated. The roles of television and other traditional media as aggregators, packagers and presenters are being reiterated and also brought to the Web with increasing success. The Web, the aficionados are now saying, is about finding things ('tell-me' medium) and the television is still a 'show-me' medium.

Compared with other developed media, Web experiences are still hampered by the nature of the access system – broadly the PC and telephone line – and all the faults that are still inherent in them, especially when used together. Slowness, unreliability, complexity and high access costs (in the UK at least) are all factors which Web users live with, but this is not to deny that the Web is growing, and phenomenally fast pundits. All graphs of growth produced by new media industry watchers look broadly like that in Figure 4.1, and there is significant growth in the publishing environment into which these new recruits to the Web can enter (see Figure 4.2).

In assessing the Web's growth and impact on media libraries and journalism we must not forget that, in the immediate future, many more users are going to access the Web, or its derivatives, through television, and this is bound to have an impact on the nature of the journalism provided. In the UK, BSkyB has launched its digital offering, and its digital

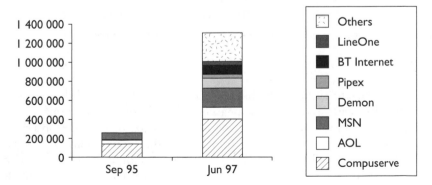

Figure 4.1 **UK Internet access accounts. Source: Durlacher, Quarterly Internet report Q2/97: The residential market 1997**

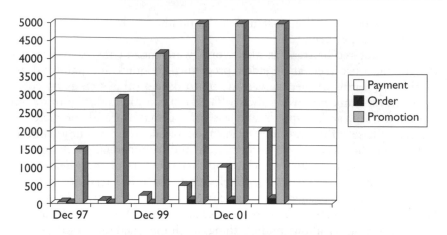

Figure 4.2 **Global Web domains by capacity 1997–2002. Source: Datamonitor**

terrestrial rival OnDigital has launched at the end of 1998. All predictions for take-up must therefore be used guardedly. One view is show in Figure 4.3.

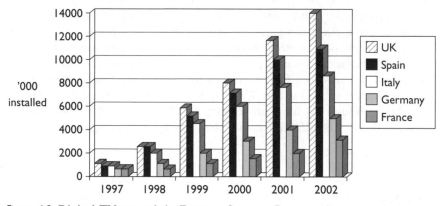

Figure 4.3 **Digital TV growth in Europe. Source: Datamonitor**

The current situation is that the pioneer work to establish a base of connectivity with relatively easy access, has been or is about to be achieved, and most future users have at least heard of it. Most observers agree that this work is about to translate to the living room, via television. Most households in the developed world should have access to a wide range of interactive entertainment and information-based content within one generation. They will have access via PC, if at work, or via PC/TV if at home, or via Personal Digital Assistants (PDAs) if travelling.

There will be a huge range of content available, it will be largely device-independent, and journalists will be feeding it. In one area at least, the rapid growth of online we have seen, and particularly the Web, has given rise to an entirely new type of data gathering and story assembly: Computer Assisted Reporting.

▶ COMPUTER ASSISTED REPORTING

The growth of personal and portable computing has led, in the USA at least, but increasingly in Europe, to journalists finding their own sources, often without the aid of librarians, through a variety of online media. The inestimable Nora Paul (1995), of the Poynter Institute, identified a wide range of source portals into which journalists can tap, in a paper entitled 'C.A.R. on the Beat: An introduction to information needs and where to go to fill them', presented at the IRE Conference, June 1995. These include:

- e-mail;
- listservs;
- newsgroups;
- bulletin boards;
- news filters;
- forums and Special Interest Groups (SIGs);
- commercial databases;
- gophers;
- Web sites.

Prior to the mid-1990s, the only relatively well-used source from those listed above was commercial databases, and this often through intermediaries such as librarians. Only the most wired journalists were using bulletin boards and gophers until very recently, even though they predate the Web by several years. In fact this list represents much more than a range of new resources available to journalists: it reflects a change in mindset about the role of the journalist in data gathering.

In some ways, these sources can be said to replicate, in electronic form, some of the more traditional sources and data feeds for journalists. The listserv, for example, is to some extent the online version of the journalist's card index of expert contacts (though far more fluid and volatile in its composition, and definitely much more driven by opinion than pure fact). The most far-reaching change brought about by these new methods of information gathering, however, is that they combine processes. Previously, the journalist kept in very separate compartments the processes involved in generating story ideas and the processes involved in researching them. These have now come together on one platform.

Some argue that the use and exploitation of Computer Assisted Reporting is at one and the same time the most important threat and the biggest opportunity facing the media industry. It is a threat, they argue, because firstly, computer access to information allows a much more level playing field between small and large media players. Even a cursory examination of the development of the Web over the last five years would tend to support this view. Relatively invisible media brands and (in UK terms anyway) small circulation newspapers have been able to establish themselves as at least equal to and in some cases much better than their larger print rivals in this aspect of their business. Moreover, they have been able to do this in front of a global audience.

Secondly, new players have entered the field and established huge brand presence through the Web almost overnight. Examples are well known, sometimes even to those who have yet to use the Web: Yahoo, Excite, America Online. (AOL was a player in the consumer online market before the Web arrived, but they have used it very effectively to gain market dominance in this field.) Interestingly, too, they all started as something other than media players, even in their own view of the business, but now increasingly feel obliged to enter the content game directly or indirectly. Microsoft have also exploited their position as a gatekeeper carefully to gain huge Web presence (despite a late realization of the importance of this). Bill Gates often denies the intention of his company to become a media player, but it really depends what is meant by 'media'.

The third threat is that readers and viewers increasingly expect online information, and the Web in particular, to be part of the media mix. Demographics of young consumers especially indicate that the public obtains news and information increasingly from online sources and they are much more willing than their predecessors to use multimedia and mixed media in their daily lives. Two examples illustrate this: even a casual glance at *The Times*' letters page shows that a good proportion of published letters are now received by e-mail and are published with their e-mail address. This is typical of most quality newspapers. A recent travel promotion in *The Times* received over 30 per cent of its response via the Web. This is despite the fact that the promotion was voucher-based, and there was no significant advantage, from the point of view of the offer itself, in using the Web to respond. It seems that users/readers simply found it more convenient.

So the threat to existing media could be characterized as a situation in which consumers are increasingly asking for online and the Web to be part of the media offered. New media players are responding to this by providing access to large banks of interesting content never previously available to the public at large, and the smaller media companies are responding by getting into the action early and becoming global media presences, after a fashion. It is a virtual, or vicious, circle, depending on your view.

The opportunities presented by these developments are, fortunately, of a similar size. As increasing numbers of print and broadcast media companies establish Web sites, they are moving away from and beyond the early experiments which involved re-purposing their old media product to develop new content and ways of reaching their customers. This is not an insignificant task, bearing in mind the scale of some of these operations and can mean:

- a move away from the tyranny of the deadline. As more traditional media outlets realize the potential to reach customers any time, anywhere, they are reacting with 24-hour rolling news, e-mail alerts and other devices which release journalists from the restrictions that have faced them over time deadlines;
- a move away from the tyranny of space. This has been an issue that has faced more than print journalists, but is most evident in the number of spiked stories and those cut to fit. On any broadsheet UK newspaper, for example, such copy outweighs printed copy by a factor as large as ten to one;
- a fusion of print and broadcast values and methodologies. It is a truism that no new media format has ever entirely replaced any previous one, but each new one has tended to do different things, in a different way, from its predecessors. Online, and the Web in particular, could well turn out to be the medium that incorporates most previous media formats. The potential this gives the journalist to exploit new methodologies for exciting readers/viewers with their content has yet to be imagined.

To summarize, it seems likely that if journalists do not exploit the opportunities afforded to them by Computer Assisted Reporting then others will, to the possible detriment of their relationship with their viewers and readers, and possibly their livelihoods too.

▶ THE EFFECTS ON LIBRARIES AND LIBRARIANS

Two of the more unusual books advertized in the *Times Literary Supplement* recently were specialist guides for librarians on using the Web for research. Inevitably, these were American, emanating from a reputable Chicago-based Academic publisher. In fact, even the most cursory research on the Web itself reveals a relatively high level of activity in the US in relation both to preparing librarians for use of the Web and, one step further on, making tools and techniques available for those who will interface with users. InterNIC, for example, in collaboration with the Library and Information Technology Association (a division of the American Library Association), provide the 15 Minute Series, a collection of Internet training materials provided for the research and education community. Subjects covered include: Internet History; E-mail; The Basics; Tools; Technology; and The Future.

In the UK, the position is far more patchy. By far the biggest initiative is taking place in the academic library community, under the aegis of the UK Electronic Libraries Programme (eLib). This programme has a budget of £15 million over three years, and its main purpose is 'to engage the Higher Education community in developing and shaping the implementation of the electronic library'. (Programme background at http://www.ukoln.ac.uk/service/elib/background/history.html).

Chris Rusbridge (1998), the programme director of the Electronic Libraries Programme at Warwick University, has written about the problems of integrating conventional library service provision with digital formats, and the need to address the issue of the hybrid library. The problems he identifies in academic libraries are all found in media information provision, and in some cases exacerbated by the nature of print journalism particularly. It is worth remembering that the peculiar problems of, say, the busy newspaper library are still pertinent in a digital environment, only more so. Considered against other professional groups who need frequent access to large bodies of data (such as scientists and financial workers) these problems include: the need to meet very tight deadlines; the spontaneous nature of the information enquiry; the lack of availability of alternative information resources; and the relative lack of information skills of journalists.

Libraries of all kinds face one overwhelming problem in the face of technology-driven research: the huge volume of material they store in book form, and the continuing need to gain access to it. Again, using the example of the academic library community's response to the growth of the hybrid library, it seems that at least that professional grouping is well down the path of thinking about the problems that the hybrid library brings, and of developing some co-ordinated response to them. In part this comes from the already very collaborative nature of the academic community, but also from their collective realization of some of the difficulties the hybrid library will impose. It would be instructive to examine where these have parallels in the world of the media library.

Rusbridge (1998) identifies a number of areas of difficulty or challenge, including:

- scaling;
- preservation;
- access;
- resources, which he breaks down into legacy resources (which I have described as analogue) and transition resources – those which have been processed into digital.

More specifically, he lists a large number of areas that the academic hybrid library customer needs to deal with:

- local OPAC (telnet/Web);
- COPAC union catalogue (telnet/Web/Z39.50);
- regional virtual union catalogue (Web/Z39.50);
- stand-alone CD-ROMs;
- off-line CD-ROMs and diskettes;
- networked CD-ROMs;
- full text services;
- electronic reserve systems;
- remote datasets at the community data centres (BIDS, EDINA and MIDAS);
- remote datasets at other universities;
- remote commercial datasets;
- local datasets e.g., bibliographies, pamphlet collections and archives;
- local Web-based documents, library and institutional;
- local Web resource gateways;
- remote Web subject/resource gateways;
- remote Web resources;
- remotely mounted electronic journals (EJs);
- local and remotely mounted e-books.

At the moment, many media libraries would find this list to be only partly applicable to them. Many are using CD-ROMs and some are networking them; remote commercial datasets have been in use for several years, sometimes delivered directly to journalists' desks; full text services are widely available in most of the national press and some regional offices. While some of the others on the list such as OPACs and their variants are not applicable, it is conceivable that most of the other applications will be widely in use in media libraries in a very short time. How will the media librarian handle these new resources as well as making traditional material available?

One of the unique dilemmas which still faces the media librarian, especially in print, is the nature of the cutting. Cuttings do not translate well from analogue to digital, despite advances in optical character recognition. There have been several attempts in national newspaper offices through the 1980's and 1990's to solve this problem which have met with limited success. In recent years, journalists could not only tolerate this, but often preferred working with cuts to working online. The early stages of the print digital revolution, at least as far as journalists were concerned, were little more than conversions of typewritten copy to computer set copy, and many journalists had little or no online access. With many of them now being given access to Web-based and other online information, however, the problem of the hybrid media library is exacerbated considerably.

Looking at some of the core problems Rusbridge identifies, there is no doubt that, for the media library, the access issue is going to have the most profound effect. Editors of newspapers from 50 years ago would not have felt uncomfortable walking into the modern news library until a few years ago. They would have seen little or no evidence of computer terminals, and the library acting as the physical focal point for all journalistic enquiry. Indeed, it is reliably alleged that, when the former home of *The Times* at Printing House Square was rebuilt in the 1960s, the then editor William Haley, erudite and library loving as he was, had the library built next to his office.

Once the transitional or hybrid library began to develop, with some remote access for journalists, this began to change: for the first time they could gain access to stories and data without going through an intermediary, and they could do it from their desk or from the field. At News International, where data from the four (once five) main newspaper titles has been captured in electronic form since the mid-1980s, journalists can search all of this data through an intranet built by library staff (see chapter 7 in this volume). To this is added a wealth of data specifically loaded to the system by librarians, to make their job and that of the journalists easier: information on celebrity dates of birth for example, or lists of major events under subject headings. Even the canteen menu and a distance chart for calculating mileages for expense claims is available. Over recent years, therefore, there has been a significant shift towards the information transaction between journalist and librarian being discrete and at one remove. Interestingly, however, this has not significantly decreased the number of face-to-face or telephone transactions taking place, so a major cuttings collection is still maintained (though the number of cuttings actually taken has reduced in recent years) and many journalists still use cuttings folders to chase leads and check facts.

The trend, therefore, at News International and in other media companies, is to continue to provide a central resource while also making online services available to all users. The big question for the next century, as the digital revolution advances and as journalists come to expect a wide range of services to be delivered to their screens, is whether it will be viable to maintain central repositories of data of any size. My judgement is that, over a set period, they will abandon much of the attempt to provide large hybrid libraries, and that the services will increasingly be provided online. This is particularly the case with print media libraries, where the kind of sources journalists tend to use are the ones which are in the avant-garde of digital conversion: news sources, periodical sources and human sources. As we have already seen, the availability of the Web is giving journalists wide access to these resources. Certainly validity and substantiation of leads are still an issue with Web sources, for the Web is still too anarchic, but as more leading brands treat it as a route to market, this will inevitably improve. The fact is, the bulk of resources used by journalists are already there or nearly there. The Electronic Library, for example (http://www.elibrary.com) claims: 'The Electric Library currently contains 9 764 810 newspaper articles, 861 957 magazine articles, over 428 002 book chapters, 1103 maps, 104 422 television and radio transcripts, and 60 618 photos and images!' With this as only one of many developing sources for journalists to use, it is difficult to imagine a situation where the journalist in 2020 for instance is not using the Web or its derivatives for most of research and also possibly for much of the distribution.

It is possible therefore that the hybrid media library, bearing in mind the rather transient nature of much media research in relation to other disciplines, will itself be a transient phenomenon. It is unlikely, too, that preservation will be a significant issue, except for the media archive and for national news collections, which are not considered here, but which will face considerable difficulties and hard decisions. One worrying factor is related, and that is storage and its near relative, retrieval. Over the past dozen years, libraries have been faced with a myriad of different digital storage media, from various sizes of floppy disc, through CD-ROM to erasable CD and DVD, to various WORM (Write Once Read Many) devices. Many of these have been a passing fancy, or if they have survived have proved inadequate responses to the problem of large-scale storage. Small wonder that many media libraries have been reluctant to invest in systems, and of those that have, some have found themselves up a digital cul-de-sac with no hope of transfer to the information super highway. Along the way they have disoriented and disenchanted journalists at a critical stage of their digital education. When it comes to retrieval systems, the picture is even more confusing, with librarians being sold expensive software that is over-engineered for the relatively simple needs of the media. A quick straw poll of 'Fleet Street' libraries reveals little commonality between systems in use to control data or images, despite a well-organized network of media librarians and a well-established data exchange scheme. Too often the librarians have had little or no influence on the final decision over installed systems, with the views of IT staff, remote from the user, sometimes prevailing.

This will change over the course of the next few years. As media properties become true digital creations (as opposed to the blended mix of analogue and digital they have been up to now) it will become increasingly easy to export data in rich text format from the production page rips produced by newspaper systems. The recent launch of digital TV will provide similar advantages for broadcast librarians.

Having watched the growth of the Web with some trepidation, experimented with uncertainty and examined their core strengths for signs of weakness in the face of the threat from new players, there is no doubt that media companies are now beginning to embrace the digital revolution. In the UK, the digital television revolution has just started and will probably produce some turbulent business seas before it stabilizes. On the Web, print media have been encouraged to see how many sites are essentially text driven, but are now also embracing the new strategies behind multimedia formats and content. Even the sceptical could predict with confidence that the UK media industry will essentially go fully digital over the next ten to fifteen years: even if a significant market for print products remains, they will be produced from a digital base. The analogue television and radio bandwidths will be switched off.

When analogue goes dark and silent, will there be any significant media libraries which do not closely echo their journalists' needs? I do not think so: just as today's media libraries are carefully geared to meet the demands of their customers, despite the difficulties of managing legacy archives alongside transitional formats, so they will be in future. The difference will be that in future the reader will be online, the journalist will be online, and the librarian will be both online and facilitating the online transaction. While this means that librarians may be less visible, it does not mean they will be any less important.

► REFERENCE

Rusbridge, C (1998) Towards the hybrid library. *D-Lib magazine*, July-August. http://mirrored.ukoln.ac.uk/lis-journals/dlib/dlib/dlib/july98/rusbridge/07rusbridge.html

5 The changing role of the news librarian

Nora Paul

First, we worked in the 'morgue', that place where old clips went to be buried in envelopes and interred in drawers. Our role was to try to guess where people might want to dig up old information and make sure a copy of any appropriate story was filed that way.

Then came the shift from hot type to cold type publishing and the analogue clip became digital. We became data processors, checking the electronic files against the published version, chasing down missing stories, recreating the old clip file headings by assigning 'keywords' to the electronic archives. This change in clip storage added a new role – information intermediary. While we had always had a delivery role in the newsroom (the reporters would ask for the clip file, we would find it and give it to them), the new electronic storage of clips made this an even more important role. Many newsrooms did not have a lot of terminals available – they had to call the library to retrieve the stories they needed. The software used to retrieve from the database was often anything but intuitive, requiring strange symbols and Boolean logic to retrieve effectively the desired articles. The librarian became more of a go-between, a necessary link between the data and the end-user.

At the same time news libraries were building their in-house electronic archives and other information resources were becoming available in electronic form, usually at high, per-minute or per-search charge. The intermediary role of the news librarian grew. Often, the budget for electronic research was in the library's control (and responsibility), providing a strong incentive for keeping control and access to these electronic resources in the library's area. The relationship between the library as server and the newsroom as client was established.

It is that server–client relationship which helped make the library more visible and clearer in the newsroom. We became the essential, critical link between the newsroom and the information it needed. It was our hands on the keyboard which provided the access to information our newsroom needed. We had it all, we knew it all, we were the key to access. It was a powerful role, an important role and now it must end.

WHAT? END!!?!!

Yes, it must end. As we move into a new information space with computer aided access to records and their analysis, and as the resources available on the World Wide Web through the Internet grow, the role we play must change with the resources now available to our newsrooms. The Internet is an essential information resource and it must be used by and understood by the people who will seek and use the information found in it. Computer assisted reporting techniques can change the type of reporting it is possible to do. But it is only through end-user understanding and use of information resources that news organizations, and the products they make, will evolve from the industrial age to the information age. Improved access to and use by journalists of the vast information age resources will allow journalism to change in important and radical ways.

What are these changing directions for journalism, what resources will be necessary to effect this change and what will be the news librarian's/news researcher's role to ensure the change happens? Let us look first at the changes in journalism and the resources required for the change. Then the news researcher's vital, but evolving, role will be discussed.

From event reporting to emphasis on context/ significance

In an age when anyone with a digital video camera and a word processor can post to a Web site all about some event, news organizations will only stand out if they can provide greater context to the mere detailing of the event. In order to do so there will need to be greater access to databases/ records that can track trends and supply statistics. Let us say there is an auto accident on the highway outside of town. You can not just report, 'Well, there's been another accident outside of town'. You will want access to a database of accidents so you can tell just how many there have been at this particular intersection.

Phil Meyer, the godfather of Computer Assisted Reporting in the US, says there are three levels of reporting. The first level is event reporting (and basically, anyone can do that): 'There was an accident at the corner of Central and Main'. Good journalism goes to the second level which is putting the event into a broader context: 'This is the third fatal accident at this intersection in the past two months.' The third level, great journalism, then explains why it is as it is – it seeks change. Are the traffic lights poorly sequenced on that corner, have the road conditions deteriorated, or have the oleander bushes grown too tall and now obstruct the view?

Information age journalism will have context and you'll need improved access to data to be able to do that. The news researcher's role as acquirer, maintainer and explainer of the data will be essential for improving end-user use of these resources.

From transcription to explanation

To stand out from the rest of the purveyors of news, journalists will have to go beyond mere recitation of the facts to providing an explanation of the events. In order to do this, more background will be required, plus quick access to the primary documents so that the reporter can do their own analysis and interpretation. Reporters will need to have the tools of analysis at hand. Instead of duly reporting the city financial officer's annual budget, information age journalists will do their own analysis of the budget numbers and see what they say.

From follow the leads to lead the pack

News organizations will need to keep ahead of what is happening rather than following the lead of other newsrooms, and this will require being alert. Some of the new resources and communication possible because of the Internet will help journalists keep ahead, and researchers can help by getting reporters on the right listservs and setting up news filtering services. Also, developing new leads through interviewing data can get you ahead of the pack; for example, the *Associated Press* ran a story about medical doctors who have government-awarded rights to grow tobacco. It started with an idea, and led to their acquisition of US Department of Agriculture records on tobacco growers which they cross-checked against medical practitioner databases in 12 states. This was a new angle, they broke the story, and led the pack.

Make the local global and the global local

With the new ways news consumers can get the latest information, it will not do just to be another outlet saying that something happened somewhere – your news will stand out if you make sure that a sense of what this means to your local readers is part of the report. In the same way, if there is something going on locally, make sure that you tie it in to larger, national or global trends – is this the only place this is happening, or is it happening in other places? Sometimes knowing this will change your whole story. Access to the world's newspapers, radio and television outlets through the World Wide Web is an unprecedented resource to make sure that the scope of reporting is not provincial but international.

Multiple angles

Journalism is too often about telling the black and white of a story. Information Age journalism will cover the shades of grey as well – it will not be just truth telling but truths telling. Finding the angles, the groups, the multiple attitudes that any complex situation has will create a new kind of coverage. The fact that seemingly every possible fringe, faction and interest group has a Web site makes the representation of varying viewpoints not just an option, but an imperative.

Let readers go deep

Print journalism has been two dimensional – there is length and width – but new journalism, particularly the types of reporting and story telling reporters will increasingly be doing on the Web, will be three dimensional. In addition to length and width, there will be depth. This ability to give readers more, to link to background and previously reported stories, will require a greater contribution by the researchers to pull together a three-dimensional package to go along with the news report.

A new style of journalism, with greater reliance on information resources to tell the story with context, explanation, angles and scope is going to require journalists' savvy about the availability and use of these information age resources. And this is where the news researcher comes in.

The furrowed brows and heavy hearts of news researchers worrying that moving to end-user research will be a move to ending their jobs should unfurrow those brows and have a song in their hearts. Their job security has never been brighter. But their jobs will be different, and their attitudes will need changing. Their roles will be expanding but only if they spur on the expansion.

As with all things there is a dark side and a light side. With the Internet and the World Wide Web, the good news is that there is so much information available. However, that is also the bad news.

One hundred and sixty years before the World Wide Web made its way to newsroom computers Johann Wolfgang von Goethe said in 1832 'The modern age has a false sense of security because of the great mass of data at its disposal. But the valid issue is the extent to which man knows how to form and master the material at his command'. The news librarian, with their training in understanding, evaluating, cataloguing and compiling information, will be the key partner in helping reporters to know how to form and master the material at their command.

This is not to say that the research role will be totally abdicated to the reporter. In a partnership, those with the greatest skills do the part of the job they can best get done. In a reporting crunch or for research requiring detailed and in-depth searching, the librarian/researcher's role will be an important contribution to the newsgathering.

Reporters are wanting this sort of guidance. I asked reporters and editors on the Investigative Reporters and Editors listserv to fill in the following, 'When thinking about how the news library operates and what it could do I wish . . .' Here are some of the responses:

- I wish our librarians had more time and inclination to go beyond cataloguing the stories for the library and do research for stories. Right now, the two of them have very little ability to point any reporter to a clip from the old system, in part because the clip catalogue was designed by a now-dead woman who apparently wanted job security so she didn't share her filing logic.

- I wish our librarians could dig out that fact or figure of background that would give a story perspective. One example: tonight we had a story about an old golf course being sold and redeveloped. We said this was a good thing because of the number of new courses opening in the area. It would have been nice if a librarian were able to find the number of golfers in the area. Our assistant managing editor found it in our marketing department's reference books.

- I wish our library would be the repository for databases that we use as reference materials, and I wish our librarian were able to put in place an interface so reporters could use it easily.

- I wish researchers and librarians would really listen to the story I'm working on; care about that story and take enough interest in it, to be empathetic with me when they are doing searches for me.

- I wish I had got direct NEXIS access earlier; our librarian recently gave us direct access and it was amazing to me how much more stuff I found than I used to find when a librarian was doing the searching for me . . . as a search progresses you get new ideas for other related things to search for and that, of course, seldom happened when the librarian was doing the search for me.

- I wish technology was improved that could help in the creation of the electronic archives because, increasingly, the librarians have to do additional data coding and/or key entry to maintain archives, Web libraries, etc. As a result, the library staff is left with little time and less energy to help reporters. Sadly, the 'new role' of the news librarian is not as a researcher, but as a keyboard slave.

● I wish we had a news researcher sitting at the Metro desk like they do at some papers. She could hear the chatter among editors and between editors and reporters and butt in with things like, 'I can get that'. 'We may be able to find that out', etc. Just by sitting there she would improve the scope and depth of the news product and, at the same time, would make editors and reporters more aware of the many, many tools available.

One reporter summed up the evolution, and the librarian's critical role, this way: 'Just when the technology and information access is getting to the point where a journalist wonders how to make sense of it all and find the information he/she requires, up steps the news librarian ... a job which was designed specifically for that purpose decades ago – and who is now able to step into the forefront of journalistic service.'

Journalists want assistance through the morass of information available, they need the support and training that will allow them to do some of their own searching and need to have the back-up of the researcher there for more complicated searching and for their knowledge of the range of resources available. As the news library moves from intermediary to partner, the roles will be enhanced and the journalism will be improved.

6 Internet use at *The Guardian* and *The Observer*: a case study

Helen Martin

Internet use at *The Guardian* and *The Observer* started in 1992 and it is hard to imagine, now it is a daily occurrence and as common as going online or pulling a book of a shelf, that life ever existed without it. Indeed the latter has suffered by comparison. Books need to be ordered, often lack currency and indexes are sometimes poor. Even online hosts, despite their search engines' efficiency, tend to be more expensive and can appear perversely limited in types of sources. Nevertheless, do not sound the death knell yet. The advantage of cross-file structured searching of several newspapers on a data host, using an efficient search engine, is a hard act to follow and so far Web use at *The Guardian* and *The Observer* supplements this feature, displacing only hard copy sources and less frequently used databases. Yet the simple act of pulling a useful book off the shelf must not be undervalued; it is fast and it is also comforting.

▶ GETTING STARTED

We had read the hype of course, but the growing realization that the Internet was going to be another hurdle to cross, like the introduction of online hosts, acted as a catalyst in encouraging further exploration. We had to be in the forefront of the revolution again, ahead of the end-users, or risk being left behind. The knowledge that those senior staff who worked from PCs, rather than creaky ATEX terminals which would not support Internet access, and who had few budget problems, were already getting hooked up, provided the real impetus for us to start agitating for browsers and new equipment.

Information issues have a tendency to move slowly at *The Guardian*, however, and it was not until April 1993 that a modem connection finally arrived and we detailed an assistant librarian to get to grips with Internet use. We felt frustrated by the length of time it had taken, but on contacting media library colleagues to ask advice on our new toy, we were surprised to learn that few had yet taken the plunge. One weary response was 'The Internet? We don't even have a fax machine yet!' Budgetary control – the first priority of all media libraries! We started by sending our allotted librarian to conferences and seminars on 'how-to-get-the-best-out-of-the-Internet' and reading a great deal, but the vaguaries of the modem connection were so exasperating that by the end of 1994 only one other assistant librarian had become hooked.

In an attempt to create further interest we hired a consultant for the day and, splitting it in two, sent the entire Research and Information (R&I) staff in two groups on a half-day session, which was a cheaper option than sending everyone to outside courses individually. We would normally limit training to the relevant assistant librarian, but the Web we felt was different – everyone had to be familiar with it in the same way that we were all familiar with various online hosts.

Interest, however, was already stirring outside the library. We read an article by Harry Evans enthusing about Internet use in American newsrooms and redoubled our efforts, seeing this as a sign of things to come. (Ironically, this is the same Harry Evans who in the summer of '98 was waxing rather less lyrical about the Web and American journalists' reliance on its inaccuracies.) Even a few reporters were beginning to bring confused requests about 'a massive database that can answer questions on any subject'.

We faced, and not for the first time, *The Guardian*'s lack of information policy that had by now allowed ISDN connections arbitrarily to senior staff, (some of whom rarely, used the Internet) but denied it to the R&I staff working on behalf of both *Guardian* and *Observer* reporters – around 450 staff journalists.

We were attempting to do a weekly research job for *The Guardian*'s, 'The Week', which involved searching through the regional press, but progress was slow as we struggled to gain access in the late afternoon; the work needed to be done as late in the day as possible. A sympathetic IT director came to our rescue and early in 1997 R&I got its first ISDN link. Internet use had finally come home! If 'location, location and location' is the estate agent's sobriquet, then maybe the librarian's (and indeed the end user's) is 'access, access and access'.

The ISDN link proved to be a boon. Fast and easy access made all the difference to interest levels in the department and soon we had a growing bookmark list and idle moments saw a queue of librarians waiting to surf and search, something we could not do from our ATEX terminals. Feeling more familiar with things we began to offer 'how-to' training to reporters but there were few takers.

Our own use of it was, in those early days, confined to the World Wide Web and to the quirky (such as UFO sites) and very often subjects that were sourced in America. One of the first successful searches we did was to retrieve an article from a newspaper produced on the Internet by striking journalists at the *San Francisco Chronicle* (http://www.sfgate. com). The best searches tended to be the serendipity ones, where we stumbled across useful sites by accident, such as a Scandals In Justice site highlighting unreported miscarriages of justices. Other examples of searches included:

- lyrics searches;
- a journalist desperate for a State Department human rights report – the story was based on the fact that he managed to view the report full-text. This would have been difficult to achieve for a daily paper in pre-Internet days;
- up-to-date statistics on the world Aids situation;
- use of a Movie database to check out nannies in the movies and various other queries;
- lines from an obscure Oscar Wilde poem. Neither our own books of quotations nor outside libraries could help;
- tracking down an article in *Columbia Journalism Review*. Columbia University's homepage included a contents page for the journal and to see full-text you have to subscribe, but with the information we managed to acquire a copy from the library at the University of Central Lancashire which has a journalism school;
- searching sources on Dubrovnik to find out details of a summer festival;
- information on McDonalds for the environment correspondent;
- Northern Ireland casualty list;
- BSE statistics – cost of disease.

We relied heavily (and still do at the time of writing) on FT PROFILE to which all reporters at *The Guardian* and *The Observer*, along with R&I staff, have access at their desk, for the searching of newspapers and journals. Much of this end-user PROFILE searching (around 81 per cent) is delegated, however, just as in the days of cuttings we had started to slip in the results of a PROFILE search, we now began to hand over a printout from a Web site along with our downloaded online search.

Yet things still felt unstructured and we welcomed an approach from City University's Department of Information Science to participate in a British Library-funded study: 'The changing information environment: the Media and the Internet', April 1997-March 1998, (City University, 1998) led by Dr David Nicholas and examining journalists' use of the Internet. This we thought would be a means of extending our own understanding of how to proceed (See the Web site at http://www.soi.city.ac.uk./~pw/ji-home.html). The announcement of the City University project coincided with plans of senior members of the R&I staff to visit the European School of Journalism at Maastricht, Holland, for a week's seminar led by Nora Paul, Library Director of the Poynter Institute in Florida, studying all aspects of news information provision.

▶ TRAINING

We returned from Holland laden with notes and advice, and a grim realization that our current training programme did not even begin to touch on any of the points that others felt salient – how to evaluate sites, how to compare search engines. Two assistant librarians with responsibility for the Internet were detailed to examine these issues and after much discussion and several dummy runs, we produced our first proper training programme.

Along with the quick 'how-to' section we now added lengthy advice on evaluating Web sites along suggested lines of authority, accuracy, objectivity, currency and coverage, what one could tell of a site by its universal resource locator (URL), how American and UK URLs differed and the importance of re-evaluating with every link.

We warned of pitfalls and fake sites, of how journalists should follow up online interviews with telephone calls. We warned that they should be wary of expressing views in newsgroups thought to be representative of *The Guardian* (whose name appeared in their e-mail address). We ran them through e-mail, mailing lists, listservs, news groups, Internet relay chat, how to bookmark and search engines. Interestingly, as a daily paper we found there was little interest in news groups – they simply did not work to our timescale, though they may have potential for the features department or on long-term projects.

The search engine issue was revised again in March 1998 when *The Guardian*'s Editor Alan Rusbridger, a committed and enthusiastic Internet user, expressed an interest. Today, we hand over a table showing which sites use full Boolean, which use partial, which require quotation marks round a phrase, etc. and when demonstrating we try to include sites pertinent to the person being trained. If their searching of FT PROFILE is anything to go by, then the training advice is water off a duck's back!

An attempt to offer a kind of SDI service (or push technology in its current jargon) to specialists proved less successful, just as it had in the early days of online, probably because journalists prefer to do their own monitoring and the results are too general. While the British Library survey made much of journalists accessing press releases on the Web, many of our own specialists simply asked why they would want to do this when they were on the mailing list in any case. For once, speed did not seem to be an issue here. Access, however, probably was. At that time these journalists had to leave their desks to search sites, although there is now desk-top access to the Internet.

▶ BOOKMARKING

Of all the things we show reporters, the facility that causes most perceptible interest is bookmarking – how to save actual sites. When our own bookmark list hit the 500 level and crashed the elderly PC, we started to organize it around a thesaurus to allow for expansion and fast access. With the entire department bookmarking sites every day, we leave the final decision of what to keep to one of the two Internet librarians, who tries to bookmark only top level sites and to carry out regular spring cleaning. The bookmark list is gold dust, not only to us but also to others. If there is one thing in the entire library capable of exciting a diverse range of users, it is the bookmark list. We began to see it as an instrument of power and grew quietly proprietorial about it! We also used it as a marketing ploy – advertising daily topical sites on our internal messaging system. This list has been transferred with a thesaurus to our intranet launched in June 1999. Some examples are included in the references section.

With the British Library/City University project well under way examining Internet use in newspapers around the country, we grew increasingly aware of our own use and logged all searches, partly for the purposes of the project and partly in order to give ourselves an idea of the Internet's strengths and weaknesses compared to other sources. We also logged comments by people we trained and found a wide variety of views:

- some wanted simply to compare search engines;
- one person worried that traditional sources of information might disappear in favour of technology. He thought that the Internet was overhyped and rubbish but his attitude became more positive after training;
- some showed signs of great frustration if results were not produced instantaneously, even though they had insisted on an inadequate search term;
- some wanted very specific searches, e.g. how many bus passes each London borough provides – we were successful by and large;
- many were overwhelmed and fascinated by the wealth of material.

At the same time we sought to alert the rest of the office to its potential and to our training programme, by advertising it on the ATEX electronic noticeboard and by word of mouth. Turn-out was steady, but slow and with the course lasting more than an hour many people deferred until another day that never dawned. By the summer of 1998 we had only trained around 70 people. Nevertheless, the Internet could advertise itself in a way the online hosts could not and the turn-out, ironically for a virtually free resource where bad searching had no financial consequences, was always higher than for PROFILE.

The Editor, meanwhile, keen to persuade use of what he saw as a vital journalistic tool, had parked access points on each of *The Guardian*'s two editorial floors. However, no printers were provided and people had to sit mid-floor with all their ignorance exposed. Moreover, with nowhere to practise they forgot their training. It was not ideal.

► MARKETING

Along with advertising our training programme and a daily topical site on the ATEX notice board we sought out other ways of marketing the Internet. To this end we organized a series of 'library lunches' (wine and sandwiches) examining the Internet from three different perspectives. The first session, which attracted the most people, was a practical demonstration of the Web – what it looked like, how to use it and examples of general all purpose sites. The second was an explanation by Dr David Nicholas of City University of the 'Media and the Internet' project (City University, 1998), that touched on preliminary findings and, lastly, we held a session by Nora Paul dealing with Internet use on American papers.

The common theme that ran through the three sessions was 'you-may-not-have-realized-yet-but-this-thing-is-going-to-change-your-working-life'. We felt that whilst the meetings proved to be a good tactic for alerting interest, one-to-one training was far more useful. Nevertheless, take up was still slow and some reporters were even decidedly hostile to the whole idea of the Internet. It was associated, we gathered, with the possible introduction of 24-hour deadlines and a 'dumbing-down' of their working practises, and out of this grew the visceral hostility of the ignorant. On occasion, when we suggested looking on the Web for answers to obscure questions, we were met with hysterically angry replies – 'load of rubbish, don't waste my time or yours'. However, success brought muted and grudging interest even if people also complained about speed and information overload.

The Internet is now well established as a research tool in R&I. We have graduated from searching for quirky sites to searching for anything at all, provided it is free, from official things like *Hansard* parliamentary reports to football hooligan sites. There is even evidence of some displacement; our LEXIS-NEXIS bill has been cut by half as a direct result of Web usage and we now buy only one hard copy of *Hansard*.

On some occasions we have neatly reversed the journalist/librarian role, telephoning through to our reporter in Lima the live Tupac-Amaru reports emanating from inside the besieged Japanese embassy, outside which he was sitting. Who is dealing with primary sources then? In future years of course, and even now, the reporter will sit outside with Web access on his knee.

▶ THE FUTURE

Our training course will evolve with the introduction of new search engines and R&I will hopefully undertake what amounts to compulsory training of journalists with the introduction of our new Mac-based editorial system, QPS, which gives end-user/desktop access to the Web. Reporters also have access to the intranet we have built which developed from an existing service we operate on ATEX, lib-wir. This consists of several mini-databases constructed by R&I covering subjects that are recurring. Thus there are lists of IRA bombs, air accidents, top libel awards, chronologies, anything that reporters might need access to in a hurry. Maintenance, however, is a concern and rather than continue to build these lists ourselves, we will now create hyper-text links through to good Web sites wherever possible. A slight irritation is that the serious sites which we build are copied by our own *Guardian* Media Lab, with whom we cannot compete when it comes to design. We hope to develop stronger ties with the lab to prevent duplication of work and to co-operate on intranet design. In truth it is not a serious problem; we simply link through to our own Web site and the learning curve involved in building difficult sites has been a useful one.

Other plans for the future involve the development of our Computer Assisted Reporting programme which, no doubt, will include downloading sites from the Web and marrying the data with other sources. We also plan to have cybrarians on the various desks alongside some monitoring of specific sites and subject areas. This latter plan is crucial as the Web is increasingly being chosen as the place to release information. The 1998 David Shayler case of alleged MI5 surveillance of Labour politicians highlights one use of information released onto the Internet, for Shayler, whilst situated in Paris, used it to air his allegations. The British Government meanwhile has been attempting to have him extradited to the UK on charges of breaching the Official Secrets Act. Thus, the Internet is here to stay.

▶ THE CHANGING INFORMATION ENVIRONMENT: THE MEDIA AND THE INTERNET

How was Internet use developing in other papers? Did it follow a similar pattern to *The Guardian*? The City University project (1998) had several concerns. What about the much touted question of information overload? What impact would growing end-use have on the information professional, on journalists themselves and on the commercial online hosts and more traditional information sources? Were users worried by the alleged lack of authority and quality of data on the Internet? Does the Internet herald the dawn of a new information age or have we been here before with online, CD-ROM and even the telephone?

These were the issues that the group involved – a multi-disciplinary one of journalists, librarians and academic information specialists – thought to study when they started on the interviewing process of over 150 journalists in both the national and regional press and broadcast media. But the concerns actually voiced were rather different and centred round fears that news was being 'dumbed down'; that readers may suffer from 'information malnutrition' as a result of being force-fed information from a vast array of sources; that Web publishing hours might impact negatively on their job. The group was even less concerned about the issues that fill library periodicals – are search engines efficient enough, and are intelligent agents intelligent enough?

Indeed the results at large were rather surprising. Firstly, use of the Internet was found to be low and extremely patchy amongst journalists. This seemed to be for a number of reasons – editorial systems at the time of the study were not always PC-based so there was a lack of desk-top access that the authors thought significant. Time constraints played a part too; most journalists do not feel information-impoverished, although often librarians would use the Internet to answer queries on their behalf, a fact of which they remained unaware. By and large the Internet seemed marginal and even e-mail was only used to seek, rather than share information, and to communicate across time zones. Several journalists complained that they wanted the instant response which they maintained the telephone gave them, along with information difficult to ascertain by e-mail, such as a hesitancy in answering questions perhaps, or the ability to press a question home. News groups, as reflected at *The Guardian*, were largely ignored, although most journalists, unlike those at *The Guardian*, were delighted to be able to have access to press releases online.

The much touted 'information overload' hardly seemed to register with journalists, though they worried about it for their readers. Journalists are used to filtering out information quickly as part of a daily routine and the Internet, if they used it, was just one more information source. They examined the first few hits and set ruthless time limits on the information searched. Only a few expressed concern about this. Perhaps the lack of a tradition of academic journalism in the UK is significant here. It was rare for people to expound the consequences of such searching methods on their profession, and whilst dumbing down was seen as an Internet trait, few equated that with their own searching methods.

Similarly, the authority of sites was rarely questioned. Once again reporters stressed that they are fast assimilators and disseminators used to making judgments of this kind. This is undoubtedly true but the researchers, in this case, were less confident. There seemed to be little awareness of the possibility of fake sites, of a necessity to verify information and of a need to look for dated updates.

Journalists were not at all concerned with the displacement of online by the Internet; the Internet was seen as a niche provider reaching parts that other services did not. Media librarians, however, did notice the beginning of some slight displacement – of both books and some online databases. This changing scenario is good for information professionals as a whole; the more information which exists, the more reporters seem to want to rely on an intermediary filtering it for them.

Perhaps the most surprising finding, however, was that of age. With the exception of freelance and young new media types, culturally committed people working in new media labs (who were the exception of the trend at every stage of the analysis), the typical enthusiastic Internet user on newspapers was aged 40 plus. Moreover the impetus for use came typically from the top down rather than the bottom up.

There are two theories as to why this was the case. One is economic: editors and managers may want to save money, but most journalists want to save time and the Internet can seem like an imposition rather than a time saver. Secondly it was thought that people in senior positions may travel in a business capacity to countries like America where use is more widespread, have more time, easier access, planning roles, more money with which to buy expensive PCs for home use and most importantly have keen children to stir their enthusiasm.

These findings, interestingly enough, were borne out at the International Online Conference in December of 1997 where the research group gave a paper. A similar study conducted amongst academic staff had discovered exactly the same age profile. Bright young things, it seems, are too busy working and holding down a job, and are very often on short-term contracts. For once the oldies triumph, but not, in the opinion of the research group, for very long. If they want to hold on to their lead they will have to start some serious surfing.

As with online, however, it was the librarians who were leading the way – mostly. There were still some papers where the Internet had made no impact whatsoever, with neither librarians nor journalists biting the bullet and there was one, the failed *Sunday Business*, which used the Internet instead of a library. Also – and this was the positive bit – it was the activities of the in-house librarians that tended to set the tone. In papers where librarians were Internet aware, this seemed to spill over on to journalists.

▶ CONCLUSIONS

What conclusions can we draw from all this and will end use of the Internet be the final nail in the coffin of the media librarian? Frankly it depends on the day! The death of the media librarian has been predicted for a long time and it is true that our numbers overall have decreased in the UK. Yet, history has shown that, thus far, those libraries which embrace new technology and accommodate the end-user are usually, though not always, the ones to survive; this was particularly true of online innovations.

There are signs that journalists are also in the front line this time round, but although there are indications from media labs of a new appreciation of information specialists' skills and even the odd brave soul who predicts the death of journalism and the rise and rise of the librarian, it is hard to envisage librarians triumphing over the gigantic ego of the national press in a face to face conflict with journalists, particularly if they themselves come under pressure.

An article in *UK Press Gazette* (1998) about the shortage of journalists in new media labs points out that they do not search for journalists with tekkie skills: 'When journalists arrive at the *Electronic Telegraph* they generally have no online training other than the ability to navigate round the Internet for research purposes'. This simply becomes a gradual and integral part of their lives in the way that editorial systems and online hosts have. The job evolves. It is the journalistic skills they want, not necessarily the technical ones. (One wonders though if these journalists have ever had evaluative Internet training.)

As far as hard copy goes, newspaper managements like the sound of end-users if this means saving on library costs, particularly when a recession is predicted. Whether this is ill-advised or not is almost irrelevant. The results of the City University study were exceedingly optimistic and in line with previous studies and we just have to hope that people other than librarians read them. The conclusion was that the more information there is, the more filtering by professional staff is needed. And arguably our status increases with each new wave of technology. It is interesting to note that the status of the librarian has risen by three points in recent years putting them on a par with doctors and lawyers (Bain, 1998) and this would seem to reflect those predictions. However, librarians themselves are divided about the outcome – even in this book.

If one casts one's mind back some fifteen years or so one realizes just how much the media librarian's job has changed and how far we have come, whether or not the mobile profession of journalism has real-ized it. *The Guardian* R&I Unit is almost unrecognizable from the passive paper-based library it once was. The skills we have acquired, the qualifi-cations we ask for, are top of the range.

Nevertheless how does one measure status? Our jobs are more inter-esting certainly. We feel more confident in our role. We are co-opted on to more meetings and committees perhaps. Editors, or some of them, are more aware of their library's existence even if the groans of boredom at the sight of yet another library memo are barely stifled. Newspapers which devote whole sections to the subject of journalism have a notable attack of dyslexia when it comes to editorial management reading three para-graphs about an information policy even when such a policy would reduce duplication of work patterns.

But promotion, when it comes, tends to move us further from our library roots and there are few, if any, librarians sitting on boards. Knowledge Management is being wrested from us by Human Resources departments (a group of people which has changed its name, status and salary level rather more successfully than librarians). IT departments steal our clothes. Our salaries are often less than half the average journalistic one, even though our staff tend to be better qualified. Journalists are often put in charge of teams to set up electronic archives and look surprised when you volunteer to do the compulsory Internet training, even if they autho-rized the cheque that sent you off to learn how to do it in the first place.

Maybe that is where the rub comes, for journalists are consummate assimilators and disseminators; their whole job and one of their main and most enviable skills is the fast mastering of a brief, any brief, no matter how complicated. It is hard for such people, used to dumbing down infor-mation for the rest of us, to place much value on exclusive skills or expertise.

Now, however, journalists are up against expertise themselves. With the Internet comes the ability for readers, who are also experts in their own field, to put their views direct, to dictate the nature of the paper they would like to read. Journalists, always middlemen, could possibly find themselves bypassed by the new technology allied to the end-user, but it is not very likely. They will simply adapt as librarians have had to since the development of online technology.

Librarians however, do slot more readily perhaps into the media labs than they do into the hard copy paper. Web sites are about facts, research, search engines and archiving as well as about writing and jour-nalism, and there are a few smart librarians heading new media labs. The electronic nature of media labs requires information skills – they need a thesaurus to order their massive bookmark lists, they need someone trained in evaluation to sift through Web sites for recommendation and use. (We just knew all those years of 'cutting up' papers had to come into its own! No one ever recognized the skill involved in that.) They need, but do not always have, librarians to advise on search engines, a vital element in something as impossibly enormous as the Internet; on archiving and interfaces; on information management in short. Some Web masters go so far as to say that search engines are replacing individual newspapers and broadcasters as they can aggregate information from different sources and it is therefore information managers, not journalists, who will be the news providers. But to profit from the advantages we are going to have to buck up our ideas and keep one step ahead of the game and most importantly this role is one that only appeals to a certain kind of librarian; the human element is vanishing.

The library's day as we knew it, the passive cuttings collection, is nearly done. It may well make financial and administrative sense to organize activities centrally but the people themselves, released from their library desks by the discarding of the paper cutting, will have to move beyond the parameters of the library if they are to survive.

The rise and rise of the 'researcher' in newspaper offices, working alongside the infinitely more skilled ones in the library (to whom they, ironically and extremely financially inefficiently, bring their queries) is no accident. Quality is not always the byword associated with research so much as convenience, familiarity and – whisper the word – dogsbody. In chapter 4 in this volume Nora Paul writes enthusiastically and even inspiringly about new age journalism requiring new age news researchers, and if ever you feel jaded and disillusioned about your job take yourself off to one of Nora's talks to be reborn. Nevertheless, British information professionals are entitled to feel a little wary about this futuristic vision of the research part of their job in a country where the party that promised us our long awaited Freedom of Information Act is backing off at the speed of light. Computer Assisted Reporting (CAR) of the kind practised in the vastness of America, with its essentially local press, is extremely hard to translate into British national press terms, being too parochial for its needs. There is really only a handful of regional papers, where huge opportunities lie in this type of CAR, with the resources or nous to employ researcher librarians, or enough of them.

The kind of CAR that could take place in a national press concerned with national issues is heavily dependent on government information being available digitally. This may be beginning to happen slowly, but we still seem light years away from the situation in the US.

We are currently suffocating under the weight of newsprint generated by Ken Starr's report on the Clinton–Lewinsky scandal. Fun reading no doubt, allied perhaps to a certain European cynicism on matters sexual, but had it been Judge Blogs's report on Tony Blair's philandering it is hard to imagine that it would have been released on the Internet – the People's Report perhaps.

Our own position, as subjects to be kept in the dark, will make the most ardently monarchist librarian look enviously towards the citizen news researcher in the States, with a right to know and the means to find out. Without the endless possibilities of CAR at our disposal, and only the exciting possibilities of the intranet to lead us into the twenty-first century, is our future less assured? Possibly. The kind of future is envisaged by Richard Withey (chapter 4 in this volume), and Hunt and Nichols (1998). Technical librarian as backroom boy/girl is the most likely future scenario in the UK, but there will be many who regret the human intervention of the news researcher and who again look enviously towards America.

It is easy for a UK librarian to wax lyrical about information overload, and filtering and quality research, about how we will train and guide people through listservs and news groups and the like. It is easy for them to see the opportunities available in intranet construction and management (an interest we share with IT, new media labs and even the new personnel departments), harder for cost-cutting managements to be convinced.

We are dependent to some extent on enlightened editors, but that is where the lack of an academic tradition of journalism in the UK works against us – the links we are forging with schools of journalism go unnoticed. Our role in the news room is generally unrecognized in any structured way. And editors, of course, are also busy people. Nora Paul in chapter 5 is right. The balance of the journalist/librarian relationship in the news room must and will change if it is to survive at all; it ought to become more of a partnership; and will be more accepting of the end-user. That in itself should not prove to be a problem. Many British media libraries embraced the end-user over a decade ago and in that same decade change and adaptation have become our middle names. The real question is, in an area where results are hard to quantify, will the men in suits recognize its worth?

▶ REFERENCES

Bain, C. (1998) Our 15-class society: prof's social scale for the next century. *Daily Mirror*, 14 September 1998

City University (1998) *The changing information environment: the media and the Internet*, April 1997-March 1998. http://www.soi.city.ac.uk/pw/ji3/5Mi_3/5M0home.html

From paint to pixel (1998) *UK Press Gazette*, 23 October 1998

Hunt, R. and Nicholas, D. (1998) Withering news. *Online Information 98. Proceedings of the 22nd International Online Information Meeting*, pp. 91–94. Oxford: Learned Information

▶ FURTHER READING

Garrison, B. (1997) The Web in the newsroom 1997.
    http://www.miami.edu/com/car/spj-97/index.htm

Jenkins, S. (1995) The death of the written word. *Journal of Information Science*, **21**(6),
    407–412

Nicholas, D. and Martin, H. (1993) Should journalists search themselves? (And what
    happens if they do?). *Online Information 93. Proceedings of the 17th International
    Online Information Meeting*, pp.227–234. Oxford: Learned Information

Nicholas, D. and Martin, H. (1997) Assessing information needs: a case study of
    journalists. *Aslib Proceedings*, **49**(2), 43–52

▶ USEFUL WEB SITES TO BOOKMARK

http://jurist.law.pitt.edu/impeach.htm
    From Jurist, the law Professors' Network, this site includes guides to
    impeachments in US history and general information.

http://www.pbs.org/wgbh/pages/frontline/shows/ira/inside/weapons.html
    Offers an IRA weapons assessment inventory by Jane's Intelligence Review. This
    is not up to date (1996) but does include locations of arms dumps.

http://www.pmel.noaa.gov/toga-tao/el-nino/home.html
    El Nino theme page from US National Oceanic and Atmospheric Administration
    Web site.

http://www/cagle.com
    Cannes film festival official.

http://www.albanian.com/main/countries/kosova/index.html
    For information on Kosova.

http://www.2000.co.uk
    Millennium site.

7 The News International newspapers' intranet experience: a case study*

Gertrud Erbach and Lynda Iley

▶ HOW IT ALL STARTED

Since 1985, News International has maintained an in-house database providing access to the text of *The Times* and *The Sunday Times*. Full text of *Times* supplements was added in October 1994. Since 1996, there has also been access to the text of *The Sun* and *News of the World*. In addition, News International exchange text with several other newspaper proprietors. With the addition of other daily and Sunday nationals, the Editorial Services database has developed into a powerful research tool for librarians and journalists at News International.

The Editorial Services database originally ran on Information Dimension's BASISK, but was migrated to BASISPlus. Migration was completed by the end of 1996. The front end for the new version was a result of co-operation between an experienced online searcher from the Reference Library and the Editorial Services Database Administrator. Their combined efforts resulted in a user-friendly and flexible front end and led to increased use of the database. As part of the migration, it was planned that the new version should have a Windows and a character cell front end with different levels of use for different types of users. The Windows front end would have used BASIS Desktop software while the character cell front end was running using FQM procedures.

Desktop was never introduced for this purpose as it did not provide all of the functionality requested. It had some compatibility problems with the network software being used and was difficult to customize. Many changes required reconfiguration of each user's PC, and licences were relatively expensive. An alternative Windows-type front end was still required.

*This piece first appeared in *Aslib Proceedings* 51(1), pp.30–4

In 1996, Information Dimensions released and strongly promoted their BASIS Intranet Solutions WEBserver – enhanced versions of the BASIS products designed to support the use of WWW technologies in intranet applications (http://www.basisopentext.co.uk). BASIS WEBserver was shipped in combination with the Netscape Commerce Server. BASIS Release 8 fully incorporated BASIS Web products and included BASIS Document Manager; BASIS WEBserver Gateway and Netscape Enterprise Server supporting document delivery across the Web and CIC (Corporate Information Centre), a rapid prototyping framework for intranet development. This software seemed the obvious choice as it was developed by the suppliers of the database software.

▶ DEFINING THE PROJECT

By the end of 1996, the largest part of the News International migration project was complete and the path was clear to implement the Web-based front end. A project was set up whose primary purpose was the provision of intranet access to the editorial database. Browser software was initially Netscape but we have since migrated to Microsoft Explorer.

The project's aim was the creation of an 'Editorial Services intranet' to provide:

- access to the editorial database through a user-friendly Graphical User Interface (GUI) front end;
- access to other relevant sources of information. This would include material from the Reference Library as a minimum; information from other departments would be desirable;
- access for all PC users;
- compatibility with the new News International production system, Hermes and its DocCenter archival function.

Some expected benefits were:

- the software was relatively inexpensive and News International already had a site licence for browser software;
- ease of administration as configuration of each user's PC would not be necessary;
- intranet access would provide the user-friendly Windows-type interface most people are becoming used to and little user training would be required;
- this interface could provide access not just to the database, but to other useful information such as Reference Library materials;

- the information would be constantly up-to-date;
- potential cost savings due to a reduced need for printed information;
- potential for improving lines of communication within the company;
- potential for integration with Hermes archival function.

▶ ESTABLISHING THE PROJECT TEAM

The project was driven by staff from two departments within Editorial Services – the Reference Library and the Information & Database Services Department. Additional help was provided by one member from the IT department.

The team which came together to develop the intranet brought different skills to the project. The project leader, the Database Administrator, had BASIS and Unix skills; the Electronic Information Manager managed the content and the Internet Librarian had some design and HTML skills.

However, the intranet was a huge learning experience for everyone involved. Each member attended the Informed Business Services course 'Creating Web Pages'. The Database Administrator taught the Electronic Information Manager the Unix vi editor and directory structure on the server. This allowed the librarians freedom to create pages, add HTML and edit files.

HTML editors could have been used but we decided against this as they tend to generate browser specific HTML and also can produce 'non-human readable' HTML; i.e. it can be very cluttered. A simple word-processing package could also have been used but Unix vi proved quick and efficient.

The Electronic Information Manager and Internet Librarian attended the Information Dimensions course 'BASIS intranet DBA' to gain an insight into database administration and managing databases for the intranet.

▶ DEVELOPING AND UPDATING CONTENT FOR THE EDITORIAL RESEARCH INTRANET

Initially, content for the intranet was planned with editorial users in mind in line with company policy to increase direct access to information for journalists on their desktops. Direct access to the editorial database via a simple, intuitive front end allowing journalists to search without much need for training was the first priority.

The Reference Library at News International is a very busy department. Operating 19 hours a day, seven days a week, the department provides an information and research service for journalists from News International's four titles and corporate staff. Between 600 and 700 enquiries are handled on an average weekday.

Much of the library's work is reactive – finding background material to breaking news stories for reporters or checking facts and figures for sub-editors. However, certain types of enquiries are recurring, such as requests for the spelling of names, basic information on a country, the chronology of events of an ongoing story such as the Northern Ireland Peace Process or economic indicators. In anticipation of these recurring enquiries, library staff over the years have compiled chronologies, lists and indices to make some of the information available quickly to allow for a more efficient service. Some information was available as Cardbox databases.

The intranet seemed the ideal medium to make these information resources directly available to journalists' desktops, giving them speedier access to certain types of information and reducing pressure on the library staff.

Editorial database

The database has been split into two due to its size. The first database stores data from 1985–1994 and the second data from 1995 to date. The priority for the intranet was a search screen for the editorial database.

Librarians access the database via a telnet session using the BASIS command language. It is very powerful but users need a high level of training. While the command language does not pose a problem for experienced researchers it can be difficult for end-users. The Web front end was designed so that anyone could use the database. Context-sensitive help is provided on each screen just in case there are problems.

The Web front end uses a Perl CGI script which sits in front of the standard BASIS Webserver CGI binary. It uses cookies* to keep the search terms available to the server when each request is performed and when refining searches. The search screens are generated dynamically by the Perl script depending on which database is being searched. Users on the intranet can choose between the two databases. It also performs manipulation of the search terms (dates and publications) so that they are understood by the standard BASIS Webserver gateway.

The database is made up of approximately 35 fields, some of which are used for searching. The Web front end initially used only four of these

---

*A cookie is a tiny file placed on a PC by a Web site to allow it to recognize the machine when the Web site is revisited.

fields – date, headline, byline and story. The default was to search all available titles but the user also had the choice of restricting a search to tabloids, broadsheets or supplements.

In January 1998 an advanced Web front end was introduced which allowed users to choose individual titles and search using the headline and first two paragraphs of text only. The dates on the search screen appear as drop down menus.

Headline, byline and story are text fields and users only need to enter words or phrases then click on search to retrieve a list of headlines. The headline is then used as a link to the full text of the article.

One advantage for the journalists is that they can take extracts from retrieved articles, edit or rewrite these extracts and paste them into their current stories rather than having to print or download into a file first. Journalists prefer searching the editorial database via the Web front end despite the fact that speed of retrieval is rather slower than through a telnet session.

Reference Library databases

The next project phase aimed to make some of the Reference Library material available. The Reference Library had used Cardbox Plus software to compile five small databases. These included a record of all aviation disasters and a record of murders of police officers in Britain.

The team decided to combine these databases into one large BASIS database. The first step was to create a database definition list (ddl) or a set of fields which made up the database. There were several common fields for each of the small databases, e.g. name. A number of fields overlapped and some could be combined. There was also a number of unique fields for each database.

One of these unique fields was used from each of the Cardbox databases to establish the view. For example, 'police force' only appeared in the police murders database and this field identified records which should appear in the Police view of the database. It was decided that there should be one 'reflib' ddl and a number of different views so that the user would see five 'different' databases even though there was only one underlying database. The five views were then made available through BASIS Desktop for staff to enter new records and make any amendments. Help sheets were written to ensure consistency of data input.

A new format was then designed on Cardbox Plus to enter the correct fields for the new BASISPlus database and take into account the new and combined fields. The records were dumped into a text file out of Cardbox. This file was then transferred to the server using Onnet file transfer protocol (FTP).

A copy of the file was made on the server and the Database Administrator split them using a script and ran a series of perl scripts to tidy the files. This ensured the data was displayed in the same format; e.g. on some of the databases block capitals had been used, so a script replaced these with lower case except for names or first words of sentences.

The new files were then loaded using High Volume Upload (HVU) on BASIS. Records which failed validation, that is those which had incorrect date formats or had empty unique fields, were placed in separate files and passed to the Electronic Information Manager for correction. These were then copied to a retry directory and loaded.

Default BASISPlus Webserver forms were generated using bwgenform – this provides default forms for searching and displaying using a browser. These were then edited: for example the default search and help buttons were changed, the search forms appeared as a table, several superfluous buttons were removed, fields which were not used for searching were removed and the remaining fields were arranged in a logical order. The same procedure was followed for the book catalogue.

New databases have been added over the past year including motor racing accidents and rail disasters. Work is ongoing on a country database with basic information on each country and a contacts database giving telephone numbers of organizations.

Reference Library research material

Reference Library research projects ranged from the life and times of various celebrities to a list of all IRA attacks on mainland Britain, a history of the Peace Process in Northern Ireland, a complete list of all ministerial resignations and sackings since 1900 and various histories of the Royal Family. There were 62 of these, all available as Word documents. The files were saved as text files and then moved onto the server using ftp. HTML was added including appropriate links – for example a link from IRA Attacks to the Peace Process and vice versa.

In the past year around 15 new projects have been added including a history of the FA Cup and a complete guide to the World Cup. The World Cup pages were updated daily to give match results, scorers and attendances.

Miscellaneous content

Conversion tables

Metric/Imperial conversion tables are provided. There is some Java script which enables users to calculate distances (what is 565 kilometres in miles and vice versa), weights and measures.

Public Libraries

The Reference Library has a record of major public reference libraries holding copies of News International titles on microfilm or in hard copy, allowing the Library to direct callers enquiring about availability of news-paper material to their nearest public library. This was made available on the intranet for all departments who receive readers' requests.

Associations

Journalists often need to telephone trade associations to gain facts or soundbites for stories. Rather than ringing the library to find a name and telephone number, a list of associations arranged by subject was made available. Therefore, if a story is being written on asthma and the jour-nalist needs accurate numbers, they can look up the National Asthma Society without ringing the library and holding on in the queuing system.

Internet links

Searching the Internet for accurate, useful information is still a time-consuming task. The Internet Librarian originally spent some time trawling the Web and finding such sites. A list of links was then produced which was divided by subject, e.g. Government, Entertainment, etc.

Style guides

Newspapers have their own in-house style guides which aim to provide writers and sub-editors with a quick reference to points of grammar and spelling and to guide them through protocols in specialized areas where confusion may arise. *The Times* style guide was added to the intranet site and has since been updated, ensuring that the electronic guide is always more current than is possible in the hard copy version. The style guide is complemented by a list of frequently asked spellings not covered in the guide and prepared by library staff.

Maintaining and updating the content

Keeping content up to date is one of the most common problems identi-fied for intranets (Morton, 1998). There were two areas of updates to consider. The first was that much of the initial content on the intranet would become unreliable without regular updates and would lose credi-bility with journalists.

It was unrealistic to expect one person to keep up with updating all research projects and five dynamic databases. We decided to give an intro-duction to BASIS Desktop to each of the staff who had compiled the databases initially. Staff were then given the responsibility for keeping the databases up to date. The research projects are updated by one member of staff who has been allocated three hours each day to scan newspapers and update where relevant. Updating is fairly straightforward. The information is entered and automatically updated on the server.

Secondly, it quickly became apparent that without new content the service would stagnate. Reference Library staff have continued to develop research topics and databases and these have been added. A 'What's New' section has been established on the Home Page to attract the users' attention.

Promoting the intranet

Once the initial content was complete, the intranet was named Edse-Web (Editorial Services Web) and was successfully promoted within the company as a valuable research tool for journalists.

► TRAINING

Edse-Web has been available since July 1997. At that time journalists at News International were still all using dumb terminals which did not support Internet/intranet access. In September 1997 *The Sunday Times* became the first title to move to the new NT environment; the other three News International titles have since followed.

Journalists are busy people and are often reluctant to make time for training. The Reference Library's online training strategy acknowledges this and training is largely done on an *ad hoc* basis.

With this in mind, the intranet was specifically designed to be as simple as possible. There are help screens where appropriate. There are easy menus. All pages are displayed within a frame with a side menu to ensure quick, simple navigation. However, it is still useful to sit with users for 15 minutes and take them through the options open to them. Help sheets and leaflets detailing what is available via the intranet have been distributed.

However, a more structured approach has been possible on *The Times*. The paper recently moved to new offices and onto an NT platform. As part of a compulsory programme of NT training, journalists were given an introduction to the intranet which has been followed up by librarians. Although the training was minimal, the benefits of increased and more effective use of the editorial database are visible.

Library staff have also made training visits to the company's bureaux in Glasgow and Manchester, offering a flexible training timetable. Two trainers offered short training slots throughout the day giving journalists the flexibility to be trained when they could find the time. We can give a broad overview of the intranet in 15 minutes but once the journalists sit down and realize the benefits, they tend to stay for an hour asking questions and offering suggestions.

▶ FUTURE DEVELOPMENTS

Content for Edse-Web will continue to be developed and managed by the Editorial Services Department. New databases are already under construction and Reference Library staff are working on information packages relating to forthcoming events. It is hoped that, as access to the intranet becomes more widely available, users will recognize its value to the organization and submit their own contributions for inclusion. An e-mail link invites users to send comments and suggestions.

▶ ACKNOWLEDGEMENTS

The authors wish to express their special thanks to Graine Milner.

▶ REFERENCES

Morton, C. (1998) Intranets: some problems and solutions. *Managing Information*, **5**(4), 26–27

▶ USEFUL WEB SITES

IBS (Informed Business Services, now trading as Keep Informed) has a good intranet help site which lists all useful links: http/www.informed-ibs.com/training/pages/link/INTRANET.html

News Librarians Division of the Special Library Association site provides further articles, links to useful Web sites and examples of intranets at various US newspapers: http://metalab.unc.edu/slanews/intranets

Mark Toner, Connecting with intranets: http://www.naa.org.presstime/1912/intranet.html

Phil Bradley: http://www.philb.com

To view an example of a newspaper intranet, edited for public viewing, see:
http://express-news.net/research

8 Good news, bad news: credibility of information and data gathered from the Internet and the World Wide Web

Barbara P. Semonche

▶ INTRODUCTION

This chapter will discuss information quality on the Web. It will also address Web search engines and offer some useful Web sites for evaluating Web site accuracy and credibility. Examples of bias, rumours, hoaxes and fraud on the Internet are shown as illustrations of pervasive disinformation. Examples of Web sites showcasing trustworthy data will also be offered. Journalists, editors, and news researchers are not only consumers of information, but they are also information providers and as such share a heightened responsibility to combat vigorously the errors that infiltrate the pre- and post-publishing process. Journalistic accuracy and news researchers' contributions to journalistic excellence are discussed.

▶ IN INTERNET WE TRUST?

'The Information Age has one nagging problem: much of the information is not true. We live in a time besotted with bad information.' Joel Achenbach (1996)

That the Web is dynamic, seductive, often disorganized, and includes information of dubious quality is hardly a surprise even to Internet neophytes. With the vast, ever-growing amount of material on the Internet, separating the valid from the questionable is difficult. Internet searchers soon discover that academic information is retrieved along with humour, advertisements, and personal Web pages. None can be trusted without subsequent verification. Having no hard and fast rules by which to separate the 'infojunk' from reliable information, one must rely upon common sense and experience. There are, however, reliable subject guides, pathfinders and information professionals or cyber scouts, known in earlier life as 'librarians,' who can and do help with the verification and evaluation of sources and data.

The Internet, and in particular the World Wide Web, affords a global platform to anyone who has access to the technology. The Internet Index compiled by Win Treese (http://www.openmarket.com/intindex/index.cfm) estimates that the number of Web pages in April 1998 was 320 million. According to the Newspaper Association of America's 'Facts About Newspapers' (http://www.naa.org) there are more than 750 North American daily newspapers that have launched online services, including Web sites, as of April 1998. Worldwide, there are more than 2800 daily, weekly and other newspapers online. And more than 75 per cent of the daily newspapers on the Web have circulations under 50 000. The number of newspaper archives on the Web is estimated to be much smaller, but it is growing. Media organizations have a tradition of careful fact-checking and editing, but they are not without problems in accuracy and credibility of what they publish and broadcast. Individuals or groups engaged in cyberpublishing may or may not have this tradition or commitment to high standards of accuracy. Therefore, on the Internet, universal trust and a too ready acceptance of the reliability of information found there is not only unwise, but it may be dangerous as well. The savvy Internet user is wary of all information and data presented and makes the effort and acquires the skills to become an astute evaluator of information quality.

Anecdotes abound about the kinds of erroneous material discovered on the Internet. Examples of rumours, fraud and hoaxes are plentiful. Still, even sophisticated Internet users, including professional journalists, can get caught trusting false 'information' which has thoughtlessly and sometimes deliberately been launched in electronic mail messages, chat rooms and Web sites.

Financial gossip and rumours posted about companies via electronic message boards can spread malicious misinformation (Goldstein, 1998). In 1998, federal regulators expressed concern publicly about the intent of some investors to pump up the price of thinly traded stocks they own or drive down the price of those they have sold short. Also in 1998, *The Cincinnati Enquirer* and Chiquita Brands came to legal blows over a reporter's unauthorized access to corporate e-mail messages (Franz, 1998). Again in 1998, Cable News Network (CNN) retracted its Operation Tailwind story when veterans with Internet access quickly mobilized a counter attack on the charge that Air Force pilots dropped sarin gas on a Laotian village (see for example, McMenamin, 1998). In 1997, Matt Drudge's online 'Drudge Report' repeated rumours that White House adviser Sidney Blumenthal had abused his wife. Drudge later retracted the item, but not before Blumenthal filed a $30 million libel suit (Zaslow, 1998). Also in 1997, there was the hoax perpetrated on the Web by some as yet anonymous jokester misrepresenting a column by *Chicago Tribune* writer Mary Schmich. The Internet version credited Schmich's published column to author Kurt Vonnegut's graduation speech at Massachusetts Institute of Technology. Vonnegut never spoke at MIT's graduation ceremony (Young, 1997). In 1996, Pierre Salinger unwisely trusted flawed information he found on the Internet about the calamitous crash of Trans World Airlines Flight 800 (see for example, Goldman and Dahlburg, 1997), and one of the most troubling incidents of journalistic unethical behaviour was during the 1994 Winter Olympics when sports reporters snooped in skater Tonya Harding's e-mail account (Brand-Williams and St. John, 1994).

These hoaxes and serious lapses of journalistic trustworthiness received considerable publicity. Doubtless there are other examples, perhaps not as well known, but just as crucial to the quality and accuracy of information circulating on the Internet. What is most troubling is that it is impossible to expurgate misinformation completely. Searchers must be willing to search carefully and thoroughly, or they too will discover that they may be responsible for perpetuating errors, fraud and hoaxes on the Internet.

A prime example of 'hoax busting', is revealed in this story by a news library researcher and a reporter from *The Miami Herald*. This article is reprinted with permission from *The Miami Herald*.

> Published: Friday, August 2, 1996
> Section: FRONT
> Page: 1A
> CYBERHOAX: HOW A LIE
> GOT LIFE ON THE INTERNET
>
> CURTIS MORGAN and ELISABETH DONOVAN
> *Herald* Staff Writers
>
> In cyberspace, they call it trolling.
> Post something outrageous online and see who bites.
> Someone went trolling last week, placing a bogus message about the downing of TWA Flight 800, using the hot-button words 'Bill Clinton' and a credible source, '*The Miami Herald*.'
> The result: fodder for anti-government conspiracy buffs, a rumor that spread like electronic wildfire, a flood of inquiries to *The Herald* – and some questions about the power of the Internet.
> 'There is a lot of fear going on around that this kind of thing could have serious ramifications', said Charles Green, a journalism professor at Florida International University.

On July 24, a short message appeared in the alt.conspiracy newsgroup, one of thousands of discussion forums on the Internet, about the TWA crash off Long Island that killed all 230 people aboard.

It read: 'It was reported in *The Miami Herald* today that two of the passengers were former Arkansas state troopers that were on Bill Clinton's security detail. They were on their way to Paris to be interviewed by *Le Monde* in Paris, as well as the *News of the World* in London.'

Some ex-troopers who guarded Clinton when he was governor of Arkansas have alleged that they helped him meet women and book hotel rooms for illicit liaisons. Clinton has repeatedly denied the allegations.

But there were no troopers aboard the flight. *The Herald* never carried such a story. Nor did any other major media.

The posting sat three days before another user calling himself Rambo copied it to other Web sites whose addresses include telltale words like activism.militia, survivalism and impeach.clinton. By Thursday, the message was on at least a dozen news groups frequented by anti-government users, and it drew immediate response. Most scoffed or emphasized that it was an unverified report, but some swallowed the bait. They viewed it as an extension of tragic events – which they consider suspicious – that included the suicide of presidential adviser Vincent Foster and the death of Commerce Secretary Ron Brown in a plane crash in Bosnia.

'Read the reports', one entry says, 'so far over 100 people that worked for him in Ark. are dead.' Another rebuffs a doubter this way: 'Why do you say conspiracy theory? I thought this was a mention of a fact seen in *The Miami Herald*. You can make your own conclusions.'

On the airwaves

The hoax also reached both short-wave and talk radio. *The Herald* received calls from Idaho, California, Virginia, Maryland and elsewhere from people seeking copies of the article.

Robert Wilson, who does radio commentary for Wake Up America, a Washington, D.C.-based programme that broadcasts on five stations covering 20 states, called *The Herald* to verify the story. He heard it on tape from another radio show, reported as fact. Wilson called the fabrication 'poisonous information from a poisoned well'.

The hoax does raise questions about the 'Net. No one can say how many bogus messages are sent out every day, but the TWA hoax underlines how easily the 'Net can be misused.

Hilbert Levitz, a computer-science professor at Florida State University and president of the city's free online system, says pranks have not created widespread problems but have been mostly simple annoyances.

'It doesn't seem to be as serious as it could be, but the potential is there,' Levitz said.

Green, the FIU professor, likens the 'Net to a street corner. 'Anyone can come along and say what they want.'

Most people will take 'Net discussions with a grain of salt, but others simply believe what they read. That poses some dangers.

Hypothetical case

'Take a company stock, for example,' Green said. Say someone posts that *The Wall Street Journal* has reported that the president of a major multinational corporation has absconded with the company funds.

There is already heated debate over the issue of privacy on the 'Net. Pranks like this will only add fuel to the fire. Green expects the Internet will eventually have to find a way to deal with such problems. For now, though, no one can agree on how – or if – to police the 'Net.

The Herald traced the original posting to the Internet address of Gene Hilsheimer, who supervises a military flight simulator in Panama City. Hilsheimer denied creating it.

'Well, gosh, it's amazing what goes out there and is picked up,' said Hilsheimer, a former Homestead resident who moved to the Panhandle after he was displaced by Hurricane Andrew in 1992.

But in electronic mail to *The Herald*, he played coy: 'I am certain that the person or persons who posted this . . . had no idea how many difficulties they may have created for both of us. However, if it was a simple troll, then whoever it was must be amazed at the effect they have had. Probably well beyond their original expectations.'

'Whoever they are, they should be ashamed of themselves and advised to pick a more fictitious source if they ever decide to go trolling in the future.'

Carol Ebbinghouse (1998), Director of the College of Law Library at Western State University, lists some useful Web sites for fighting the disinformation that bombards us all in April 1998's *Searcher* magazine. They are provided here.

Hoaxes: sites that fight the fakes
http://ciac.ln.gov/ciac/CIACHoaxes.html

Myths (and urban legends)
        http://www.urbanlegends.com
Frauds: investment fraud
        http://www.sec.gov/consumer/cyberfr.htm

Ebbinghouse also offers some recommendations to defuse and reduce the spread of disinformation. They include:

- think before you forward e-mail;
- never, never forward e-mail just because someone asks or encourages you to do so;
- investigate before you believe what is in your e-mail or on the Internet. If it sounds too good, bad or sad to be true, it probably is not true. There are plenty of resources to check out virus scares without forwarding a warning message any further. See http://www.2meta.com/april-fools for a collection of these types of virus hoaxes.

► QUALITY INFORMATION OR 'INFO JUNK'?

Information quality is a slippery subject. Truth is elusive. In many cases what is truth to one person may be nonsense or irrelevant to another. Within the morass of Internetworked data there are both valuable nuggets and an incredible amount of junk.

As a first step, it is possible to recognize that there are hallmarks of what is consistently 'good' information. The most basic requirements of good information are:

- objectivity – that the information is presented in a manner free from propaganda or disinformation;
- completeness – that the information is a complete as possible;
- viewpoint – that all aspects of the information are given and not restricted to present a particular viewpoint unless clearly identified as an advocacy or promotional source.

In evaluating information quality on the Web, there are several eloquent spokespersons. One is Hope N. Tillman, Director of Libraries, Babson College, Babson Park, Massachusetts. While her Web site (http://www.tiac.net/users/hope/findqual.html) is probably most appropriate for scholarly research, the criteria she outlines for evaluating information on the Internet are more generally applicable. Essentially Tillman advocates using common sense. The critical evaluative skills useful in critiquing books, reports and databases are the same ones required in sorting through the information found on the Internet. Other cybersavvy sleuths support this general checklist for measuring information quality on the Web:

Scope – what is the purpose of the site? Does it advocate a particular point of view? Is the information primary or secondary in nature? Do the pages include links to support its central ideas? Is the site inward-focused or outward-directed in its linking? (Disinformation is often self-referencing.)

Audience – for whom is the site intended? Is there a clear indication of the intended audience? Information needs to be at a level that the user can understand and assimilate. Information that is too complex or too simple is often useless. Is the site research oriented or is it meant to be informational or even entertaining?

Author – what is known about the author? Does the site offer credentials as to the background, education, experience or training of the Web site's creator? Can these references be validated? If the author is not well recognized, there are verification tools on the Web, such as Finger or WHOIS (http://www.network.solutions.com/cgi-bin/whois/whois), which may offer some help.

Publisher – as commercial activity has increased on the Web, marketing has also increased. Many 'information' sites are thinly disguised marketing or public relations efforts created by interested corporations. Bias, if there is any, should be apparent. Be advised that it is not just corporations who offer 'selected' information. Any agency, private or public, corporate or government, can (and frequently does) have its own agenda to promote and should be evaluated with the same care as any other source of information.

Currency – being up to date is vitally important in researching and collecting data. Is it clear when the site was created? When was it last updated? Is there a copyright date? Is there a publication date from a conference or journal? Are the links still active?

Accuracy – are misspellings evident? Are people, places and events correctly identified? Are numbers, percentages, statistics and polling data incomplete or suspect?

Archive – some dated or historical information is still valuable depending upon the researcher's purpose. Does the Web site offer access to earlier data? Can it be found easily and acquired legally? Is there a contact from which further information can be obtained?

Treatment – for a research document there should be an explanation of the data that was gathered and an explanation of the research methods used to gather and interpret it. Sources that the data rely upon should be cited fully. A bibliography should be included or be available.

Ease of Use – does the site require proprietary software or passwords to access the information? Are these easy to obtain? Is there a cost? Is the information presented in a logical, ordered manner? Is there a site map or index? Do graphics and multimedia enhance or detract from the quality of the site? Is a non-graphics display available? Can one navigate the site easily? Is there a way to exit the site easily?

'Isn't there a simpler way to evaluate digital data? In our brave new electronic age is there any software to help identify "info junk"?' Jean Ward, now retired from the University of Minnesota's School of Journalism and Mass Communication, asked this question in the Summer 1995 *Poynter Report*. Ward proposed, humorously, that software could come to the rescue of filtering out bad information. Specifically she suggested the creation of new applications such as:

- 'Accu-Meter' to give the accuracy score for each electronic file accessed;
- 'Stat-Check' to ring a loud bell on the computer when statistics err;
- 'Fact-Check' to flag sentences containing flawed facts;
- 'Plagia-Alert' to make copied phrases, sentences and paragraphs flash red when they are too close for comfort to another's work.

While such 'dream applications' may be a bit fanciful, the frustration journalists and researchers endure in finding and evaluating information is genuine. Reporters use the Internet and the Web for discovering news-worthy issues and topics, for following trends, finding potential inter-viewees, uncovering data for further investigation and for gaining leads to other useful sources. All of these methods are as essential to the news-gathering process as are telephone tips, press conferences, press releases, public records, expert testimony, news leaks and so-called authoritative publications. In short, the Internet and the Web are places where alert jour-nalists and librarians launch, not conclude, their research. These profes-sional researchers recognize that digital warehouses are primarily for browsing, not for scooping up factoids and running to press with them. Ward highlights the information quality issues that emerge in this process:

- Database dilemmas – search results often acquire more credibility than they deserve. Dirty data looks exactly the same as clean data (errors are endemic, they are endlessly perpetuated and indeed, they have been known to have an inexhaustible shelf life);
- Who said that? – cyberspace resembles gossip in some respects; anyone can say anything. And they do so without identifying clearly what is a rumour or humour;
- Corrections, anyone? – only a small fraction of the errors made by even respectable newspapers will be corrected in print. This is not to say that newspapers do not have corrections policies and procedures. They do, but implementing them, even in errors of fact, is challenging. This can lead to the newspaper making 'beta errors correcting

alpha mistakes'. This problem is exacerbated when some
published errors do not make it into the online databases or
into the Web archives. Consult this Web site for research and
policies on online database accuracy and corrections:
http://metalab.unc.edu/journalism/databasequality.html;

- Who's an expert? – discovering qualified persons willing to be
interviewed for publication or broadcast is difficult at best.
Relying upon earlier published stories, either on the Web or in
print, is a risky business without checking further;

- What about those numbers? – in our statistics-driven world,
many in the media have been too quick to accept numbers
from a wide variety of sources without adequately assessing
their reliability. Journalists and researchers have been burned
here and have developed suitably suspicious attitudes, even
about so-called official public records. (One praiseworthy
example: in a NewsLib e-mail message dated June 9, 1998,
Kitty Bennett, news researcher for the *St. Petersburg Times*
(FL), reported errors discovered in the United States Social
Security Death Index by a journalist working on a voter fraud
series.) For useful insight regarding numerical errors, consult
John Allen Paulos' (1996) book, *A mathematician reads the
newspaper*;

- Whose interpretation? – if the facts can be accepted, the
interview sources reused and statistics repeated from
previously published sources, is it any wonder that news
becomes stale and, perhaps, even prone to information that is
incomplete, out of date, and simply wrong?

- Who wrote this first? – plagiarism and the unethical invention
of quotes, data and events is not typical in journalism, but
there are some notable exceptions. Explanations offered
include deadline pressure, carelessness, and burnout. Most
journalists battle these demons daily and win. A few do not.
See Harry Amana's Web site for detailed accounts of these
and other examples of lapses in journalistic ethics:
http://www.unc.edu/~haman/news.htm.

Ward concludes with this challenge: 'If these are the questions, what
are the answers? Continued professional training in the ethical and knowledgeable search for information on the Internet and Web is a place to
begin. Recognize criteria for information quality. Encourage skepticism.
Punish plagiarism. And enlist news librarians' co-operation with editors
and reporters in identifying and supporting quality control programmes'.
In short, do not wait for 'dream software' to do the job.

For examples of Web pages that can be used to discuss authority
and accuracy, objectivity and currency and coverage in Internet training

sessions, please consult Janet Alexander and Marsha Tate's Web site: http://www2.widener.edu/Wolfgram-Memorial-Library/examples.htm. For even more information on this topic, a list of Web sites on evaluating information on the Web is provided in the appendix.

► WEB SEARCH ENGINES

Unless one has the exact location of a desired Web site, the URL (uniform resource locator), then one must either browse the Web or undertake to search cyberspace via a search engine. There are many of these with different search protocols and content affecting the amount and quality of search results.

There are basically two types of retrieval protocols functioning on the Web: indexes (sometimes referred to as directories) and search engines. *Multimedia Magazine* runs an annual 'Search Robot Test' to determine which type is the best (http://cyber-ventures.com/mh/paper/search98.htm). Of course, what is determined to be the 'best' is, in the final analysis, in the eyes of the searcher. As Internet guru Reva Basch has said repeatedly in her seminar, 'There is more to searching the Web than Web search engines'.

Susan Feldman (1997) offers some good, practical advice in evaluating Web search engines and services. She provides a major search engine feature chart that compares coverage, what is indexed, major commands, searching capabilities and special features. Reviewed are AltaVista, Excite, HotBot, Infoseek Ultra, Lycos and Open Text. Essentially Feldman analyses the search engines' results from selected queries. She emphasizes that all search engines (and there are more than 1800 on the Web) vary in many functions. One must read the FAQs (Frequently Asked Questions) and the search help guides, otherwise it is difficult, if not impossible, to take advantage of the power and sophistication of the search engines. Feldman concludes, 'Every search engine will give you good search results some of the time. Every search engine will give you surprisingly bad search results some of the time. No search engine will give you good results all of the time'.

Another useful Web site comparing and evaluating these search engines belongs to Hope Tillman and Walt Howe. The Web site is: http://www.delphi.com/navnet/faq/search.html. A good introductory paper explaining the concepts of information retrieval, followed by an evaluation of the major search engines can be found at Mark Lager's Web site: http://www.library.ucsb.edu/untangle/lager.html.

▶ INTERNET SCOUTS

Indexes, directories and search engines are all effective ways of discovering useful and credible information on the Web. Equally important is knowing where the good, reliable Web sites are to begin with. 'Scouts', some of whom are skilled news researchers, search and compile subject speciality lists and links. They are frequently invaluable sources of information. For journalists and news researchers, the following list of URLs is a good place to start.

Leitce, C. *Librarians' index to the Internet.*
http://sunsite.berkeley.edu/InternetIndex/
Bennett, K. *Sources and experts.*
http://metalab.unc.edu/slanews/internet/experts.html
Barbara Gillis Shapiro's Web site
http://www.gate.net/~barbara/index.html
SLA News Division Top Internet sites for journalists.
http://metalab.unc.edu/slanews/internet/topten.html
SLA News Division US Newspaper archives on the Web.
http://metalab.unc.edu/slanews/internet/archives.html
Poynter Institute for Media Studies' Research Centre
http://www.poynter.org/research/research.htm
This site offers rich research sources in a variety of forms including bibliographies (organized by format, e.g., print, online), 'Hot Research' and journalism education and training.
National Press Club Library's Internet resources for journalists
http://npc.press.org/library/reporter.htm
This site offers access to biographies, phone books, expert locators, print and broadcast news sources, media organizations, maps, writing sources, Internet searching tutorials, Reporters' Internet guide, and specialized subject resources.
Dean Tudor's Web site for Computer Assisted Reporting
http://www.ryerson.ca/~dtudor/carcarr.htm
Gunaratne, S. *Internet journalism resources.*
http://www.moorhead.msus.edu/~gunarat/ijr/
John Makulovitch's Web site for journalists
http://209.8.151.142/vlj.htm
Lycos Search Engine's Top 5 per cent of the Web
http://point.lycos.com/categories/index.html
The Freedom Forum http://www.freedomforum.org/
This site offers excellent sources on the First Amendment, media ethics and international media issues.
Deadline Online:
http://www.deadlineonline.com/

This site offers practical tips on the sites best able to yield results on people-finding, source-finding, document-finding, fact-finding, business tools, and finding background on newsworthy topics.

► NEWS WEB ARCHIVES

Susan Feldman, in her 1997 *Searcher* article, stated, 'If you want yesterday's news, the Web is an uncertain source'. Nora Paul offers a helping hand. In Paul's article (1998), 'News archives: one-stop shopping, boutique hopping and the specialty news search site', she compares selected news Web search engines. The list is included in the appendix.

All the news about Web archives is not bad or disappointing. But there are important questions about quality and accuracy in the post-production and 'repackaging' or 're-purposing' of the news. Consult Neuwirth's article (1998) for an in-depth report on how 'old news is good news for newspapers'.

Electronic newspaper clipping files just may produce handsome rewards for publishers, but the investment and talent required to create this electronic marvel is not trivial. There are other concerns as well. For example, will Web archives managed and distributed by individual news-papers or newspaper groups have a negative impact on the large and long-time collections of full-text databases offered by such commercial vendors as LEXIS-NEXIS? Can newspapers support the competitive marketing, long-term storage and quality controls for Web archives? It will be interesting to watch. Developments during the next few years may well answer such questions.

► NEWSPAPER ACCURACY

'In journalism there has always been a tension between getting it first and getting it right.' Ellen Goodman (1994)

The media, journalists in particular, have long been targets for criticism con-cerning accuracy. This criticism, frequently self-generated, is justified. There is ample historical evidence of newspaper inaccuracy. Obviously, the strug-gle to report news accurately did not begin with the advent of the Internet.

Thomas Jefferson, the United States' third president, was frequently irked by the Press' 'abandoned spirit of falsehood' and suggested that '. . . the four sections of newspapers should be labelled: Truths, Probabilities, Possibilities, and Lies'.

By the time of the United States Civil War, the Press began the more frequent use of 'qualifiers' in their news reports. For example, accounts of military actions were sometimes subheaded 'Important if true', a disclaimer on its way to evolving into the World War II use by the *Boston Globe* of 'Unconfirmed' over its unverified reports.

During the late 19th and early 20th centuries, journalism schools were launched and books were being written about good, ethical journalistic practices. In 1903 Edwin Shuman warned in his book, *Practical journalism*, 'While even the best newspapers contain some errors of fact, habitual misrepresentation and inaccuracy will kill any paper'.

How newspapers ventured from admitting occasional mistakes to printing correction notices in a standardized format is difficult to trace. No law was passed. No decree was issued. Correction policies seem to have evolved over time to the point where the media is increasingly held accountable for its reporting. Accuracy has become central to journalism's ethical foundation.

Michael Singletary (1980) undertook a review of news reporting accuracy cited in scholarly literature. His report examines some potential causes of inaccuracy. The causes ran the gamut from poorly prepared reporters and hasty coverage of breaking news to a relatively new rationale, the psychological foundations for accuracy.

Fred C. Berry, Jr., in a *Journalism Quarterly* article published in 1967, reported the number of errors in terms of the source of the story. Stories obtained as press releases were found to be the most accurate (62 per cent had no errors). Percentages for other sources were: personal interview – 55 per cent accurate; reporters at event – 45 per cent; telephone interview – 36 per cent; and police, letters, court records, magazines and other newspapers – 45 per cent. About 82 per cent of stories which relied on law enforcement personnel for information had one or more errors, while only 18 per cent of stories that relied on court records had one or more errors.

What is missing in this research, besides the obvious lack of current data, is the accuracy rate of in-depth, long-term investigative reports. Not simply 'shoot-from-the-hip' exposés, these investigative reports are seriously undertaken and carefully researched. Typically they are produced by special teams of highly experienced reporters, editors and news librarians, who spend weeks, if not months, carefully gathering and analysing the material before writing the articles. They then undertake the painstaking 'line-by-line' editing and fact-checking required to document every critical element. Two top proponents of this kind of investigative research and reporting are *The News & Observer*'s (Raleigh, NC) reporter, Pat Stith and former special projects editor for *The Minneapolis Star-Tribune*, John Ullmann, who were responsible for their papers receiving Pulitzer Prizes.

In the 1990s, articles and speeches by Andrew Schneider and Louis Boccardi warned of the downside of technology in journalism. They and other media specialists believed that the use of computers to gain access to information carries hazards as well as rewards for reporters. Some editors feel that database information is relied upon too much and used as a crutch to support poor writing. These critics claim that people, not statistical data, should be central to the well-written story. The accuracy of the information must be checked carefully since raw statistics are easy to misinterpret. No journalist or researcher would disagree.

Audiences are increasingly noticing factual mistakes by journalists. The news industry is anguishing over its crumbling credibility. And who can blame media consumers? According to a July 1998 poll conducted by Princeton Survey Research Associates a majority of Americans (62 per cent) profess to losing faith in news media accuracy following recent confessions of incorrect and fabricated reporting. The sensational 'confessions' involved Stephen Glass at the *New Republic* and Patricia Smith, a *Boston Globe* columnist. (Consult Prof. Harry Amana's Web page for more detailed information: http://www.unc.edu/~haman/news.htm). Obviously, misinformation, even if corrected later, is likely to find its way into other re-formatted sources such as online databases and the World Wide Web.

Discussed here has been the accuracy, or more to the point, inaccuracy in the media. It seems appropriate to identify the standard journalistic practices for assessing the credibility of information sources. In short, what are professional journalists trained to do to ensure the accuracy and credibility of their reporting? At the very least, they accept and follow the guidelines below in the pre-publication news gathering process.

- Double-check the spelling and accuracy of all names, dates, 'facts', and events and be fully aware that conflicting information on these elements is likely. Standard print reference materials, recognized 'experts', online commercial databases, e-mail, Internet and World Wide Web sources may disagree with one another. Keep checking until reasonable doubt is eliminated;
- Be suspicious of all 'facts' regardless of their source (individual or print/digital record). 'Dirty data' does not look any different from clean data at first (or even second) glance. This skepticism serves journalists particularly well when interviewing so-called 'experts', searching online commercial databases, browsing Internet lists or navigating the World Wide Web;
- Believe that all data has the potential, even the likelihood, of being incomplete, out of date or incorrect. This includes so-called scholarly reference materials;
- Understand that there are no 'reliable' experts, only people who think that they know what they are talking about at any given time. Everyone's credentials and statements must be corroborated and, if necessary, challenged;

- Enlist the services of news researchers (also called news librarians) to aid in the investigation of the accuracy and reliability of print and electronic resources;
- Behave fairly and honestly with all the information discovered;
- Recognize and report when information is incomplete, incorrect or out of date. Take special care with polls. Recognize that stories about public opinion polls and surveys should include, at the very least, margin of error, types of questions used, audience surveyed, poll sponsor, and the date and time of the survey;
- Exercise all due care when crediting a source, whether it is an individual, group or publication. Journalists can never know when their work will be challenged. A wise journalist will keep copies of all data;
- Actively seek rigorous editorial review of work for accuracy and clarity, as well as for newsworthiness;
- Recognize that prior information in one's own papers or broadcast tapes may not be complete or even accurate, particularly if proper follow up on stories has not been done. Remember that most news stories are printed in increments and gaps are likely.

While these guidelines for journalistic behaviour are universally accepted, journalists do not always follow them. Verification of information and data is nearly always time-consuming and challenging. Not even scholars and researchers, unburdened by daily deadlines for publication, can claim perfection in accuracy of data collection and analysis. Clearly, credibility has been the Web's Achilles' heel. The only protection for journalists is to continue to check their sources in the old-fashioned way. The first step is to enlist the skilled reference and research services of news researchers.

▶ NEWS RESEARCHERS' ROLE

'Our responsibilities [as news researchers and librarians] are to discover, nurture, cultivate information; harvest it, keep it clean, store it, protect it, and share it'. Sharon Ostmann Clairemont (1993)

This mission statement can be expanded to make room for the trend toward Internet training and cyber coaching of journalists by news researchers. Prime examples of this trend include *St. Petersburg Times*' Internet trainer Debbie Wolfe and BBC's *Panorama* programme information researcher Annabel Colley (chapter 3 in this volume). There are others.

Not specifically mentioned in Clairemont's statement is the task of 'cultivating information'. More and more news researchers are playing major roles as 'intranet' developers for their news organizations. Intranets are private (usually password-protected) Internetworks that take Internet-related tools and standards (Web browsers, search engines, and HTML) and turn them inward allowing news staff to share information in-house and at remote sites. News research centres are typically the content providers. Included in these intranets is everything from local government statistics to local biographies, area maps, phone contacts, crime chronologies, weather charts, and much more. Excellent examples of news research intranets can be found at this Web site: http://metalab.unc.edu/slanews/intranets.

Another Web site offers further examples of the news researcher partnership with reporters in the news gathering process and provides details on award-winning research performance. The Web site is: http://metalab.unc.edu/journalism/awnwslib.html

Collecting information and verifying its factual accuracy is central to journalism. The importance which journalism places on verification can be seen in the practice of double checking facts or getting more than one source for a story. Verification gives journalistic communication credibility and believability. These intranets are at the core of the rapid, accurate access to local, hard-to-collate information. News research staff collaborate with reporters, editors, photographers, network administrators and data analysts to keep the information on these intranets current, accurate and comprehensive.

At nearly all stages of the pre-production news gathering process, from story conception and assignment, to research, to finding and interviewing sources, to establishing source credibility, to information analysis and presentation and even to the distribution of the finished articles, the control and management is done with computers. This includes the use of in-house and commercial databases, graphical and statistical software packages and the Internet, both its text versions and its graphical interface, the World Wide Web.

Often overlooked in this newsgathering process is the concern for quality controls in the post-production stage. This stage involves the accuracy, credibility, currency and comprehensiveness of archived records, specifically microfilmed backfiles of newspapers, as well as the bibliographic and full-text files on commercial databases and, most recently, the archives of news Web editions. The correction of information in these archival records is crucial, but such corrections are not always timely and definitive. The rationale frequently offered is that newspapers are 'history in a hurry'. Necessary factual corrections will follow ... eventually. Obviously, this is not always the case.

This is an area of great concern to news librarians and media researchers because they are frequently the professionals who detect post-publication errors in completing their jobs preparing articles and records for loading into the archived media, databases, Web sites and microfilm. The most successful of these archival quality control programmes involve the close co-operation of news librarians, copy editors, photographers, graphics designers, computer Internetwork administrators and commercial online database vendors. Quality and accuracy are everyone's concern in today's multimedia news world.

Errors come into print or broadcasts in two ways: pre-publication and post-publication. Pre-publication errors result from inaccurate information delivered or collected by journalists or misconstrued subsequently in any of a large number and variety of ways. If the original data is contaminated and uncorrected, the final product, whether print, electronic, or microfilm, is unreliable and nearly impossible to correct.

While considerable effort is expended in pre-production fact checking (some might argue effectively that it is still not enough), less is being done to secure high quality control in post-publication.

The post-publication errors come in those instances when one format is converted into another, such as from a print format into an electronic one, either a full-text online database or a Web archive. These conversions offer special challenges to journalists, editors, cyberscouts and news researchers in maintaining the quality and accuracy of original sources. Errors are exacerbated.

Can news media articles archived on the Web be trusted? That is one of the questions *Arkansas Online* editor Bruce Oakley undertook to research in 1997. A Knight Editing Fellow at the University of North Carolina at Chapel Hill, Oakley studied the accuracy in electronic archives, including online commercial databases such as LEXIS-NEXIS. The full report of his research, 'Accuracy in electronic archives: an investigation', is available at this Web site: http://metalab.unc.edu/journalism/oaktre.html

While at UNC-CH, Oakley communicated with Jackie Chamberlain, Library Director for the Riverside, CA *Press Enterprise* on the news library electronic mailing list, NewsLib. Together, they started comparing notes, virtually, and decided to widen the research to include newspaper databases. Chamberlain's survey can be found at this Web site which served also as a gathering place for panellists preparing a programme on database quality for the 1998 annual conference of the Special Libraries Association. The Web site is: http://metalab.unc.edu/journalism/databasequality.html

This site will continue to be maintained to cover additional research and trends on quality control in Web and database archives. Oakley, Chamberlain and the other panellists have identified where errors enter the news gathering process. Errors of all types can be made anywhere between the initial draft of a news article to the final storage medium. How to prevent, reduce, detect and correct these errors is a never-ending challenge involving the entire news staff, reporters, editors, researchers, Internetwork administrators, software producers and database vendors.

▶ SUMMARY

Assessing information quality from the Internet and the Web is a never-ending chore. The electronic flood of text, sounds, and images taxes our understanding to the fullest. A cautionary sign, such as 'Public-service warning: the Internet is not a news service. Read what is there with care and be your own editor' would be helpful, but no guarantee of information quality. The Internet is simply not able to judge the quality of what it offers.

Everyone is involved at one time or another when searching and retrieving information in this graphical digital format. One cannot simply assume that everything found, no matter how attractive or seemingly reliable, is trustworthy. The Internet is indeed riddled with gossip, rumours, hoaxes, hyperboles, lies, trickeries and scams, but it is just as true that the network also provides important information that is factual. Therefore, the admonition is clear: Be wary. Take time to check out who is responsible for the information posted as well as the content provided. In large measure, the responsibility for evaluating Internet and Web quality belongs with individuals. Quality is your call. If you have doubts, but do not know where to turn, consult an experienced Web searcher. Several examples of evaluating information quality can be found using the Yahoo! search engine under the heading 'Internet evaluation'.

Web search engines are useful, to a point, but are still not as refined as carefully edited abstracts and indexes. Still, valuable information can be found on the Internet and Web, particularly if one follows the lead of Internet scouts and Web gurus who track closely the source and content of what is offered. These dedicated information professionals typically carve out a subject specialty and then proceed to assess critically the digital landscape it covers.

In addition, practical guides for evaluating Web information are easy to find and understand. They bear striking resemblance to the common sense approach long used by scholars and researchers testing the accuracy and reliability of information in print sources.

Take advantage of e-mail, listservs, and newsgroups. Enjoy browsing the Web, but always beware of what is found in all those digital sources. It might be quality information or infojunk. Withhold trust until you can test the data with confidence. Misinformation is artfully woven into the Web. Journalists and news librarians must learn to recognize incomplete, inaccurate and out-of-date information and then join forces to combat it. Such is their professional heritage and responsibility.

▶ ACKNOWLEDGEMENTS

The author gratefully acknowledges the contributions of Sheila Denn, UNC-CH School of Information and Library Science graduate student, in researching information for this chapter.

▶ APPENDIX

Web sites on evaluation of Web sources

Based on a list compiled by: J. Alexander & M. Tate: March 1997

Tillman, H. *Evaluating quality on the Net.*
  http://www.tiac.net/users/hope/findqual.html

Widener University/Wolfgram Memorial Library. *Evaluating Web resources.*
  http://www2.widener.edu/Wolfgram-Memorial-Library/webeval.htm

Auer, N. *Bibliography on evaluating Web resources.*
  http://refserver.lib.vt.edu/libinst/critTHINK.HTM

Ciolek, T. M. (ed.) Australian National University. *Information Quality WWW virtual library.* http://www.ciolek.com/WWWVL-InfoQuality.html

Grassian, E. *Thinking critically about World Wide Web resources.*
  http://www.library.ucla.edu/libraries/college/instruct/critical.htm

Harris, R. *Evaluating Internet research sources.*
  http://www.sccu.edu/faculty/R_Harris/evalu8it.htm

Hinchliffe, L. *Resource selection and information evaluation.*
  http://alexia.lis.uiuc.edu/~janicke/Evaluate.html

Libraries of Purdue University. *Why we need to evaluate what we find on the Internet.*
  http://thorplus.lib.purdue.edu/~techman/eval.html

Libraries of Purdue University. *Evaluating World Wide Web information.* http://
  thorplus.lib.purdue.edu/research/classes/gs175/3gs175/evaluation.html

Ormondroyd, J., Engle, M., and Cosgrave, T. *How to critically analyse information sources.*
  http://www.library.cornell.edu/okuref/research/skill26.htm

Schrock, K. (Ed.). *Kathy Schrock's guide for educators: critical evaluation information.*
  http://discoveryschool.com/schrockguide/eval.html

University at Albany Libraries. *Evaluating Internet resources.*
  http://www.albany.edu/library/internet/evaluate.html

Current major search engines

AltaVista	http://altavista.digital.com
Infoseek	http://www.infoseek.com
Northern Light	http://www.nlsearch.com
Google	http://google.com
Excite	http://www.excite.com
Lycos	http://www.lycos.com
HotBot	http://www.hotbot.com
DejaNews	http://www.deja.com
Yahoo!	http://www.yahoo.com

Specialized collections of search engines

Argus Clearinghouse for Subject-oriented Internet Resource Guides
http://www.clearinghouse.net/

Gopher Search gopher://gopher.cuis.edu/77:nosort:gopher_root:
[000000]_search.shell per cent20gopher_root:[searcjodx]stumpers-l*

The World Wide Web Virtual Library
http://vlib.org/Overview.html

Usenet Search the FAQs
http://www.cis.ohio-state.edu/Excite/AT-faqsquery.html

eBLAST
http://www.eblast.com
eBLAST is one of the news Internet directories. It includes 125 000 annotated
and rated sites in 17 top-level and 140 second-level subject areas. You can
browse down 8 levels in some areas. You can also have the option to search
just eBLASTís directory or to include the Alta Vista search engine database.
The Encyclopaedia Britannica offers eBLAST as a free service to search the
entire 32-volume set of its encyclopaedias. EBLAST offers advanced search
options, combining the features of several search engines. Also included are
celebrity bookmarks and a 'Web site of the Day'.

Major news media Web archives

Sites on the Internet that help locate individual archives from news sites and
provide one-search services for news. The original is taken from Paul (1998).

NewBot	http://www.wired.com/newsbot
NewsHub	http://www.newshub.com
News Index	http://www.newsindex.com
NewsTracker	http://nt.excite.com
Total News	http://www.totalnews.com
Yahoo	http://headlines.yahoo.com/Full_Coverage/

Scout pages (listings of individual news sites with archives available)

News Hunt
   http://www.newshunt.com

Special Libraries Association / News Division
   Newspaper Archives on the Web
   http://metalab.unc.edu/slanews/internet/archives.html

▶ REFERENCES

Achenbach, J. (1996) Bad news. *Los Angeles Times*, 31 December 1996

Berry, F.C. Jr. (1967) A study of accuracy in local news stories of three dailies. *Journalism Quarterly*, **54**(3), 482–490

Brand-Williams, O. and St. John, P. (1994) Free press writer busts into Harding's e-mail. *Detroit News*, 25 February 1994

Clairemount, S.O. (1993) The Orange County register, 1993. *Poynter Report*, Winter

Ebbinghouse, C. (1998) Frauds, hoaxes, myths, and chain letters: or, what's this doing in my e-mail box? *Searcher*, **6**(4), 50–55

Feldman, S. (1997) Web Search Engines. *Searcher*, **5**(5), 44–57

Frantz, D. (1998) Despite newspaper's apology, Chiquita accusations linger. *The News & Observer* (Raleigh, NC), 18 July 1998

Goldman, J.J. and Dahlburg, J.-T. (1997) Salinger revives missile theory in Flight 800 crash. *Los Angeles Times*, 14 March 1997

Goldstein, A. (1998) Message boards breed financial cybergossip. *The News & Observer* (Raleigh, NC), 23 August 1998

Goodman, E. as quoted in Marshal, B. (1994) Corrections: a history of getting it right. *Media History Digest*, **14**(1), 53–56

McMenamin, B. (1998) Humbled by the Internet. *Forbes*, **162**(2), 48ff

Neuwirth, R. (1998) Old news makes new business sense. *Editor & Publisher*, **131**(17), 14ff

Paul, N. (1998) News archives: one-stop shopping, boutique hopping and the specialty news search site. *Searcher*, **6**(1), 64–70

Shuman, E. (1903) *Practical journalism: a complete manual of the best newspaper methods.* New York: D. Appleton & Co.

Singletary, M. (1980) Accuracy in News Reporting: A Review of the Research. *ANPA News Research Report*, (25)

Ward, J. (1995) Information quality or info junk. *Poynter Report*, Summer, 4–5

Young, J.R. (1997) Purported MIT commencement speech turns out to be another Internet hoax. *The Chronicle of Higher Education*, **43**(49), A20

Zaslow, J. (1998) Straight talk: Matt Drudge. *USA Weekend*, July 3–5, 15

▶ BIBLIOGRAPHY

A tangled Web (1996) *Arizona Republic*, 18 November 1996

Associated Press (1996) Navy, FBI deny missile shot down jet; Salinger offers to share details. *Chicago Tribune*, 8 November 1996

Borden, D.L. and Kerric, H. (1998) *The electronic grapevine: rumor, reputation, and reporting in the new on-line environment.* Maywah, NJ: Lawrence Erlbaum

Salinger isn't the only one to be duped by bogus 'info' (1996) *Atlanta Journal-Constitution*, 14 November 1996

Brandt, S. (1996) Evaluating information on the Internet. *Computers in Libraries*, **16**(5), 44–47

Calcari, S. and Solock, J. (1997) The Internet Scout Project: filtering for quality. *Choice*, (34), 25–30

Campbell, D. (1997) Untapped sources. *The Guardian*, 10 July 1997

Clyde, A. (1998) Evaluating and selecting Internet resources. *Emergency Librarian*, **25**(4), 32–34

Coates, J. (1996) Internet is thick with false webs of conspiracy. *Chicago Tribune*, 10 November 1996

Cohen, J.B. (1996) Surfing for sources. *Editor & Publisher*, June 29, 34–35

Collins, B.R. (1996) Beyond cruising: reviewing. *Library Journal*, **121**(3), 122–125

Dempsey, B.J. and Jones, P. (1998) (eds) *Internet Issues & applications, 1997–1998*. Lanahm, MD: Scarecrow Press

Dickey, C. and Hosenball, M. (1996) A conspiratorial turn of mind. *Newsweek*, November 25, 93

Dine, P. (1996) Officials dismiss Salinger's theory. *St. Louis Post-Dispatch*, November 9, 3

Eisenberg, A. (1997) Disliking the Internet. *Scientific American*, **276**(6), 44–45

Evaluating Web resources (1998) http://www2.widener.edu/Wolfgram-Memorial-Library/webeval.htm

Fitzgerald, M.A. (1997) Misinformation on the Internet: applying evaluation skills to online information. *Emergency Librarian*, **24**(3), 9

Gilster, P. (1997) Information posted on the Net may lack facts. *The News & Observer* (Raleigh, NC), 2 September 1997

Gilster, P. (1998) Use the Net to check a Net author's credibility. *The News & Observer* (Raleigh, NC), 24 March 1998

Goldsborough, R. (1997) Information on the Internet often bears a double check. *CMA – The Management Accounting Magazine*, **71**(7), 28–30

Gunaratne, S.A, and Lee, B.S. (1996) Integration of Internet resources into curriculum and instruction. *Journalism & Mass Communication Educator*, **51**(2), 25–35

Gunnison, R.B. (1998) Drudge dredges up the dirt first. *The San Francisco Chronicle*, 24 January 1998

Hahn, S.E. (1997) Internet: let the user beware. *Reference Services Review*, **25**(2), 7

Himmelfarb, G. (1996) A Neo-Luddite reflects on the Internet. *The Chronicle of Higher Education*, **43**(10), A56

Hoax? Scholarly research? Personal opinion? You decide! (1998). http://www.library.ucla.edu/libraries/college/instruct/hoax/evlinfo.htm

The Internet Newsroom: Your guide to the world of electronic fact-gathering. http://www.editors-service.com

Jadad, A.R. and Gagliardi, A. (1998) Rating health information on the Internet: navigating to knowledge or to Babel? *Journal of the American Medical Association*, **279**(8), 611–614

Jacso, P. (1997) Content evaluation of databases. *Annual Review of Information Science and Technology*, 32, 231–267

Junion-Metz, G. (1998) The art of evaluation. *School Library Journal*, **44**(5), 57

Kennedy, S.D. (1997) Finding the gems among the garbage – not everything is on the Internet, but there's something for everyone. *Information Today*, **14**(1), 43–45

Ketterer, S. (1998) Ethical considerations in the development of journalistic guidelines for Web use. June 2, 1998. http://www.math.luc.edu/ethics97/papers/Ketterer.txt

Ketterer, S. (1998) Teaching students how to evaluate and use online resources. *Journalism & Mass Communication Educator*, **52**(4), 4–14

Lowes, R.L. (1997) QuackNet: medical misinformation awaits your patients on the Internet. *Medical Economics*, **74**(2), 178–180

Makulowich, J. (1996) Quality control on the Internet. *Database*, February, 93–94

Marshall, L. (1997) Health and medical industry research information on the World Wide Web. *Database*, **20**(2), 57–58,60

Mauro, T. (1995) Reporters must learn to use the Net wisely. *ASNE Bulletin*, February 14

McMurdo, G. (1998) Evaluating Web information and design. *Journal of Information Science*, **24**(3), 192–204

McNab, A. (1996) Data on the Internet: criteria for evaluation. In *UK Online User Group State-of-the-Art Conference*, **123**–126

Miller, E.D. and Boyd, W.M. II (1994) *Technology and journalism: do they fit?* Special report on converging technologies, pp.2–4. St. Petersburg, FL: The Poynter Institute for Media Studies

Miller, S.H. (1996) Mergers, the Internet and college journalism. *The American Editor*, (777), 29–30

Moeller, P. (1995) The digitized newsroom. *American Journalism Review*, Jan/Feb, 42

Morehead, J. (1997) A patent saga: from print to CD-ROM to the Internet. *Reference Librarian*, (58), 107–119

Murphy, K. (1997) News organization balk at effort to rate online content. *WebWeek*, **3**(28), 5

Naughton, J. (1998) The Internet: he admits most of his stories are lies. But this time he's wrong. *The Observer*, 1 February 1998

Noack, D. (1996) Gathering news online. *Editor & Publisher*, September 21, 31–33

Oakley, B. (1997) Accuracy in electronic archives: an investigation. http://sunsite.unc.edu/journalism/oaktre.html

Oliver, K.M., Wilkinson, G.L. and Bennett, L.T. (1997) Evaluating the quality of Internet information sources. Paper presented at ED-MEDIA/ED-TELECOM (Calgary, AB, Canada, 1997)

Pagell, R.A. (1995) Quality and the Internet: an open letter. *Online*, Jul/Aug, 7–9

Reddick, R. and King, E. (1996) *The online journalist: using the Internet and other electronic resources*, Chapters 10 and 11. San Diego: Harcourt Brace College Publishers

Salinger's recklessness (1997) *Rocky Mountain News*, 15 March 1997

Rundell, T. and Stevenson, V. (1996) Evaluation of legal information resources on the World Wide Web. *The Law Librarian*, (27), 183–184

Salinger's sad obsession (1997) *San Francisco Examiner*, 16 March 1997

Sanders, R.L. and Penn, I.A. (1998) It isn't worth your time: a critical look at the Internet. *Records Management Quarterly*, **32**(2), 38–44

Semonche, B. (1996) Finding the good stuff on line. *TUNE-IN*, (3), 1,9–10

Sipe, J.R. (1997) Although the Net runneth over, info seekers had best beware. *Insight on the News*, **13**(23), 40–42

Smith, A. (1998) *Evaluation of information sources*. June 24, 1998. http://www.vuw.ac.nz/~agsmith/evaln/evaln.htm

Soloway, E. and Wallace, R. (1997) Does the Internet support student inquiry? Don't ask. *Communications of the ACM*, **40**(5), 11–17

Sowards, S.W. (1997) Save the time of the surfer: evaluating Websites for users. *Library Hi Tech*, **15**(3–4), 155–158

Steele, B. and Cochran, W. (1995) Computer-assisted reporting challenges traditional news-gathering safeguards. *ASNE Bulletin*, January, 12–16

Turner, R. (1996) When rumors make news. *Newsweek*, Dec 30/Jan 6, 72

Wall Street Journal, 7 August 1997. http://www.freerepublic.com/forum/a1006379.htm

Wehmeyer, L.B. (1997) Evaluating Internet research. *Syllabus*, September, 46–50

Wilkinson, G.L. et al. (1997) Evaluation criteria and indicators of quality for Internet resources. *Educational Technology*, **37**(3), 52–58

Young, J.R. (1997) Wave of the future or a waste? UCLA requires Web page for every class. *The Chronicle of Higher Education*, August 1, A21–22

9 How long will it take you to digitize all these pictures?: creating the electronic picture library

Patricia M. Baird

▶ INTRODUCTION

The first edition of this book published in 1991 had a chapter on still pictures which concentrated on sources, type and usage. There was no mention of the words 'electronic', 'digital' or 'database'.

In these short eight years, the picture industry has changed dramatically, and still picture technology is now an integral part of the electronic newspaper production process. Many aspects of the usage of still images persist – for instance captioning, copyright, rights usage, publication history and reproduction costs. However, the methods by which most media libraries, particularly newspaper libraries, receive, access, use, send, deliver and archive still images have altered so extensively that electronic handling of digital images is now the *de facto* standard. The new technology which transformed the national press in the 1980s has encapsulated electronic picture production, and many newspapers are now produced using fully integrated digital processes.

This chapter will look at pictures as they have been digitally integrated into the newspaper production process, and specifically at the creation of an electronic picture library and how that has repositioned the role of the picture library and information service – not a case study, but an examination of the paradigm shift in production and management of still images, and a review of the major hurdles which have to be overcome.

▶ PICTURE COLLECTIONS

Newspapers and broadcasting agencies often have massive collections of pictures which are used in paper products or broadcast transmissions.

Management, storage and use of these still collections have been documented extensively, particularly in the first edition of this book, so rather than cover that ground again, it will be more productive to examine how these pictures can be digitized and incorporated into the electronic production environment, alongside the influx of digital pictures which are sent daily around networks. Retrospective scanning is the answer. But that single sentence suggests too facile a solution. Selecting what has to be scanned from a collection of perhaps 10–20 million picture items is no small task. Ensuring that the captioning information which accompanies the hard copy is accurate and sufficient and then entering that data into a database to accompany the picture should also not be under-estimated. There are then the questions of acquisition of hardware, scanning training, colour appreciation and finding staff with the appropriate set of skills to do the job.

The title of this chapter – 'How long will it take you to digitize all these pictures?' – was an actual question, seriously posed. As soon as a technological solution to a specific problem is produced, it then becomes an urgent requirement, with scant time for reflection on the whole new set of problems which would pave the way to the solution.

In this chapter, therefore, it is necessary to consider the new set of challenges, problems and technological demands which the electronic environment imposes, and to make the mental leap required when considering a digital as opposed to a hard copy set-up. Traditional workflow procedures must give way to new processes and new ways of thinking, since it is not sufficient simply to decant the contents of the hard copy picture library into an electronic environment. We must consider what the technology will do for the picture library over the traditional set-up, and the opportunities it affords to management, distribution, storage and retrieval as well as multi-user access. Consideration must also be given to new concepts – optimum picture size, compression, storage, back-up, integration with picture desk, copyright and, probably most important of all, indexing procedures – since, for the moment, interrogating a system using words in combination is still the best way of retrieving a picture. However, indexing electronic pictures is a very different exercise from indexing hard copy collections, as will be discussed later.

The temptation once the technology is in place (and there is no prescriptive package for that configuration, since it depends on users, intended products, cost, distributed or local working environments, etc.) is to scan as much and as quickly as possible from the hard copy collection. This is too simplistic a notion and consideration should be given at the outset to questions such as what are the organization's priorities? What is to be scanned? What will give the organization most immediate benefit? Should in-house copyright only be scanned? And is the intention to hold high resolution online or offline? Careful planning and discussion with Editorial, on how the pictures are to be retrieved and used, and with the

IT department which will be responsible for the networked support and dissemination of the pictures, will ensure an optimum solution. Once the parameters have been set, an intensive scanning operation, with established database and indexing procedures, integrated with the daily digital feeds coming into the picture desk from external sources, will also ensure rapid growth. The system should be progressively rolled out to some key users who can test and provide feedback. It is also important to monitor the loading effect on the network, probably a local area network in the first instance, before full roll-out is contemplated. Users beyond the local network present other problems, depending on the mode of transmission and the specification of the receiving workstations.

▶ TRANSMISSION

The convergence and the increasing sophistication of the computing and telecommunications industries and the proliferation of networks in the past few years have improved the speed of transmission of electronic data. Text retrieval has been successful over networks, both local and wide, for many years as the growth of the online industry shows. But only in recent years have the conditions been improved sufficiently for the transmission of pictures. Network bandwidth has increased so that the large volumes of digital data which comprise the picture can be transmitted without gumming up the lines and causing severe frustration to the recipient who may be waiting anxiously for the picture for a deadline. In other words, to transfer pictures over a network link, the data traffic must be compressed to an acceptable minimum so that pictures can be sent and received speedily. A great deal of work has gone into compression or how to package the picture in such a way that redundant or unrequired binary information is minimized in transmission.

▶ SIZE

The question of size of the digital file has to be raised at the outset and should be determined within the commercial context. This is not something which can be prescribed for all. In most cases, within the newspaper industry, a raw file of between 8–10 Mb is sufficient for most day-to-day purposes. However, the primary use of pictures within the environment – print-on-paper – is by no means its sole use. The picture may be required at a later stage to fit a centre spread or to be used for a quality publication (magazine or book), to be sold as a glossy print or made available as an online resource or on the Internet. For these purposes, size may prove to be problematic. There are two ways in which the picture can reside within the system. Either the picture is received in digital format, or the picture is scanned from hard copy, negative or positive. If the latter, then, at any time, the image can be re-scanned from the original raw material to a larger size to suit other purposes; if the former, then resourcing from the originator is the only answer. However, where the copyright resides with the newspaper, there is usually an accompanying set of negatives from which larger scans can be obtained. The implication of this is that, once scanned to a standard size, original hard copy should not be discarded, in case the picture is required as a larger file. Whatever the original scanned size, the digitized images do not have to be stored at that size. The data which comprises the picture can be compressed so that the storage overhead and the transmission times are minimized. An appropriate compression ratio has to be set for the database and for the intended uses of the pictures. This has to be done in conjunction with the colour print specialists within the editorial department who can assess pictures for resolution, depth and authenticity of colour. These standards for the database must be explored and tested within the production environment prior to set-up.

▶ COMPRESSION

When the picture is retrieved and decompressed all significant data should still be available for whatever the picture's intended use. Rather than explore technical specifications, it is enough to ponder how a compression ratio of 20:1 or 10:1 will speed up the transmission and indeed the retrieval of a picture. The database may in the first instance be for use only within a local area network, but its use could gradually extend beyond. The compression ratio will also often determine how a picture is transmitted externally – over a dedicated network link, an ISDN line or a normal telephone line etc. Standards have been set up for the transmission of compressed pictures and the JPEG standard is the best known. The Joint Photographic Experts Group met in the early years of this decade to discuss and agree standards for the compression of images – the JPEG standard. This work was further developed by the ISO (International Standards Organization) and JPEG now represents a whole range of compression techniques which deal with technical details such as lossy and lossless compression. A detailed account with examples is available in an IFRA (INCA–FIEJ Research Association) Special Report 2.17.

► FORMATS

The electronic picture library should be capable of receiving, managing and retrieving digital images – whether from external sources, scanning from retrospective hard copy collections or scanning for production from negative film. The system should be sufficiently extensible to handle pictures of different sizes (since we cannot dictate the size in Mb of pictures from external sources – although that perhaps is something for the future). Whatever their size, the pictures have to be stored in RGB format (Red, Green, Blue), the minimum number of colours required to view the picture. RGB format is the raw state of the picture before it is manipulated for print purposes, by using software such as Photoshop, which enables the user to sharpen, clean-up, add/change colour, crop, remove blemishes etc. – in other words make the picture suitable for print-on-paper production. The image is then saved into the production system in CMYK format (Cyan, Magenta, Yellow, Black) which allows millions of colour combinations and also contains sufficient encoded information to run on a specific press. The original picture, of course, remains in the database in its original RGB format for future use. The digital integrity of the picture remains and black outlines and china clay marks are a thing of the past.

► DISPLAY

Pictures are stored for display purposes within the database in various sizes – stamp, thumbnail, preview and high-resolution. The smaller sizes are excellent for displaying an array of pictures on the subject and may be sufficient to differentiate for intended use. The preview size is larger, but still low-resolution, and is often used at the page planning stage and at subsequent stages prior to production. This ensures that high-resolution pictures are not in the production chain sooner than necessary, since they would have an adverse affect on the network if they were constantly being moved around.

► STORAGE

All versions of the picture have to be stored and, leaving aside high-resolution material for the moment, searching the database should retrieve pictures as quickly as possible. Therefore local storage and speed of display are vital: stamp size is about 10 Kb; thumbnail 60 Kb; preview 100 Kb. Costs of hard drives have been reducing steadily over the past few years and at the same time capacity has been growing. Single hard drives quickly reach capacity and have no in-built resilience. If they fail at a critical time, it may affect production dramatically. RAID drives (redundant arrays of independent disks) are gaining in popularity, offer resilience and increased capacity, even as prices are decreasing. If one disk fails, then a spare can be inserted almost without the users being aware that there has been a failure. More importantly, the database continues in use since the data is spread across several disks. RAID boxes – a few years ago 16 Gb; 32 Gb and 48 Gb were common but expensive – are now available in hundreds of Gb and for a fraction of the cost. Therefore a fairly powerful server driving several RAID boxes and output being delivered to reliable, current specification machines, with sufficient RAM (dependent on the size of the database) will deliver a good result. Again, there is no definitive solution, since there are so many variables.

▶ HIGH RESOLUTION STORAGE

High resolution pictures – presuming the optimum to be 10 Mb, or 1 Mb compressed using the ratio 10:1, are the versions of the picture least accessed and least retrieved overall in the production process. But since they are the ultimate version for production, they probably present the greatest difficulties. At production peaks, delivery has to be fast as deadlines have to be met. Held on RAID, delivery is speedy, but boxes fill up very quickly and an unending supply of capital expenditure is not often available. Therefore cheaper storage media, although there is an overhead on delivery, may have to be contemplated. For instance, CD-ROM or MO (Magnetic Optical) discs held in an appropriate jukebox offer an alternative. Jukeboxes can, for example, hold 500 discs and with each CD-ROM capable of holding approximately 600 Mb, the storage costs are very low. Jukeboxes however, whether holding CD-ROM or MO discs, are mechanical devices and are subject to mechanical break-downs and failures. The scenario of all versions of the picture being held on hard drives of some description with high-resolution pictures on some form of optical media within a jukebox is a perfectly acceptable one as long as there is sufficient and instant help, should it become necessary, from a supporting IT department. In fact, there has to be an alliance between the information service hosting the database and the IT department – perhaps more than an alliance – an IT Business Manager with special responsibility for the service is an essential. Electronic databases are continually evolving and continuous dialogue on new developments is essential between provider, users and the IT department.

► BACK-UP

From the outset, a secure and reliable back-up to the database and picture storage is vital. Everything again comes down to cost and there are various back-up configurations ranging from a complete set of kit mirroring the original kit, or all high resolution on RAID with optical storage as back-up to everything backed up to tape (restoration from this medium needs to be tried, tested and speedy). The most important factor, however, is that back-up is essential, both on-site and off-site, preferably as optical or tape storage. In a digitized library, pictures are multi-access, can be sent easily across networks, do not get lost, cannot be a substitute for a coaster and do not get dog-eared, torn or abused in other ways. However, if it is the only version of the picture available and something goes wrong with the network, power supply, jukebox or the database itself the library can find itself in a very vulnerable position which not only incurs user-wrath, but could affect production of the newspaper which inflames user-wrath even further. So back-up, back-up, back-up! Figure 9.1 shows a possible configuration.

► DATABASE

It may seem that too many 'hard' issues have been discussed so far without concentrating on what are arguably the most important aspects of any media collection – indexing, searching and database management of the system. Pictures can be digitized and held on the most elaborate configuration

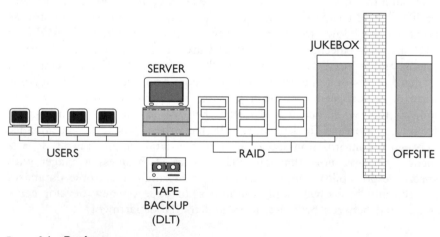

Figure 9.1 **Back-up**

of hardware and in enormous volumes, but unless retrieval is swift and accurate, the collection is impenetrable and useless. Pictures, in the main, can only be retrieved using text – single words or combinations of words. And until we have reached the stage where it is commonplace to speak to the system and request a picture of the Queen in a blue coat at a pub in Devon holding a bottle of beer, then we have to rely on indexing terms which comprise the database. The database management system of course controls indices, input/output, where data resides on the system, security, delivery, and many other aspects which, unless the system has been created in-house, are the prerogative of the system designer or supplier. The search engine to be used determines the type of indexing techniques to be followed in the database. If full-text searching and fuzzy searching are both available, then few restrictions need be applied at the input stage and most users require minimal training in searching the database.

Picture databases within newspapers to a great degree have become central repositories for picture collections. So where is the difference between that and the role of the traditional hard copy picture library? The difference lies in the fact that, in the traditional library, processes have to be involved beyond hard copy – editorial scanning to obtain a digital file to incorporate the picture into the production process. The hard copy is returned to the library and the procedure is repeated when the picture is required again. In an electronic picture archive, the high resolution digital file is already held online in the library's database, is chosen when required, does not need to be re-scanned each time it is used, and to that extent, the library has acquired a front-line production role. Pictures are searched for and exported when required, already digitized and ready for manipulation according to how they are to be used in that day's publication.

The administration of the system belongs to whoever 'owns' the database. In many cases, that role belongs to the library. Someone has to take responsibility for the control and evolution of the database because it will not be a *fait acompli* at the outset. As it is used day by day, users and administrators alike identify improvements, create wish-lists, identify commercial possibilities and see potential for repurposing the data – little of which was originally intended. The entire system is a growing, living entity. As technologies develop, questions must always be asked regarding how a new scenario can improve access, retrieval, speed, quality, delivery and integration with the entire editorial process, where uses of pictures and pagination are increasing as newspapers compete with one another for bigger, better, eye-catching products in the perpetual battle for circulation. Before discussing indexing procedures, the latter concept – integration with the editorial process – is worth examining.

► INTEGRATION WITH PICTURE DESK

At present within many newspaper editorial departments, picture desk and archive activities are separate. There is no reason why this artificial separation should continue, since the technology is now there to support the integration of what is essentially two sides of a coin. As mentioned at the outset, the majority of pictures are received daily in digital format by picture desks. Picture feeds are transmitted from wire services such as PA, Reuters or AP to electronic picture desks, as well as from picture agencies, photographers in the field, or scanned from negatives or other hard copy on-site. All flow through the picture desk and must be captioned sufficiently to be identified. Most agencies now include IPTC (International Press and Telecommunications Council) headings on pictures. This is text information which remains with the picture wherever it goes in the publication cycle. IPTC has established standard headers for pictures which are transmitted electronically. There are around 40 headers (or fields) which can take information concerning all aspects of a picture, but for most practical purposes within newspapers, perhaps six are essential. The picture has to be captioned – who, where, when, taken by whom, date and copyright – and these form the irreducible minimum number of headers for clear identification. The real importance of these headers for many picture databases is that pictures with IPTC headers, transmitted into a picture desk with database integration, are received, loaded, indexed 'on-the-fly' and are instantly searchable by anyone with access to the dynamic database. All information is retained with the image, and published pictures can be tracked throughout the publication process. Depending on the storage capacity of the dynamic database (can be 14, 30 or 60 days), this is the main picture working area for on-going stories. The picture archive (traditional library) is the final repository for that selection of pictures which have been published or which are considered worth keeping by the picture editor as shown in Figure 9.2.

► BENEFITS OF INTEGRATION

The benefits of an integrated system are many and are self-evident. All feeds, irrespective of origin, go through the picture desk. Feeds can also be taken from ISDN or from modems and, with IPTC captioning, are instantly available to all. Intermediaries are unnecessary at this stage. Pictures which are then chosen for publication have the appropriate additional information included by the journalist responsible – date of publication, publication title, page number, size used, colour or black and white, position on page and, if necessary, reproduction cost – all of which

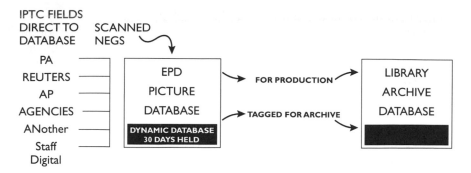

Figure 9.2 **Integrated picture desk**

accompany the picture through the publication process. High resolution traffic is kept to a minimum during the production cycle, networks are relieved, and picture editors are provided with a simple mechanism for selection of material for the archive, with all relevant information still intact. On-the-day publication information, including size and where published in the newspaper, also contributes to the pricing of the paper and is pertinent data for the next time the picture is published. The archive, in this scenario, therefore takes one step away from front-line production where it had been repositioned, by default, over the past few years, and assumes its rightful position as back-end electronic archive. This is not to suggest that the library is a backwater and has no role to play in the editorial process. On the contrary, the library is still the owner of the database and, taking the long view, has to ensure that the minimal IPTC captioning is checked and enhanced so that multiple and varied approaches can still retrieve the picture. The library also has a proactive role in the exploitation of the archive, in the research and support it can give to the picture desk and in scanning on demand from the hard copy collection. Having a democratic dynamic database at the front end, however, relieves the networks and eases the production process.

▶ COPYRIGHT

One of the most important elements in the captioning information of the picture is the copyright statement. Who owns the picture? How much does it cost to reproduce? Is it to be used under licence? Has there been an assignation of copyright? Can the picture be syndicated? If the answer to any of these questions is unclear, then there may be repercussions for the newspaper. The more pictures which are owned by the company producing the newspaper, the lower the cost to the title; pictures can be used for purposes other than first print use and they can be distributed and controlled by the company. If the copyright is not owned in-house, then it is very important that the copyright is clearly indicated in order that the owner is adequately remunerated for the rights to reproduce the picture. With the proliferation of networks and the relative ease with which pictures can be transmitted, copyright is more important than ever before. Owners are very mindful of their rights and are quick to move to litigation if they feel their rights are being infringed. It is not too dogmatic to say that pictures should not be held in the database unless the copyright is known and clearly indicated. Sadly this does not always happen.

► INDEXING

In a traditional picture library, pictures are indexed and filed according to name, place or subject – these being given usually in accordance with a naming convention or an approved list of subject headings. And unless there is a significant investment in time and money to duplicate pictures, there is only one copy which is filed in one folder. If someone has that folder out for use, then, obviously no one else can use the picture simultaneously. No such restrictions exist in an electronic library. Perhaps only one electronic version of the picture exists, but many users can have simultaneous access and the picture can be indexed in such a way that many different approaches can retrieve it. There is no necessity to follow a rigid set of subject headings. Although there is a temptation when setting up an electronic picture library to mimic the indexing system used previously, this must be avoided and the mental leap made to the new paradigm. Replicating traditional subject headings in an electronic system will under-utilize the power of the search engine used to interrogate the database. Many systems currently use full-text searching and even fuzzy searching which will deliver an approximation of what the user requests if the request is not specific. The golden rule, however, for the person responsible for inputting indexing information relating to the picture is to describe the picture. It is not sufficient merely to describe the news event to which the picture relates. All significant elements in the picture must be described, since the picture may be used in many different ways and for purposes other that the original intention. This is especially true as the picture database grows. The user can only achieve a level of specificity if sufficient indexing terms are included. The earlier example is a case in point. In the database in question, there are almost 7000 pictures including index term 'Queen': 3912 of them relate to Queen Elizabeth II; eight include the term 'blue coat'; six include the place name Devon and five show her holding a bottle of beer and smiling. Better than searching through many hard copies, but it is only possible if all indexing terms are included.

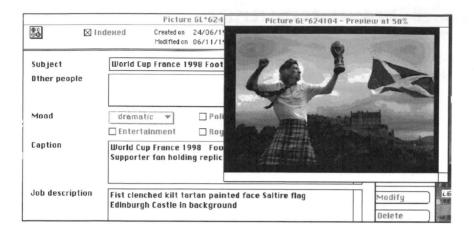

Figure 9.3 **Describing pictures**

Natural language can be used on modern systems since most search engines can incorporate all terms into their indexing structures. So conforming to a pre-defined list of terms at input level is a procedure of the past. Features of the most familiar search engines include single word or name searches, before and after a certain date, soundex, Boolean operators and positional operators. To these can be added other features which can also be searched and which are only relevant when describing pictures e.g. mood, distinguishing features, gesticulation – pointing, sneezing, head in hands – colours, full descriptions of dress, location and so on. It may be that at some future date, a particular element of the picture (which is not the dominant subject matter of the picture) can be cropped and used satisfactorily. Figure 9.3 is a case in point.

▶ USERS

Databases do not exist independently of their users and care should be taken to ensure that what is being produced is what is actually required and not something which those who are producing the database think will be 'good for' the users. A consultation process will determine intended uses, peak production times, permissions and levels of access, workflow and responsibilities, and the dialogue has to be continuous since picture database access and use is evolving as new developments take place.

► COMMERCIAL POSSIBILITIES

Apart from their primary use within the print medium (or depicted on a screen) pictures can be used for many other purposes. If the collection of in-house-owned copyright material is sufficiently large, then the picture library assumes a role other than support for Editorial and becomes a commodity in itself. Pictures can be sold to the public, can be reproduced in many formats, licensed to others for specific use, syndicated, can be reproduced as CD-ROMs and can be transmitted via a modem link, or even quicker by ISDN line. Until now there has been no obvious electronic market place, but the growth of the Internet and the e-commerce developments which are taking place daily, suggest that browsing, buying and selling and receiving pictures in digital format is the way forward. An article in *The Observer* (Doward, 1998), quotes Martin Ellis, General Manager of Corbis UK (owned by Microsoft's Bill Gates), describing the picture library: 'The conventional model is of an office with rows and rows of filing cabinets containing transparencies. With digital you don't need to physically trudge around libraries. You can view everything over the Internet'.

The stills archives industry (and note, it is now being referred to as an industry) has, according to *The Observer* article, a turnover of around £1.4 billion a year and the figure is likely to rise 'as the idea of making money from intellectual property rights takes off and the full impact of digital becomes clear'. Corporate alliances, mergers, acquisitions and other deals are likely, since in the digital picture market, big is best – big in the sense of content covering as many subjects as possible, which is why Corbis is buying stock libraries to add to its own massive collection. However, to labour a theme already discussed, indexing and classification are vital and even more so as volumes increase. Otherwise, how would you easily get pictures of lightning at night in the rain over fields, or royals in pensive mood wearing black and pearls, or firemen in green wellies, or Cannes in the sun with parasols, sand, yachts and beach huts, or a herd of sheep in a lane in Tuscany, or, to go back to the original example, the Queen wearing a blue coat in a pub in Devon and holding a bottle of beer. The examples may sound rather obscure, but just wait until someone asks for such an item from a hard copy library and the case for digital becomes clear.

The immediacy of the Internet gives the picture library a proactive sales arm which has never been possible until now. Today's copyright pictures can be 'pushed' to likely markets almost before the print run starts, can be requested, paid for and received in digital format ready for use in the global market place which the Internet has created. Archive pictures also can be accessed at the same one-stop shopping site, and, as nostalgia never goes out of fashion, are always in demand.

▶ CONCLUSION

The conclusion? There is none. The electronic picture library is a growing, evolving entity within the organization which is developing in line with computing power, networks, new products and telecommunications. The current electronic production processes in newspapers in particular extend now to picture handling and manipulation. Pictures are an integral part of the production cycle. Therefore it follows that the archiving of these pictures should also be done on an electronic platform – scanned and loaded once for many, varied uses and always available. Careful management of the electronic archive not only satisfies the demands of today's journalists, but also contributes to the commercial activity of the organization, as additional uses and new customers are found for repurposed pictures. The Internet is destined to be the marketplace for digital transmission of still and moving images in the new millennium. There are 4.2 million UK adults accessing the Internet every week (mid-1998), and with household penetration of 6 per cent since launch three years ago, this makes the Internet one of the fastest growing media (NOP July 1998). Global penetration is that writ large.

▶ END NOTE

This has not been a case study, but it may be useful to indicate that Mirror Group's picture library has been developing electronically since late 1993; it operates on Picdar's Fastfoto platform and is a networked service to newspaper titles in London, Glasgow, Birmingham, Coventry, Belfast and Derry. The system logs over 12 000 transactions per day; has 850 000 high-resolution pictures online; its library input is around 1000 pictures per day and it services around 500 journalists with responsibility for pictures. The picture library provides the raw material for Mirror Group's sales arm, MSI (Mirror Syndication International) and researches and provides content for Mirror Media Web sites, both of which operate commercially on the Internet in the global market place.

▶ REFERENCES

Doward, J. (1998) Drink a cup of profit to auld lang syne. *The Observer*, 1 November 1998.

IFRA (1996) *Efficiency of file formats and data compression for storage and data transmission*. Special Report 2.17. Darmstadt: IFRA Publications

National Opinion Poll July 1998.

10 Written archives in broadcasting with particular reference to the BBC

Jacqueline Kavanagh

▶ INTRODUCTION

The value and uses of the working documents created in the normal course of business are increasingly being recognized across many sectors, including the broadcasting industry. The drive to exploit the programme product through repeats, sales, release on video, audio and multimedia has strengthened the importance of keeping and being able to retrieve vital information, particularly about ownership of legal rights. Archives are often thought of as 'old historical information' but they were all at one time current records kept for business reasons and later for reference. The relatively recent distinction made between records as 'current and useful' and archives as 'old and only kept for historical reasons' is largely artificial. Records/archives will be retained for a variety of often overlapping reasons – some legal, some for the corporate memory, some purely historical. Whether the need to manage these records effectively is regarded as the province of records managers, archivists or others is often a matter of chance, but it is important constantly to bear in mind what records across the whole spectrum might be needed, for whatever purpose, in the future.

▶ THE RECORDS OF BROADCASTING IN THE UK

The oldest broadcasting organization in the United Kingdom is the BBC. The British Broadcasting Company was formed by a group of radio manufacturers in 1922 as a commercial radio broadcasting company and given a broadcasting monopoly. It became a Corporation by royal charter on the 1st January 1927 (Briggs, 1995). The Television Act, which came into force on 30 July 1954, broke the BBC's monopoly in television by allowing the creation of independent television companies and the Independent Television Commission, ITC (formerly Independent Television Authority, ITA). For a full account of the history of independent television, see Sendall 1982, 1983 and Potter 1989, 1990. Some companies have retained the records they created themselves. When others ceased trading on the re-allocation of franchises some records were lost, but in other cases records were transferred to successor companies, or to the National Film and Television Archive at the British Film Institute, or the Library of the Independent Television Commission (the successor body to the ITA), who may be able to offer advice on the whereabouts and accessibility of particular archives. The records of some individual television programme makers have also been deposited with the library of the British Film Institute. The BBC's monopoly of radio broadcasting continued in the UK until 1973, when independent local radio companies began broadcasting, although it always had to compete with stations which were based in Europe but broadcast in English, such as Radio Luxembourg, or the offshore pirate radio stations. The BBC's own archives contain substantial information on many other broadcasters across the world.

▶ THE BBC'S RECORDS

The BBC's written records have been organized on a formal basis since the late 1920s, when a system of filing registries was gradually introduced throughout the Corporation. These registries took in and held both current and back correspondence, minutes of meetings, memoranda and other papers relating to every aspect of the BBC's work. In particular they ensured complete sets of the records directly related to programmes – contracts, scripts and the daily log (known as the 'programme-as-broadcast') of the content of each broadcast service.

The BBC realized from an early period that its work and the position it occupied were important and in many ways unique. Attempts were made to gather relevant papers and information about the early days of broadcasting even before the Corporation moved across London from Savoy Hill to Broadcasting House in 1932. Miss Edwin, secretary to the head of administration, Admiral Carpendale, wrote to long serving staff in London and the regional stations asking them to 'write the archives' by which she meant brief histories of their areas. Her efforts were delayed by the move and still more hampered by the outbreak of World War 2. Anxious memoranda show that the precious files had been sent to some unknown destination which eventually proved to be the cellars of Woodnorton Hall in rural Worcestershire, one of the BBC's wartime evacuation centres. In the wake of the crucial role broadcasting played in the war, it was decided that a history of the BBC should be written and an archives section of Registry was set up prior to the appointment of Asa Briggs as historian in 1957. This became the BBC's Historical Record Office. It was moved to more spacious accommodation in the grounds of BBC Monitoring at Caversham some 40 miles west of London and renamed the Written Archives Centre (WAC) in 1970. The Registry Service has continued and a records management unit, now called the Records and Programme Information Centre (RAPIC), was incorporated in 1979 to handle the appraisal of records before transfer to WAC. The BBC therefore has a virtually unbroken sequence of records keeping from the late 1920s onwards.

The different records management areas work closely together: they are interdependent and the enquiries they receive from within the BBC are often similar, differing only in the dates of the information required. Together they have developed and implemented a core records policy, endorsed by the BBC Board of Governors, setting out those areas of records which should be kept in the long term, either because they relate to the BBC's core business of making programmes, or for the Corporation's other needs, and also to fulfil the BBC's Charter obligations concerning its archives. Alongside this policy a detailed retention schedule covers all the categories of record which come within the remit of the records management areas and determines how long each should be kept. This is constantly updated and revised as circumstances change.

The nature of the registries has changed over the years to meet contemporary needs. They were originally set up as the result of an early example of management consultancy. In 1927 the BBC asked Lieutenant Colonel Haldane to review their record keeping practices and make recommendations. His report stated firmly that it was a common fallacy that even if a girl knew nothing she could always file, whereas what was needed was someone with intelligence, imagination and a good general education. He recommended the setting up of filing registries on the lines of those currently used in government departments. The BBC took his strictures to heart and set up large centralized units serving an entire building or area in London, headed by university graduates. As the BBC grew and divided so the Registry Service followed and shadowed the pattern of its users. Specialized registry units were developed from the 1960s onwards to serve the needs of specific groups of staff – management, legal, education. As the administrative environment of the BBC began to change more and more frequently, in common with other similar large organizations, the Registry Service responded by setting up smaller more flexible units and by offering additional services such as 'on-site' filing, where Registry staff file the papers in people's own offices. This allows people to keep control of their own papers without the development of numerous different personal filing systems, while enabling the Registry staff to keep track of important papers and clear out ephemeral material, or files no longer required immediately to hand.

At the same time, the Registry Service decided to concentrate their skills in the most effective way by withdrawing from the filing of straight-forward material – particularly programme files, which could be done without difficulty in production offices – and concentrating on the more complex policy or legal records, which need more comprehensive classification and indexing to retrieve them quickly. The development of a records centre in cheaper accommodation also allowed the registries to concentrate on current work and save valuable space in high cost office areas by transferring out files which had been identified as of potential importance, but were no longer required on a daily basis, to await detailed appraisal.

Because archives are working papers – legal, administrative, technical – accumulated in the normal course of business and filed for reference, their original arrangement normally mirrors that of the organization which produced them, as the logical result of the way in which they were generated and used. Part of the evidence about that organization – the way its hierarchies, departments and divisions interacted – is therefore contained in the way the files were made up and kept, so it is important to preserve that arrangement (their provenance) as far as possible.

The BBC's filing registries, which were responsible for creating and maintaining all the files, created a formal structure for its papers and largely this extended right across the Corporation when the registries were set up in the regional centres in Scotland, Northern Ireland, Wales and England. However, users tend to want their own papers, so the arrangement of the files was usually first by which department sent them and only then by subject. It is important to bear this in mind when consulting the files, since it may explain what now seems illogical. Sections corresponding to the work of a department e.g. Children's Hour, talks, TV documentaries, usually contain both departmental policy discussions and files about individual programmes. Some, however, such as Policy or Countries, are more general and because Radio was the first service to develop, with the most senior managers having offices in that area, the main policy papers are usually to be found in sections which formed part of the Radio Central registry. These include the minutes and papers of the Board of Governors, the Board of Management and the main advisory committees as well as files dealing with overall programme policy.

Original indexes, covering programme output as well as the files, and finding aids are supplemented by computer-held and searchable Shelf Lists showing the file titles and their reference numbers within each section. For some of the most heavily used sections, there are more detailed Précis Lists which give a summary of the contents of the files. These are intended to give a guide as to whether the contents of particular files are likely to be relevant and are particularly useful for seeing the nature of the work handled by that department.

The key record relating to programmes is the Programme-as-Broadcast (now called Programme-as-Completed). These records exist from the summer *before* the British Broadcasting Company came into being during the time when the individual manufacturing companies were trying to promote their new services. They did this by setting up 'point-to-point' broadcasts at fashionable charity events of items of tasteful music such as classical songs, designed to appeal to people at fashionable charity events where people would hear them and buy sets. The Ps-as-B consist of an accurate daily log of every broadcast on every BBC service giving details of timings, who took part and what music was played, primarily for making payments to the participants and rights owners. The log is produced after the broadcast and is therefore far more accurate than *Radio Times*, the BBC's own listings magazine, published from 1923 onwards. There is no index to *Radio Times* but the national radio and television Ps-as-B were indexed apart from the wartime period. Programme files covering individual programmes or series will be found in the relevant departmental section but not all programmes have a file.

Programme scripts are available at the Centre once they have been transferred to microform approximately two years after transmission, but not all scripts have survived and some programmes were not scripted. Originals are retained where they have hand-written alterations or other intrinsic value – Winston Churchill set out some of his scripts almost like poetry using special large font type, clearly to aid his delivery. News bulletins for radio survive only from 1939, apart from the General Strike of 1926, with some regional and overseas, including BBC foreign language bulletins; separate television bulletins begin in 1954. News broadcasts from other parts of the world have routinely been monitored by the BBC since 1939 and are published in translation in the *Summary of World Broadcasts* (current editions available from BBC Monitoring, older material microfilmed by Bell & Howell Information and Learning, formerly known as UMI). The Centre has a complete research set.

People who took part in radio programmes, including those for the overseas services, were booked on different types of contract, filed separately – artist, scriptwriter, composer, talks, copyright – so someone like Benjamin Britten would have several different files depending on the capacity in which he was being approached. Most of the early files contain original correspondence as well as contracts. Television contributors' files form a single Television Artists sequence. Contributors such as the poet Dylan Thomas, or the singer Kathleen Ferrier, who may have been booked in a Region (usually for a Regional programme), would also have papers among the Region's files held at the WAC.

The WAC holds a comprehensive collection of BBC publications, including the Regional editions of *Radio Times*, and its overseas equivalent, *London Calling* (now called *On Air*). Articles in *Radio Times* though unindexed are an excellent source of additional information and show the breadth of vision of the broadcasters; Arthur Burrows, the Director of Programmes, in the very first edition in 1923 wrote 'and when we broadcast

Parliament – and it's bound to happen this century or next', although it was some 52 years before the ambition was achieved. From 1929 to 1990 the BBC published *The Listener*, a literary magazine with original articles and reviews as well as reprints of some radio talks. The London edition of *Radio Times* and *The Listener* are available together with BBC wartime news bulletins and other records on microfilm/fiche published by Chadwyck-Healey Ltd: Cambridge, UK. There are sets of BBC Schools Broadcasting pamphlets, BBC Handbooks (yearbooks), concert programmes and the many books accompanying particular programmes. The Centre has a collection of BBC publicity material, including concert and other posters and small leaflets which make excellent exhibition items. BBC Staff Lists were published regularly and are available in the Reading Room with a small collection of general reference books and works relating to broadcasting.

A small number of Special Collections, which include the papers of people, notably Lord Reith, closely connected with the BBC, either as staff or Governors, and small items – anything from enamelled badges given to children who were members of the Radio Circle to a tiny crystal set – donated because of their relevance to the history of the BBC, are normally available on the same basis as the Corporation's own archives.

▶ THE USES OF THE BBC'S RECORDS

The uses of this continuum of records are very varied. In the registries customers mainly require access to their own records – correspondence, minutes of meetings, agreements or case files – but they can also ask their local unit for material which ranges outside that area either in subject or date. The advantage of the integrated approach is the ability to avoid duplication and locate information across the entire system rapidly and efficiently. This pays special dividends with major policy or legal requests. These might include questions about when a particular clause was included in the BBC's Charter, the background to Party Political Broadcasts, requests for all the contracts for a specific programme, all the files about a particular property or all the papers relating to a claim involving the legal process of 'discovery', where each side must present all the relevant documents to the other's lawyers. The final selection of material, which will have saved a great deal of the legal department's time, may have been drawn from over 60 years and several different units, including RAPIC and the WAC.

As documents cease to be in current daily use, files relating to the BBC's core functions, particularly programme making, are transferred to RAPIC, where their long-term value is assessed against criteria developed in consultation with their creator departments, as well as staff from the registries and WAC. If departments want other records, required only in the short-term, to be retained (such as financial records which must be kept for 7 years), commercial storage can be arranged. Files at RAPIC which are judged to be for permanent retention are transferred to the WAC after they are approximately 20 years old, by which time their usage has normally declined to a lower level. Files held in registries or RAPIC are only available for the BBC's own purposes. Once they have been transferred to the WAC, they can be made available to others for research.

Many large organizations use their archives to research their history and to further their public relations. In addition to Asa Briggs' *The history of broadcasting in the United Kingdom* (1995), the BBC has commissioned books on many different aspects of its work (Higgens, 1983), including broadcast engineering (Pawley, 1972) and the Third Programme (Carpenter, 1996). The written archives of the BBC are drawn on for exhibitions, as part of the displays at the visitor centre in Broadcasting House – *The BBC Experience* – and for programmes, particularly those celebrating anniversaries or reviewing some part of the BBC's role in British society. These include topics such as broadcasting during World War 2, or the Henry Wood Promenade Concerts which the Corporation rescued from the threat of closure in 1927 and continues to mount every summer as one of the world's largest music festivals. Staff at the WAC also supply background material for speeches and answer enquiries from the public about the history of the BBC and its programmes, whether broadcasts for children, news, drama or popular comedies. In recognition of the BBC's public service obligations, *bona fide* researchers wishing to consult the files can book a seat in the reading room without charge unless their purpose is commercial.

The nature of the BBC's everyday work has led to the accumulation of archives which are a rich source for researchers in many fields, but particularly for biographers, historians and musicologists. The BBC has made programmes on every kind of subject, and asked leading figures from a huge range of writers, politicians, entertainers, musicians, scientists and others to take part. It employs actors, choirs and orchestras and commissions drama and music, presenting concerts and the first performances of new works. As the letters in the BBC's archives show, in September 1932 George Bernard Shaw wrote to Sir John Reith the BBC's first Director General suggesting that he should commission Sir Edward Elgar to write a symphony. Elgar accepted with delight, but on his death in 1934 only sketches for the 3rd Symphony had been composed. Many years later they were elaborated by the composer, Anthony Payne, and the symphony was given its first performance by the BBC Symphony Orchestra in February 1998.

The Corporation gathers as well as broadcasts news at local, regional, national and world level. Although it is not a government department, it has worked very closely with the government, particularly during World War 2, broadcasting both in English and in many foreign languages. The BBC has exchanged information and helped to set up and train staff for many other broadcasting organizations, particularly those in countries which have close ties with Britain, such as India, former colonies in East and West Africa and the Caribbean, Australia, Canada and South Africa.

Since the 1920s the BBC has been a major publishing house for both books and magazines, together with publications to support its broadcasts for all levels of education. Its broadcast engineers have made it a world pioneer in the field of research and development.

All these activities generate original records, which illuminate not only the history of the BBC and broadcasting, but all aspects of British culture and twentieth century social and political history. Recent research topics have included the role of the 'spiv' in television comedy, perceptions of Germany and how the North of England was viewed by other areas, as well as more obvious topics such as wartime propaganda. The present growth in media studies, increasing emphasis on the use of original records for research and the popularity of twentieth century history all point towards greater use of broadcasting archives. However, compared with the programme recordings, the richness of the written archives is not well known.

In using most archives the researcher has to use a certain amount of lateral thinking and this is particularly so with the BBC's records. The Corporation is divided into large areas, known as Directorates, but records created by one department may be used mainly by another, and areas often worked together on programmes or exchanged views. Experienced staff are needed both to answer enquiries and to lead researchers through the ramifications of this very large archives system. Researchers undertaking substantial projects need a sound grasp of their subject and some idea of the way the BBC worked at that time, before approaching the records, but the research possibilities are wide and the papers rewarding.

The process of making a radio programme is in some ways similar to that of publishing a book. From the beginning, the BBC chose knowledgeable staff who could produce a fund of good ideas for programmes, bring a wide circle to the microphone and deal with them on equal terms. The resulting exchanges were often very open and friendly, showing how people worked on the programmes. Producers had to present their ideas beforehand within their own department, argue their case and secure agreement, as well as negotiating with their contributors – encouraging, persuading and offering advice. Biographers find this whole process is often very revealing. Besides the making of programmes, there may be other papers in quite different files as a result of contacts made for other reasons – people such as George Bernard Shaw and Joyce Grenfell sat on BBC Advisory Committees or were Governors; Peter Medawar and Sir Edward Appleton gave the Reith Lectures at different times; Louis MacNeice and Sir Adrian Boult were on the staff and have personal files.

Researchers interested in 20th century history, particularly social history, whether for programmes or for academic research, find both the scripts and the internal correspondence of value (for a fuller account of the BBC's written archives, see Kavanagh, 1992). Contemporary attitudes to all kinds of issues from the status of women to health, education, jazz and disarmament are reflected both in programme output and in policy discussions (Scannell and Cardiff, 1991). The BBC takes its objectives 'to educate, inform and entertain' very seriously – the staff set out their ideas and argue with passion and intelligence; for example, the at times heated exchanges which developed between Dorothy L. Sayers and the *Children's Hour* staff over her play cycle, *The man born to be King*, range not only over theology but also over what children can be expected to understand and techniques of writing for radio. Policy files deal with all the difficult issues which face programme makers – taste, decency, political or religious bias, censorship and propaganda in wartime. Other files cover music, drama, comedy, news and sport as well as the broadcasting of major events such as the Coronation of Queen Elizabeth in 1953. Extensive systematic research from 1937 onwards gives a unique picture of what the audience thought, not only of the programmes, but also of topics such as horse racing or regional accents. These supplement the huge coverage which broadcasting received, contained in a comprehensive collection of press cuttings about every aspect including commercial broadcasting. These also offer a useful route to wartime programmes, which were not indexed.

Making these sources available presents certain problems: scripts were made to be broadcast and by definition are not private, but internal records were written for a few other staff to read. The writers spoke freely in confidence, the people concerned may still be alive, and legal considerations, particularly breach of confidence and libel, must be taken into account. Contributors could quite reasonably object to access being granted to recent contracts showing their earnings and libel applies while the subject is still alive. The BBC's policy is to make as much available as possible within these constraints, currently up to the end of 1974 but all files have to be checked before they can be used for research. It is not practical to release material on a year-by-year basis, so the closure period is normally moved forward in blocks of approximately 5 years at a time. The other main legal issue, copyright, arises when researchers want copies of documents. Letters written by BBC staff are BBC copyright, but the files are full of letters written to the BBC by numerous other people and organizations. These and the programme scripts are the copyright of the writers or their heirs not the BBC, which has no power to authorize copies without their permission. A database entitled *Writers and their copyright holders* (WATCH) held at the library of the University of Reading, UK provides a useful starting point for searching.

As organizations move more and more towards computer-based information handling, all the same considerations met in document records management apply – the need to keep and organize only what is needed for the time it is required, but at the same time to make sure important records can be found quickly and are not missing or destroyed. Data Protection legislation is in force and a Freedom of Information Act is planned. Unrecorded unstructured documents held in hundreds of personal computers and databases are already a records manager's nightmare. Paper documents can at least be re-sorted and appraised given time. It may not be possible even to identify in what software system computer held records were created, still less read them. The *Domesday Project* was one of the BBC's first ventures into interactive computer programmes. To mark the 900th anniversary of the Domesday Survey of 1086, two large disks were developed, in conjunction with major partners from industry and education. One disk allowed access to huge amounts of electronically held data including Ordnance Survey maps, land usage and population distribution. The other contained all kinds of information and images gathered by local groups about their locality. At the time almost all schools used the BBC Acorn computer with which the disks were designed to run. Ten years later how many people have either the hardware or software to access these disks?

▶ REFERENCES

Briggs, A. (1995) *The history of broadcasting in the United Kingdom* (5 Vols). Oxford: Oxford University Press

Carpenter, H. (1996) *The envy of the world: fifty years of the BBC Third Programme and Radio 3*. London: Weidenfeld & Nicholson

Higgens, G. (1983) *British broadcasting 1922–1982 – a selected and annotated bibliography*. London: BBC Data Publications

Kavanagh, J. (1992) BBC archives at Caversham. *Contemporary Record*, **6**(2), 341–9

Pawley, E. (1972) *BBC engineering 1992–1972*. London: BBC Publications

Potter, J. (1989) *History of Independent Television in Britain*. Vol. 3. London: Macmillan.

Potter, J. (1990) *History of Independent Television in Britain*. Vol. 4. London: Macmillan

Scannell, P. and Cardiff, D. (1991) *A social history of British broadcasting*. Vol. 1 1922–1939. Oxford: Basil Blackwell

Sendall, B. (1982) *History of Independent Television in Britain*. Vol. 1. London: Macmillan

Sendall, B. (1983) *History of Independent Television in Britain*. Vol. 2. London: Macmillan

► ORGANIZATIONS

BBC Written Archives Centre, Caversham Park, Reading, RG4 8TZ, UK. Tel: +44 118
   946 9281/9282. Fax: +44 118 946 1145. E-mail: wac.enquiries@bbc.co.uk

BBC Monitoring, Caversham Park, Reading, RG4 8TZ, UK. Tel: +44 118 946 9289.
   Fax: +44 118 946 3823. E-mail: Marketing@mon.bbc.co.uk.
   http://www.monitor.bbc.co.uk

Bell & Howell Information and Learning (formerly known as UMI), 300 North Zeeb
   Road, PO Box 1346, Ann Arbour, MI 48106-1346, USA. http://www.umi.com

Chadwyck-Healey Ltd., The Quorum, Barnwell Rd., Cambridge, CB5 8SW, UK.
   http://www.chadwyck.co.uk/

Independent Television Commission, 33 Foley St., London, W1P 7LB, UK.
   Tel: +44 171 255 3000. Fax: +44 171 306 7750.

National Film and Television Archive at the British Film Institute, 21 Stephen St.,
   London W1P 1PL, UK. Tel: +44 171 255 1444. Fax +44 171 436 2338. E-mail:
   library@bfi.org.uk http://www.bfi.org.uk

Writers and their copyright holders (WATCH) database, available as a free service over
   the Internet from University of Reading Library, PO Box 223, Whiteknights,
   Reading, RG6 2AE, UK and Harry Ransom Humanities Research Center, The
   University of Texas at Austin, PO Drawer 7219, Austin, TX 78713–7219, USA.

11 Sound recordings: recorded music libraries and sound archives

Sally K. Hine

▶ **INTRODUCTION**

Tony Trebble was responsible for the chapter 'Gramophone libraries and sound archives' included in the first edition of this book, published in 1991. I could not hope to duplicate his comprehensive resumé of the history of the recording industry and the early days of broadcasting and sound archives. I am therefore updating the chapter, incorporating the expansion of the new technologies now in use in the field, whilst still retaining much of his data and his words. Tony became only the second Librarian of the BBC Sound Archive in 1962; I became the fourth in 1994 and a lot of what I have learnt since then has come directly from him.

▶ **BACKGROUND**

Sound archivists, especially in the BBC, are often the recipients of such requests from professional media researchers as recordings of Disraeli and Gladstone debating in the House of Commons; Ramsay MacDonald's address to the Glasgow Chamber of Commerce in 1913; the first performance of Parsifal at Bayreuth in 1882 and of many other similarly interesting occasions. It may be prudent therefore, to begin by indicating the chronological limitations of sound recording and noting its changing technologies. In the beginning, in 1877, Thomas Alva Edison contrived his tin foil phonograph; ten years later he produced a wax cylinder phonograph. The gramophone, using discs, was developed and brought to the verge of commercial viability by Emile Berliner during the last decade of the last century; the first discs appeared for sale in 1894. The subsequent battle for supremacy between the phonograph (cylinders) and the gramophone (discs) was resolved in the latter's favour by about 1914. Acoustic recording was replaced by electrical from the mid-1920s. From that period the manufacture of gramophone records in all its processes did not change essentially until 1948, when the Columbia Broadcasting System in the USA published the first long-playing records, made possible by the development of magnetic tape. This had been pioneered in Germany during the war in response to Hitler's requirement of his scientists for a quality of recording of his broadcasts and speeches which would be indistinguishable from live broadcasting.

The new discs revolved on the turntable at 33⅓ revolutions per minute – until this development the standard speed had been 78 rpm. The general acceptance of the new speed was briefly hindered by the introduction by the Radio Corporation of America of 7-inch discs playing at 45 rpm: these became the preferred format for popular music 'singles' material. Long-playing records at 33⅓ rpm were first issued in the UK by the Decca Record Company in 1950. Stereo recording was introduced from the mid 1950s and was general from 1960.

The development of digital recording caused the introduction of compact discs (CDs) in 1983. The CD has now become the most popular and successful of all domestic recording carriers and is used for all kinds of music and speech. Another more recent digital development is the minidisc which is used in the music industry and in broadcasting but has not yet 'taken off' as a popular domestic format, although there are minidisc players on the market. The minidisc is probably more likely to be used as a home recording medium. Digital audio tape (DAT) is used for recording music for the record industry and in broadcasting and a substantial number of BBC programmes is now broadcast from this format.

These are the main technical developments of the international commercial record industry which is overwhelmingly the main provider of recorded sound material – music and speech – as we reach the end of the 20th century. The colossal range of music recorded in this period and the distinction of many of the performances require no exposition here, nor does the practice of most of the large international companies of re-issuing inimitable old performances in the new technical formats as these are introduced. The large amount of spoken or 'speech' material also published since the first appearance of the gramophone record should not be forgotten (nor should the cylinder material); sadly, items from this category of recorded sound are seldom re-issued. Eminent persons who recorded (always from scripts) for the commercial firms include Baden-Powell, Donald Bradman, Sarah Bernhardt, Winston Churchill and scores of others notable in diverse fields. Authors whose works were recorded in the early days by lustrous interpreters include Browning, Chaucer, Dickens, Donne, Hardy, Hopkins, Keats, Kipling, Milton, Pope, Shakespeare, Shelley, Tennyson, Wilde, Yeats and many other poets and dramatists. Foreign firms, and the international branches of the great

English and American companies, were also active in recording notables across the spectrum.

Nevertheless, most researchers seeking spoken material will suppose that the broadcasting organizations, and in particular the British Broadcasting Corporation (BBC), will be the most useful sources. But some disappointment may be experienced at the comparatively limited extent of the material held. It was the opinion of John Reith, the first Director-General of the BBC, that the essence of the new medium of broadcasting was its 'actuality', a term understood by decades of BBC 'wireless' persons as live, though not necessarily spontaneous, programmes. For this reason Reith did not encourage research into or the development of recording – indeed he is said to have been positively discouraging, believing that the public might demand a refund of its licence fee if it were offered pre-recorded and not live programmes (no matter how stiltedly scripted or delivered were the latter). He had no objection to the use of commercial gramophone records of music to the extent permitted by the manufacturers and other interested parties. Some slight experimental work in the late 1930s using wire and film as carriers produced unremarkable results. War reporting did create a need for mobile recording equipment, but the remaining years of the 1940s saw little interest or advance until towards the end of the decade, when magnetic tape became available to broadcasting organizations. Even this development was accepted with caution, and for some years the BBC's archival policy for sound recordings required that material of supposed permanent interest should be transferred to long-playing discs: another advantage of disc over tape was that access to the material was easier and quicker if the disc was labelled in detail and banded.

This archiving method was replaced in the early 1990s with banded CDs, which are better quality (one of the disadvantages of the vinyl discs was that after several 'plays' the quality would deteriorate and they were susceptible to scratches and to dust), hold more material; take up less storage space and can easily be 'cloned' if more copies are required. A CDR (recordable CD) is now much cheaper than a reel of ¼-inch tape and the cost of equipment needed to reproduce and edit these CDs is no longer prohibitive. A similar view to this policy of archiving onto a different and maybe more permanent medium was held by the BBC Television Service in the early years of videotape recording, introduced in the late 1950s, 'archival' items were transferred to film for permanent retention. Such caution may be justified. Simulations of longevity can never entirely convince, although several manufacturers now offer tapes for which very long durabilities and insignificant deterioration are claimed. Tests carried out on CDs suggest that they will last for maybe 100 years if treated well. There is however a question mark over the suitability of DAT as an archiving medium – there have been reports of the information disappearing after a few plays and a DAT recording machine has a very delicate mechanical system which has been known to fail. It seems to be the general view in the archiving world that DAT, while being an excellent recording medium, is unsuitable for long-term archiving.

▶ RESOURCES

The National Sound Archive

Opened in 1955 as the British Institute of Recorded Sound, the National Sound Archive (NSA) became a department of the British Library in 1983 and now holds over a million discs, 170 000 tapes and other sound and video recordings, both historic and new. It is the national repository for sound recordings of all kinds and one of the largest sound archives in the world. It describes itself as 'an invaluable resource for professional and amateur musicians, researchers, teachers, film makers, journalists and broadcasters'. Copies of all current UK commercial records are kept as well as a vast back catalogue of recordings (from as early as the 1880s), many of which are simply not available anywhere else. The NSA houses a wide range of broadcast materials including a substantial proportion of BBC Sound Archive recordings. If a BBC recording is not in the collection, it can be borrowed from the BBC Sound Archive and listened to at the NSA. There are also thousands of hours of unique unpublished recordings and a growing collection of videos. Subjects covered include recordings of all kinds of music, from classical and jazz to pop and traditional music from all over the world. Spoken word recordings span political speeches, theatre performances and many authors reading and discussing their own work. There are also collections of sound effects, documentary, industrial and mechanical sounds, as well as natural and wildlife sounds (over 100 000).

The extensive Recorded Sound Information Service complements the listening and viewing service and offers a wide range of catalogues (online, CD-ROM and microfiche), discographies, periodicals and monographs which covers every aspect of recorded sound. The National Discography is the most comprehensive database on recorded sound anywhere in the world and is kept up to date with advance details of practically all record releases in the UK. The database is used by the Music Alliance for the licensing of sound recordings, and by the British Library as its catalogue of recent releases for the NSA. The Music Alliance is the new name for what was the Mechanical Copyright Protection Society and the Performing Rights Society who joined forces in 1997. Records from this database are checked against the physical product at the NSA and a subset of the data is then converted into CADENZA, the NSA's online catalogue, which, as well as the National Discography, includes entries for more than 1.75

million published and unpublished recordings. The Recorded Sound Information Service is based in the Humanities 2 Reading Room (of the new British Library in Euston Road, London NW1) and the Listening and Viewing Service is based in the Rare Books and Music Reading Room. There is also a Northern Listening Service at the British Library's premises in Boston Spa, Yorkshire. Although it is possible to have access to and to listen to a huge amount of material at the NSA, the sometimes intractable problems of copyright and contractual law ensure that it is by no means certain that the actual use required of the material will be quickly agreed or forthcoming at all.

In all cases the researcher must be guided by the NSA's own understanding of its obligations to the owners of rights in the recordings; these rights will sometimes be complex and obscure. The researcher will need access to copyright guides such as *Copyright made easier* (Wall, 1998), and copies of the 1956 and 1988 Acts of Parliament. The uses to which the selected material will be put are crucial, as is the context in the proposed broadcasting, publication or distribution. Broadcast material is particularly difficult: usually those who participate in radio programmes are paid only for the broadcasting of their material in its original context, not for its possible re-publication in other media or in programmes produced by other broadcasting organizations. For further information on broadcasting material and the rights see the following section on the BBC Sound Archive.

The NSA's own *Directory of recorded sound resources in the United Kingdom* (Weerasinghe, 1989) comments on behalf of all collections, that 'questions of access and copyright in sound recordings are complex, but the associated problems are rarely insurmountable; it should nevertheless be noted that the *Directory* gives details of access for listening purposes only. Occasionally, information on a copying service will be provided. However, the absence of such details does not imply that copies cannot be made available, provided that any necessary clearances are obtained.' The NSA *Directory* is a valuable reference source for collections of recorded sound and includes an alphabetical list of collections; the main entries for these collections are arranged in county order and an index of subjects is included. The collections described in the *Directory* may be categorized as follows: national and university libraries and collections; local government libraries, museums, record offices, school and community projects; colleges and schools; specialist organizations and institutions; local radio stations and private collections. Out of the 489 collections listed most (about 222) are in the local government group. Another important reference source, invaluable to both historians and those involved in the history and preservation of sound recordings of all kinds is *A manual of sound archive administration* by Ward (1990), the Head of Curatorial Services at the NSA.

Oral history

Of the total 489 collections listed in the NSA Directory, 346 offer 'oral history', and because this term now looms so large, some cautious discussion of it is appropriate. In the introduction to the NSA *Directory*, its compiler and editor Lali Weerasinghe (1989) writes,

> 'Recording technology has become increasingly accessible to non-specialists as well as to recipients of professional media training, allowing greater scope for members of the community to be directly involved in generating and managing recording projects. The field of oral history in particular has grown very rapidly with large numbers of groups at grass-roots level carrying out a wide range of interviewing projects, especially in the fields of work experience and reminiscence. From the early 1970s until the end of the 1980s, the Manpower Services Commission (later known as the Training Commission) funded oral history projects on an annual basis as part of the national community scheme. Many of these projects lasted for only one or two years of funding and then disappeared from sight, leaving relatively small collections in the hands of a local museum or public library and very often sparingly documented; a great body of invaluable material was nevertheless gathered in this way. In several cases the persistence and tenacity of oral historians have ensured that small sound archives were able to benefit from a more consistent flow of funds. Some organizations, like the North West Sound Archive and the Bradford Heritage Recording Unit, have been able to establish themselves as professional creators and administrators of recordings, despite the need for them to struggle for uncertain future funding.'

Researchers requiring an academic raison d'être of oral history and a guide to its practice should read the publications of Dr Paul Thompson of the Department of Sociology of Essex University, including his contributions to *Oral History: Journal of the Oral History Society*, published since 1970. *The oral history reader*, edited by Rob Perks of the NSA (Curator of Oral History) and Alistair Thomson (lecturer in the Centre for Continuing Education, University of Sussex), is an essential resource for oral history students as well as practitioners (Perks and Thomson 1998). This book is essential reading for anyone involved in the field and is a broad-based collection of papers, from Alex Haley writing about his family passing down dialects and reminiscences that allowed him to trace his roots in the Gambia, to practical advice as to where to place the microphone while conducting an interview. But elsewhere the term 'oral history' may simply mean an interview with somebody or other, usually old: 'oral reminiscence' would be a more accurate term in many cases. Age rarely utters uniform accuracy, and a successful oral history interview requires considerable preparation by the interviewer to gauge the strengths and lacunae in the subject's material, which then must be carefully structured before the interview takes place. The facility of cassette recording and now of minidiscs and therefore the absence of careful preparation needed in the past has produced thousands of hours of interview material which, while being of interest to the researcher, are at the same time both daunting and possibly unreliable. Most successful are the projects which collect interviews around a distinct theme: for example, a history of a company or institution or a particular period in the evolution of a village or small town. The Imperial War Museum has a large collection of oral history, comprizing interviews with members of the armed forces, and the BBC has a collection of interviews conducted with retired senior members of staff which builds up a history of the corporation.

The BBC and the British Library are collaborating in a project to be called *The century speaks: BBC millennium oral history project 1900–2000*. The plan is to capture the experience of the past 100 years through the voices of the people who have lived through it. Each of the BBC's 40 local radio stations will broadcast its own series of programmes throughout the autumn of 1999 and into the new millennium, in which local people will reflect back over the last 20, 50 or 100 years. The themed programmes will be broadcast simultaneously in the different local radio station areas and every interview as well as the 40 separate series will be held at the NSA, where it will be known as the Millennium Memory Bank. It will be a unique record of the century and a fascinating legacy for future generations. An interesting aspect of this project is that the interviews will be recorded onto minidisc.

BBC gramophone library

The BBC has the major collection of commercial recordings in the UK, holding about three million recordings representing about four and a half million separate performances dating from the 1880s. The stock consists of about 130 000 78 rpm records (now increasingly being transferred onto CD after being cleaned up and digitized), vinyl LPs (over a million) and an ever growing collection of CDs (approximately 300 000). This probably makes this BBC resource one of the biggest in the world. Direct access is given only for BBC production purposes but commercial organizations concerned with broadcasting or advertizing etc. can open accounts and have access to this stock and to the research staff. There is an online catalogue which covers the complete collection, which is not at present available outside the BBC. Eventually it is envisioned that BBC production staff will be able to access commercial music directly from the record companies online, but it is likely that the historical aspects of this collection will still need to be available to the BBC for research and for use in programmes.

Mood music

'Needletime' restrictions were abolished at the end of 1989, and broadcasting organizations are now free to include as many commercial recordings in their programmes as budgets will allow. (Needletime was the 'ration' of gramophone records permitted for programme use. A figure was formally agreed with interested bodies). A cheaper source of incidental or background music is 'mood music', sometimes referred to as 'library music' – recordings made by publishers of their own music and made available on subscription to broadcasting and other entertainment enterprises without further copyright or performing fees. There are now many companies producing these: Bruton Music, Chappell, Firstcom, Atmosphere, EMI KPM, JW Media Music and Carlin are just a few examples. The catalogues and the music itself of some of these mood music companies are available on CD-ROM. MARS (Multimedia Archive Retrieval Systems plc) provides an online subscription service to enable users of mood music to make research enquiries, audition material and then download their selection as opposed to having to deliver the physical product. The first catalogue available online is the entire EMI KPM Production Music Library and this will be followed by JW Media Music and Amphonic Libraries. It is hoped eventually that MARS will include the National Discography data as well. This is the first truly digital mood music service, i.e. access to the catalogue and the delivery of music.

BBC Sound Archive

This collection consists of about 750 000 recordings, selected from the huge output of BBC Radio for future use, either as whole programmes to be re-broadcast or to be cleared and sold in the BBC Radio Collection series of audio cassettes, or as clips from news bulletins or interviews to be used in the programme-making process. The collection was started in the late 1930s, but as has been said before, much material was not recorded in those early days, so it does not really come into its own until after the Second World War. Even then there was a strict selection policy and even by the 1950s and 60s there were not the staff or resources to keep a huge amount of radio output. Nowadays nearly all the news output is kept along with much live music as well as drama and comedy. The selected material is indexed and catalogued in detail to allow instant access for production staff. The collection is kept on various formats: vinyl discs,

¼-inch tape, DAT, CD and audio cassette. Access for commercial purposes (broadcasting, feature films, advertizements, videos etc.) can be arranged through BBC Worldwide Library Sales who can license the use of Sound Archive recordings for commercial purposes. A contributor to a radio programme has usually signed a contract allowing that contribution to be used in a BBC programme and must be contacted for permission before BBC Worldwide Library Sales can issue a licence, as will anyone else who holds rights in the programme, such as writer or adaptor. These rights holders may need a payment. For example, Winston Churchill's famous war-time broadcasts must be cleared through the literary agent Curtis Brown and a fee paid before they can be used for any purpose other than broadcasting.

Researchers wishing to use the Sound Archive are usually referred to the NSA, where listening and individual research is free of charge. The NSA has a large collection of BBC material and also records material for its own use, mostly music and drama. Occasionally it is necessary for a researcher to refer to the material on BBC premises and a research charge is levied. The holdings of the Archive are catalogued into a database and searching is possible by subject, contributor, programme title, recording date, transmission date and anything else that will be of use to a researcher. Research into the Archive would normally be through either BBC Library Sales if a licence is needed, or the BBC Information & Archives Commercial Research Unit. The research is usually carried out by the expert research staff within the BBC. Broadcasting libraries are accustomed to receiving requests which are unusual or even eccentric, and researchers should always state exactly what they want, no matter how unconventional. The online catalogue is not at present available outside the BBC, but the NSA can provide catalogue access on microfiche to the older material (up to 1992). Finally, the BBC's collection of dialects and accents (useful for actors preparing roles) includes such exotica as a Russian-speaking Frenchman and a Scotsman intoning Latin (this collection is also available at the NSA).

Independent broadcasters

News and current affairs material may also be available from Independent Television News (ITN), and from Visnews Film Library, an international television news agency providing a daily syndicated news service to broadcasting organizations in over 100 countries. In addition to its own material, Visnews has acquired several important newsreel libraries: the sound material dates from 1929 to 1959. British Movietone Film Library and the Pathe Library also offer sound material from 1929. Addresses and contacts are in the *Researcher's guide to British film and television collections* (1997).

Local material

Researchers will find no uniform response from local radio stations, whether BBC or independent. Inclusion in the NSA Directory will be a hopeful sign. Local radio material, if available, will both in theory and in practice be less subject to legal restriction than programmes generated for network broadcasting; often there will be no written contract between the contributor and the station, and residual use may be at the discretion of the manager or whoever is delegated to deal with the request. Many stations deposit their material with local public libraries or record offices: this situation may facilitate access but makes the legal position no more straightforward.

Sound effects

In addition to the BBC's programme archive the BBC Sound Archive contains a large collection of sound effects. These effects have been produced through the years primarily to support the drama output of BBC Radio and are therefore somewhat different from the commercially available SFX series produced by such as Hollywood Edge and Chandos. If a scene in a drama takes place on a beach, the sound effect of the waves beating on the shore needs to be at least three or four minutes long, unlike the quick and instant sounds produced by other companies. There were 20 000 SFX in the original vinyl seven inch series, many of them available commercially through the then BBC Enterprises on vinyl LPs and very popular with public libraries. Many of these effects have now been cleaned up and digitized and transferred to CD, to compliment the BBC Sound Archive's collection of newly recorded SFX. There are now 150 CDs in the series (both newly recorded effects and remastered transfers from the vinyl series) and most dubbing theatres and studios in BBC radio and television have complete sets. BBC Worldwide now produces the first 60 of this series in what is called the 'professional' set and they can be purchased from there. It is also possible to purchase the higher numbers in the series from the archive directly. There is a printed catalogue available. The NSA has over 100 000 fully documented recordings of birds, mammals, amphibians, reptiles, insects and fish and most of these are available for purchase.

Other resources

Away from London, the North West Sound Archive at Clitheroe Castle, Lancashire is the most substantial collection of sound recordings and its practice of oral history more stringent than most. The North West Film Archive in Manchester has completed an oral history project (sound only) on the film and cinema industries in that area. The leading sound archive in Scotland is the School of Scottish Studies at Edinburgh University, in Wales it is the Welsh Folk Museum at St. Fagan's, Cardiff and in Northern Ireland it is the Ulster Folk and Transport Museum at Holywood, County Down. Of the specialist collections in London, that of the Imperial War Museum's Department of Sound Records is the largest. Its own material is remarkably unfettered by restriction on wider use: its copies of BBC recordings are sometimes restricted however. Excellent catalogues are available. The International Association of Sound Archives (IASA) publishes a *Directory of member archives* (1992) as well the *IASA Journal* (formally called Phonographic Bulletin until 1993), which will be useful for overseas collections and contacts.

Literature

The literature of the history of the commercial recording industry is small. The standard work is *The fabulous phonograph 1877–1977* by Roland Gelatt (1977). In the USA, the provenance of this book, 'phonograph' means both Edison's cylinder machine and Berliner's gramophone. In England, Compton Mackenzie founded the magazine *Gramophone* (Gramophone Publications Ltd) in 1923. The files of this continuing monthly publication provide a detailed record of the industry's progress and product not duplicated elsewhere. It also publishes catalogues of currently available material. Popular music is served by *Music Week* (Miller Freeman), less about music than those who work in the business, but indispensable in this field.

The memoirs of recording managers are useful for information relating to the professional business of recording, the expansion of the repertoire and the recording careers of musicians. Examples are:

> Batten, J. (1956) *Joe Batten's book: the story of sound recordings*. London: Rockliffe [This describes the lighter side of the business.]
> Culshaw, J. (1981) *Putting the record straight, the autobiography of John Culshaw*. London: Secker & Warburg
> Gaisberg, F. (1946) *Music on record*. [Reminscences of the author's work as Chief Recorder of the British Gramophone Co.]. London: Robert Hale
> O'Connell, C. (1946) *The other side of the record*
> Schwarzkopf, E. (1982) *On and off the record: a memoir of Walter Legg*. Discography p.244–288. London: Faber.

Publications offering assessments of currently available recordings of 'serious' music began appearing in the USA in the 1930s, but not in the

UK until 1951 when Edward Sackville-West and Desmond Shawe-Taylor began a distinguished series of surveys: *The record guide* was followed by *The record year* in the 1950s and this series was followed in the 60s (that is, just at the beginning of the stereo record era) by the *Stereo Record Guide* series, later published under various titles.

Resources and reference books used to trace recorded music and used in the 1990's in the BBC Gramophone Library include:

Bronson, F. (1992) *The billboard book of number one hits.* 3rd edn. New York: Watson-Guptill Publications

Bunting, P. (1995) *The gramophone opera catalogue.* Harrow: General Gramaphone Publications

Gilder, E. and Port, J. (1978) *Dictionary of composers and their music: every listener's companion arranged chronologically and alphabetically.* London: Paddington Press

March, I., Greenfield, E., and Layton, R. (1993) *The complete Penguin guide to compact discs and cassettes.* London: Penguin

'*Music Master*' *tracks catalogue* (1992) 5th edn. London: Retail Entertainment Data

'*Music Master*' *CD catalogue* (1998) Hastings: Music House [Continues: Music Master CD Index.]

Music Week Directory (1998) *The essential guide to Who's Who in the music industry.* London: Music Week (part of Miller Freeman Entertainment)

Preston, M. (1988) (ed) *Tele-tunes 1998.* Morecombe, UK: Preston (Mike) Music [Reference book of music for television commercials, programmes, films and shows.]

R.E.D. *classical collector catalogue* (1998) London: Retail Entertainment

Rice, T. (1996) (ed) *Guinness book of British hit albums.* London: Guinness Publishing

Smash Hits fortnightly (1978–) London: Emap Metro Publications Ltd

Strong, M.C. (1995) *The great rock discography.* 3rd edn. London: Canongate Books

Weller, H. (1997) (ed) *Guinness book of British hit singles.* 11th edn. London: Guinness Publishing

Whitburn, J. (1992) *The billboard book of top forty hits.* New York: Watson-Guptill Publications.

Comparative surveys of particular categories of the repertory are many, but often fugitive and sometimes eccentric. Jazz is still best served by Rex Harris' Jazz (1952) and his and Brian Rust's *Recorded Jazz: a critical guide* (1958). Authentic ethnic and folk music catalogues have been produced by the BBC Sound Archive and are available at the NSA. Although based upon the BBC's own collections, the catalogues provide an excellent introduction for researchers inexperienced in this field. The

NSA maintains a comprehensive library of books and journals, and all the titles cited here will be found there, together with the largest collection of discographies and associated publications in the UK.

Resources and reference books used to trace radio programmes include:

Donovan, P. (1992) *The radio companion*. London: Grafton

Gifford, D. (1985) *The golden age of radio*. London: B.T. Batsford

Wilmut, R. and Grafton, J. (1976, 1992) *The Goon Show companion: a history and goonography*. London: Robson Books

BBC Radio Programme Index 1946–1992 (unpublished but research is available at the BBC Written Archives Centre, also part of BBC Information and Archives at Caversham in Berkshire)

▶ REFERENCES

British Universities Film Council (1997) *Researcher's guide to British film and television collections*. 5th edn. British Universities Film Council

Gelatt, R. (1997) *The fabulous phonograph 1877–1977*

Harris, R. (1952) *Jazz*

Harris, R. and Rust, B. (1958) *Recorded jazz: a critical guide*

International Association of Sound Archives (1982) *Directory of member archives* International Association of Sound Archives

Perks, R. and Thomson, A. (1998) (eds) *The oral history reader*. London: Routledge

Wall, R. (1988) *Copyright made easier*. London: Aslib

Ward, A. (1990) *A manual of sound archive administration*. London: Gower

Weerasinghe, L. (1989) (ed) *Directory of recorded sound resources in the United Kindom*. Boston Spa: British Library Research and Development Department

12 Film and video libraries: the BBC experience

Sue Malden

▶ **INTRODUCTION**

The BBC Film and Videotape Library (known as Television Library) is part of the grouping 'BBC Information and Archives'. In 1993/4 all BBC libraries based in London were brought together as part of the process to create one integrated Library Service. The grouping includes the Television and Sound Archives, the Still Picture Libraries, Information Research, Music Libraries (both commercial recordings and sheet music), Pronunciation Unit and Document Archives (including the Written Archive Centre).

▶ **GROWTH AND CHANGE**

The story of film and videotape media libraries is one of growth and radical change, and of the imperative need for these libraries to be able to adjust to and manage this change, as the broadcasters introduce new formats, new programming, new channels and new services for new markets.

The variety and amount of film and videotape resources in UK broadcasting libraries are increasing at a tremendous rate with the expansion in the role played by film and videotape as a major source of information and entertainment in the daily lives of people. A greater amount of footage is being shot, more and more programmes are being made and television material is being used more frequently. The BBC Television Archives receive an additional 130 000 items each year.

Growth is inevitable in most television libraries for many other reasons than just the increased output. Significant changes in attitudes to television in recent years have influenced the rate of overall growth in many television libraries.

Firstly, the study of television output for its own sake has reached new heights. There is a recognition and encouragement of serious academic study of television's influence on public perception and understanding of issues and events in society today through news, documentary and drama output. Television series such as *Dr. Who* or the works of television playwright Dennis Potter are studied alongside the writings of Shakespeare. Television's interpretations of Shakespeare and other playwrights' work are also useful tools among the resources of schools, college teachers and students.

At the other extreme, the popular press is full of 'news' stories regarding the activities of television stars and personalities. There is a growing interest in television output and its stars for their own sake. This has resulted in the demands on libraries and potential uses of library material becoming much more varied. Chat shows want footage to illustrate careers. Series such as *Box Pops* and its precursor *Windmill* used BBC Film and Videotape material to illustrate particular themes and subjects for junior viewers. '*Heroes of Comedy*', so thoroughly researched by Cy Young, uses television performance to celebrate the work of comedians, many of whom developed their own work through television.

The history of television itself is celebrated using the archives – 1984 and 1986 saw two great series on the history of television, the first on Granada, and the second on the BBC. The BBC further celebrated its 75 years and 60 years of television in 1996 with programming and a wonderfully animated CD-ROM using content from the Archives.

Many television playwrights and drama producers/directors have made a significant contribution to 20th century culture; their work receives appropriate acclaim and status. The National Film Theatre runs seasons celebrating the works of Alan Bennett, Dennis Potter, Mike Leigh and Jack Gold, to name but a few. Also, the Millennium celebrations, and not only those on television, are bound to make demanding use of the content of our Archives.

Television is now recognized (for better or worse!) to be part of our culture and heritage and this changing perception in the value of television output is reflected in the retention policy of the BBC and other broadcasters.

▶ SELECTION POLICY

The BBC Television Archive has a most comprehensive set of archive selection criteria and procedures which is applied to output at various stages in its life: at transmission; six months after broadcasting to review the work in progress; five years after transmission where the benefit of hindsight is used to assess value of programmes; and when preservation work is necessary, either due to age, deterioration, or technological changes which result in obsolescence of replay equipment.

The following criteria are used when assessing and categorizing the archival significance of output.

- material showing performances or productions of excellence or significance in the performing arts. This category includes concerts, operas, ballets, plays, etc., recorded, presented or produced by the BBC on videotape or film;
- material of significance in the history and development of television. This covers outstanding artistic and technical achievements, new television techniques and outstanding examples of existing techniques. Also included in this category are programmes or items about television itself or containing useful compilations;
- material of sociological interest giving examples of contemporary life and attitudes. This category includes material from all forms of output, including current affairs, documentaries, drama and light entertainment;
- material in which people of historic interest from all spheres appear;
- material showing events (actuality) of historic interest in all fields;
- programmes or series which reflect the output of BBC Television and the work of individual contributors including producers, directors, writers, performers, etc;
- material showing places of geographical interest, especially related to stages of development and to wildlife;
- material of general historic interest. This includes material on current events of historic significance and documentary material on historic subjects. News bulletins are included in this category;
- temporarily retained material awaiting further identification and categorization;
- material illustrating scientific progress and research; and
- material of importance in natural history.

► HISTORICAL DEVELOPMENT OF BROADCASTING TECHNOLOGY, IMPACTS ON THE LIBRARY

Much broadcast output that may not have been retained in the past is now being kept in libraries because technological developments have made this possible.

Christine Whittaker, senior film researcher on BBC's *The people's century* series, has described with feeling the frustration experienced by film researchers at discovering how many early television programmes were live broadcasts. In the BBC library it is bemoaned that a young Denis Waterman as *Just William* in 1963 was not preserved for comparison with later performances in *The Sweeney* and *Minder*. Perhaps Denis Waterman is not so disappointed.

The rate of increase in material deposited in the BBC Television Library has grown dramatically over the years since the inception of broadcasting in 1936. In the early days of BBC broadcasting the hours of transmission were limited to only two or three hours per day, week days only, and with the schedule repeated throughout the week. Broadcasts were live. A small amount of film was being used by 1948 when the BBC's newsreel broadcasts began (replacing the earlier reliance on the spoken word and Movietone material for news programming). Prior to the break in transmission during the war, demonstrations films – compilations made to specifically illustrate what would have been seen in the programmes of the time – are some of the rare examples of television output that exist from this early period. Their titles reflect the spread of broadcasting: *Television comes to town*; *Television comes to London*.

The amount of film material was now beginning to accumulate. There are also records in the BBC Written Archives in Caversham (Kavanagh, 1992) that as early as 1937/8 the BBC was organizing the filming of stockshots for use in future programming.

Film recording

In 1947 the telerecording process began to be used. The BBC has a rather 'murky' piece of film of the 1947 Wedding of the Queen and Prince Philip, identified as 'experimental' telerecording. By the time of the Coronation in 1953, the process had been much improved. When the ITV service began in September 1955, the opening night was telerecorded. These telerecordings were 405-line, not 625-line which is currently used: the fewer the number of lines on the screen carrying the picture signal, the less clear the image.

The development of telerecording meant that there was now the means to record virtually all of these live programmes on film, recording either prior to or on transmission. Gone are the days when a repeat of the 1954 BBC Television Sunday Night Theatre production of the play *1984* meant that the whole drama had to be re-performed on the following Thursday. This was, of course, something not unusual to the actors and producers of the time with their theatrical background and experience who were used to at least two performances a day, but hard for present-day researchers of past output to comprehend!

In 1948 the BBC Film Library came into being as part of the Television Film Department which was headed by Philip Dorte and with Bill Nicklin as the first library store man. This marked the beginning of a more systematic retention of these demonstration films, early stockshots, newsreel items and telerecordings. There was an exponential growth in the Television library's holdings due in part to extended hours of broadcasting and to technological developments which enabled more programmes to be recorded. However, despite these advances, much of the broadcasting in the 1950s and 1960s remained live.

Unfortunately there are many gaps in the collection from this period. The studio or outside broadcast-based programmes went out live and were not always recorded off transmission. Consequently, much drama output, such as early work of Simon Gray, series – *Dr Who*, comedies – *Till death do us part*, music – *Top Of The Pops*, has not survived partly for this reason, partly because the limitations on the exploitation of performers' Rights, and partly due to the technical instability of early videotape recordings. Videotape was then seen as a means to 'timeshift' transmissions, not as a long-term preservation medium.

Film

Nitrate

One major problem for some film archives that the BBC Television Library has escaped is the preservation of nitrate film (the use of which ceased round about 1952). All Visnews early newsreel collections (e.g. Gaumont Graphic; Empire News Bulletin) on nitrate film were deposited at the National Film and Television Archive and the Imperial War Museum – the latter receiving material mainly covering the periods 1914–1918 and 1939–1945 – following transfer to videotape. Visnews' experience in the project is a salutary lesson to all in media libraries. The quality of many of the transfers was so poor that neither Visnews' customers nor Visnews themselves were at all happy. Visnews has since improved the quality of copies it holds of the nitrate originals.

Other libraries such as Pathé and British Movietone still have considerable vulnerable nitrate film holdings which require particularly careful handling, viewing, copying and storage conditions because of the stringent fire safety requirements for nitrate film. Therefore, instant access for television programme use is not always possible – an important factor that researchers have to bear in mind. Fortunately, the nature of the subject content of this older material tends to mean that it is more likely to be used in a programme where the researcher has a reasonable amount of time to organize access to the material and arrange for transfer to a 'safer' format.

BBC Television began on 2 November 1936 (closing down September 1939-June 1946), broadcasting nearly 10 years before the first of the Independent Television companies began in 1955. As a result, some of the BBC early footage was on nitrate stock. However, an early programme of transfer in the 1960s means that there is no nitrate in the BBC Library. It is also unlikely that any of the independent Television companies have a nitrate problem, as they began broadcasting some time after the regular use of nitrate film had ceased.

Gauge

Fortunately the BBC Television Library does not have to tackle the problems involved in storing, preserving and providing access to the wider range of film gauges, e.g. 28-mm, 9.5-mm, more prevalent in smaller archive collections. Gauge is the main issue of concern for users of other television libraries' early film holdings however, as well as ready access to machinery on which to run the film of the two major gauges – 35-mm and 16-mm.

The BBC holdings of 35-mm safety film is probably greater than other television companies, though newsreel companies such as Visnews, Pathe, and Movietone will also have considerable 35 mm holdings, as do the major archives such as the Imperial War Museum and the National Film and Television Archive. Access to 35-mm viewing facilities is often limited outside these specialist libraries.

The early 1960s saw the introduction of 16-mm cameras in television production. The cameras, the stock and the associated equipment were much lighter in weight, giving the cameramen much greater mobility. This in turn had a tremendous influence on the types of programmes made. The BBC saw the birth of travel and natural history series such as *Travellers' Tales* and *Zoo Quest*; and the documentaries of Tony Essex and Norman Swallow. The first *Tonight* programme showed some fascinating works of English eccentricities as well as international stories from Mexico, Vietnam, America, etc. These cameras could go out to meet people and record sights, scenery, events – avid viewing and vital television, despite being in black and white.

Sound

All television film sound is recorded on a separate magnetic soundtrack. This magstock is proving to pose a very serious preservation problem as it can be attacked by the 'vinegar syndrome' which results in shedding of oxide and release of acetic acid, hence the name. Some news items in the 1960s were filmed on 'mag-stripe' stock. Many early outside broadcasts and studio productions were recorded on film recording with a combined optical sound track on the edge of the picture. This process involved the recording of pictures onto film from a monitor tube set up in front of a film camera. This was a precursor to videotape as a means of recording television programmes.

Colour

Colour transmissions began in 1967 following the introduction of 625-line broadcasting, hence the title of some programmes in the late Sixties – *Jazz 625*, *Theatre 625*. The most widely used television colour film stock is Eastman negative. Programmes were shot on 16-mm colour film from 1967 onwards, although there was a transition period lasting until about 1971. The BBC began colour news broadcasts in 1968 and the News unit turned to reversal film stock such as Ektachrome. This reversal stock helped to speed up the news gathering process. Once processed, the film had a positive image, enabling editors to view and edit the images more easily and quickly, and thus get pictures on screen with greater speed.

In most BBC regional stations, it was still common practice to shoot on black and white as late as 1972/3. Vital time was saved between shooting, editing and transmission by phase-reversing the negative on transmission. The implications of this for many regional libraries is devastating. The items from regional magazine programmes often exist only in negative form and are rarely completely edited, sometimes with no synchronized sound – the commentary frequently having been added live on transmission!

Film had dominated television output from the early days in 1936 till the 1980s. The early 1980s marks the tip in the balance between film and videotape in broadcast media libraries, and now without doubt videotape in its many formats is the dominant medium. Of course, libraries still hold vast quantities of film and the significance of this great variety of gauges and formats is many-fold.

Videotape

The very first form of videotape recording was developed by the BBC engineering 'boffins', as Richard Dimbleby called them when the process was demonstrated on *Panorama* in 1956. VERA (Video Electronic Recording Apparatus) was never really more than experimental. AMPEX went on to develop the 2-inch Quad System, which became widely used from the late 1950s onwards as the method of 'timeshifting' or pre-recording programmes or inserts for later transmission. This was the first open-reel videotape format used for main studio and outside broadcast recording in the early 1960s. Telerecording on film continued in parallel as a means of recording programmes and it was also during this early period that videotape recordings were being transferred to film recordings, film being a more permanent medium than tape.

News gathering became even faster with the introduction of Electronic News Gathering (ENG) methods. The BBC News ENG holdings date back to early 1981, with the BBC regional centres quickly following. For some years now, ENG was the format used by all major news gathering and broadcasting organizations.

News operations switched to ½-inch Sony Betacam SP (BBC) and Panasonic MII (Thames Television) video cassettes. The first of the metal particle tapestocks, Betacam SP, was also used by the BBC for studio recordings of some programmes such as *The Late Show*, and *Panorama*. These are all cassette formats, varying in size of tapes and cassette, and consequently requiring different equipment for recording and replay – a very significant factor for the libraries storing and providing access to these tapes.

In 1994 with approximately 60 000 2-inch Quad tapes the BBC embarked on the lengthy process of transferring these tapes to a new format – D3 and more recently Digibeta. This had to be done as the format was obsolescent. No more machines were being manufactured and the remaining few being cannibalized for spare parts. Reworked recording heads were increasingly expensive, there was a dwindling of human expertise in the format and there were signs of deterioration in the tapes.

By late 1998 the project was nearly completed. Two copies of the quad tapes together with a VHS access copy have been made, with one of the tapes acting as the security master throughout the transfer process.

It is now necessary to start planning a similar programme to deal with the 1-inch tapes. By far the largest collections of videotape are now 1-inch C format. This has been in regular use since 1981/2 by all major UK Television companies. The BBC holdings are over 200 000, and at the height of its use were growing by a net annual rate of 30 000.

The current transmission format in use by the BBC is D3, introduced in 1991. This is a composite digital tape format and likely to be the last composite format to be used in the broadcasting environment. Plans are already being made for its replacement. As the BBC moves into the multi-channel world, it is now facing a proliferation of digital tape formats that will have significant impact on the library in terms of our role in the production process, storage and data management.

A significant factor in the television programme library business is related to the very physical nature of the holdings as outlined above. The major formats on which television programmes are made or recorded are 35-mm and 16-mm film, 2-inch Quad, 1-inch helical scan C format videotapes, ¾-inch U-matic tape, Betacam, Betacam SP cassettes and the range of Digital tape formats – D3, Digibeta and a range of DV (Digital Video) – DVCPRO and DVCAM, Digital S and Betacam SX. All digital tape cassette formats are in current use, D3 and Digibeta for studio and outside broadcast recording. The DV range is increasingly being used for location recordings for documentary and news. BBC Production is following BBC News in the digital domain and camera originals are being stored on servers for multi-access. To date, the use of servers for storage remains in the production/post-production phase and all video and audio content is archived onto tape for long-term retention. However, before long, the library will be involved in the organization and management of the programme data wholly in the digital domain – content asset management systems are the future.

▶ INTAKE

In order to take in this range of television programme material, library systems must be able to distinguish between the different formats and accommodate any new formats in their stock control and technical maintenance systems. It is essential that all the different gauges and formats are quite clearly indicated in the retrieval system both for the benefit of the potential user of the material and to assist the librarians in making the most efficient use of limited storage.

The Television Intake section of the BBC Library works very closely with the post production department documenting tapes as they are recorded and processed through the post production process. The library takes in all pre-recorded television output, all transmission standard tapes, off-air recordings of programmes, duplicates of transmitted programmes and selected rushes. Every tape has to be identified by title, date, unique BBC number, format, production code and duration. Film components of programmes are still essential for the future exploitation of the programmes, together with separate music and effects tracks either on film or as a sypher dub for videotape. Each item has its own unique number, as well as the number of the programme for which it is a component part. As the production process becomes more complex, so do the requirements of the system and the library staff.

▶ STORAGE

Film and videotape require different storage conditions, although videotape has less sensitive requirements than film. In particular, the long-term conservation requirements for the newer metal particle tapes are by no means well established or certain, but are likely to differ from those for film storage. Film is best stored flat. This ensures an even weight distribution within the storage can and reduces the chances of the film warping.

At the BBC Television Archive the Master Picture and Sound Archive holdings are stored in a self-contained vault. The temperature is kept at 55°F ±5° and at a relative humidity of 50–60%. These conditions are best described as medium-term storage, necessary because our material is regularly accessed. The National Film and Television Archives keep their master material at much lower temperatures but this necessitates a period of acclimatization prior to use of the material. These levels of humidity surrounding the film prevent the adhesive on the film from becoming too dry and brittle which causes join breaks, or too damp which leads to warping and difficulties of replay.

There are two other film vaults which contain viewing prints and tracks at a slightly warmer temperature and all vaults are protected by smoke detectors and a sprinkler system. Videotapes are suspended within their containers, and therefore need to stand upright on edge to reduce the incidence of edge damage to the tape. The storage temperature needs to be a fairly constant 67–70°F.

As a result, separate individual stores for archive film and videotape are necessary, increasing the overall space required. Different racking and shelving specifications are necessary and require painstaking planning of storage areas in media libraries. In order to maximize storage space, different-sized racking systems on which to store different-sized tapes are often necessary, e.g. it is not appropriate to store small Betacam cassettes alongside 2-inch Quad on the same racking.

With the introduction of the later video formats, i.e. Betacam, Beta SP, MII and Digibeta, there was some good news for broadcasting libraries. The formats were getting smaller and therefore lighter and easier to handle, and also occupied less space on the shelves. Compare the dimensions and weight of a 2-inch Quad videotape with an MII cassette box!

However, there is a danger now that the formats are becoming too small and too portable and therefore in greater danger of being misplaced. It is easy to lose and misplace cassettes the size of the domestic VHS; too easy for production staff to walk off with the tapes after an editing session, lend them to someone else, leave them in the office, etc. Frequently each videotape cassette or spool is a unique recording, and it is not always a compulsory part of the production costing and processes to provide two copies of each programme for the libraries. Therefore this increased 'portability' of tape format is a television media librarian's nightmare. It is hoped that such problems will disappear in the future when everything is digitized and stored on servers.

As a risk management policy duplicate copies of our holdings are stored separately on the site. There are also working stores at both Broadcasting House and Television Centre to meet the operational needs of our customers in those buildings.

► EQUIPMENT

Again, all these different gauges and tape formats have very serious cost and technological implications for television librarians. It is essential to maintain the equipment necessary to replay these films and tapes. Most film libraries have both 16-mm and 35-mm viewing facilities, however, this is not always the case. Researchers in BBC Manchester rely on the goodwill of Granada or the North West Film Archive for 35-mm viewings.

In the first edition of this book I claimed that 'film presents relatively few problems for television libraries compared with issues associated with videotape. The equipment required to replay broadcast format tapes is varied, expensive and complex to maintain. As the formats change, these media libraries must ensure that they can maintain the equipment necessary to replay the various formats'. Things have changed. There are now fewer film replay machines (Steenbecks) available to researchers and most are currently located in the Film and videotape libraries rather than in editing suites. Researchers increasingly prefer viewing cassettes over film.

As one format succeeds another, and in particular as videotape now dominates over film, many television media libraries will experience a radical change in emphasis in the way in which their holdings are used.

Many enquirers are now refusing to view film copies, expecting to find VHS access cassette copies available for the entire holdings. It will therefore be necessary to introduce a programme to create more VHS access copies of the older material.

At the BBC Library there is 2-inch Quad, 1-inch C format, ¾-inch hi-band U-matic and Betacam, Beta SP, Digibeta, D3 and D2 replay equipment and a Telecine machine to run film at transmission standard. This provision is perhaps more necessary for the BBC library than for many others, since the library is on a site separated from the main broadcasting centre in Wood Lane by at least 10 miles. There is also a line linking the library with the main control room at Television Centre and through there on to any BBC site. Consequently we can now transmit from any original format down the line to our customers who can select extracts, record them on to their preferred format or play into their programme. This is a great asset when providing access to many different formats to very tight deadlines.

Fewer and fewer ITV companies are retaining 2-inch Quad replay machinery. They have, like the BBC, been transferring from their 2-inch tape to newer media.

▶ TRAINING

Given this situation, staff working in the libraries must be fully aware of the significance of all these different gauges and formats and the implications for their users. Internal technical training is provided for librarians and there is a team of technicians to work on the material and operate the range of equipment.

Increasingly, freelance researchers are not familiar with the different formats, with which programmes are recorded on what media or format or with the facilities available for replay. As a result, the users are becoming more dependent upon the staff of the BBC library to explain these details to them. Thus the training and awareness of the staff in these libraries dealing with enquiries is becoming more detailed and complex, and their role in the efficient and effective use of their libraries' holdings is becoming more critical. Much time needs to be spent on training and familiarizing new staff with this knowledge about the technological aspects of the holdings.

The well-trained, well-informed film and videotape librarian can assist and guide the inexperienced researcher to get the best out of these media libraries. Thus, for example, in the BBC Television Library it will take at least six months of fairly intensive training and information and experience gathering before a librarian is really considered competent to work in our Enquiries area. The value of this experience is reflected in the number of librarians who are now launching themselves in freelance research areas.

As a general rule the BBC Television Library recruit a range of staff with different qualifications and experience. Technical staff must understand and have a working knowledge of film, videotape and broadcasting technology. There is a large team of staff working in the storage areas and they, like intake staff, must have a basic level of education and interest in broadcasting output. Researchers and cataloguers are usually already qualified librarians or have substantial experience of broadcasting media library work. All staff receive training in customer care as it is intended to be a very customer-focused library.

▶ STOCKSHOTS

Television directing and editing has become much more sophisticated since its early days in the 1950s and 1960s. The style is now for much faster moving programmes, a pace produced partly by short sequences and tighter edits. Sometimes electronic effects are used to move from one sequence to another – page turning, zooming in or out, etc. This means that transmitted footage is increasingly more difficult for others to re-use. Users of the future will have to re-use whole sequences cut by someone else in their programmes, rather than be able to select for themselves from long sequences. This is likely to lead to a greater emphasis on the potential value of the unedited camera original footage as a source of re-use material in stockshots.

It is this material that will yield the long sequences that give greater flexibility for future re-use. In addition, since the use of videotape cassettes (i.e. Beta SP, DVCPRO) in these areas of output is now so prevalent there is far more material from which to select. This is because all the originally shot material survives the editing process, since selected sequences are transferred from the original tape to the editing master, rather than being physically cut as in the old film editing process. The BBC News Library, ITN and BBC regional television libraries have a long tradition of collecting and processing these rushes for use in new production.

Staff selecting or cataloguing material for these library holdings must be particularly careful when making the material available for re-use, ensuring that all restrictions and clearances and/or sensitivities have been observed. It is hoped in the future to develop further this role for the librarians, so that they will be involved earlier in the production process, assisting in the logging and indexing of rushes prior to editing.

▶ RESEARCH

The way in which library film is re-used is also changing. Traditionally, the heaviest re-users of library material are the News and Current Affairs production area. As videotape is now the format of nearly all of their current programme-making output, they are increasingly less inclined to use film extracts to illustrate their stories. The difference in picture quality between film and videotape is very noticeable and awkward on the eye. Therefore, the use of film as stock footage is declining, and would now only be used in a cast where the content is of unique significance.

There is another relatively recent change in the way of research. Increasingly, details on the content of output as a valuable source of information is becoming apparent, e.g. information about the number and nature of programmes transmitted on a particular subject such as industrial disputes, or social issues. BBC News needs to be able to demonstrate for the Annual Report how many bulletin items were broadcast on specific topics. Increasingly, patterns of television broadcasting schedules are studied.

▶ CUSTOMERS

The number of our customers is growing as more and more contract staff are employed as researchers by Broadcasting and Production and as the independent production sector grows. The library now serves the needs of users who are frequently very new to the area of film research and have little technical background or knowledge. In this climate of great technical change, variety and complexity, as mentioned earlier the users are becoming increasingly dependent on the knowledge of the library staff. They will not necessarily know the hazards involved in viewing nitrate film, or realize that most footage shot before the 1960s will more than likely be 35-mm and black and white. It is not unknown to be asked for actuality footage of the American Civil War, or colour footage of the Titanic entering New York Harbour. However, experienced researchers such as those who belong to FOCAL (Federation of Commercial Audio-visual Libraries) are frequently using the library as they are employed to work on archive classics such as *The people's century*; *Cold War*; the *Omnibus* trilogy on situation comedy; or *Heroes of comedy*.

News and current affairs

Those producing the News and Current Affairs programming in all major broadcasting companies are nearly always working to the very tight transmission deadlines of daily news bulletins, nightly magazine programmes, weekly documentary/magazine programmes and the 24-hour news service.

The need to meet such constant pressing deadlines puts considerable pressure on film and videotape media libraries. ITN's library is dedicated to a fast turn-around to satisfy enquiries from many news and current affairs areas, as is the BBC Library, whose users are mainly BBC Newsroom staff – journalists or picture editors. In these areas, it is rare for the libraries to have more than a few hours' notice in which to research, physically locate and deliver the library material to the appropriate editing suite. It has been known for the BBC Library to research and find material for the bulletin whilst it is on air.

The BBC News videotape section deals with approximately 150 enquiries per day. The nature of these enquiries will, of course, vary in complexity and depth – from 'medium close-up of Blair smiling' to 'anything to illustrate discontent in Eastern Europe'. They will search their news catalogues as well as using the services of the main Television database, and any other appropriate sources.

At the BBC Television Library, the special requirements of News and Current Affairs production are also recognized in our service provision. One member of staff is dedicated to answering and researching any enquires from the news staff which are necessary to supplement the information in their own catalogues. Inevitably, when material is located in the main catalogue and store, it is needed in a great hurry for the news bulletin. A considerable store of news bulletins and rushes is kept at Television Centre to meet this demand. There is also the line linking the Television Library and the News area which comes into its own in really tight deadlines. Thus the library was able to supply *Dr Who* extracts to the *Six o'Clock News* bulletin when news was received of Jon Pertwee's death, just minutes before the bulletin went on air.

In addition, each of the major BBC Current Affairs programmes has their own member of the library staff based with the production department, to co-ordinate all their requirements of the library. This is a provision that is offered to 'heavy' users of the library, since it is a way of facilitating the most efficient and effective use of the library catalogues and holdings for the production departments, and it increases the sense of involvement of the library staff. Library staff are working directly with BBC Education and have built up a Production Village that researches, selects, views, compiles, edits and repackages programmes from the Archive for the late night educational programming *Learning Zone* and the Knowledge Channel. BBC Choice Channel was successfully launched in September 1998 with the help of library staff behind the scenes researching for the schedule planning and the repurposing of programmes. These two new channels are only part of the tremendous increase in demand for the content of the Archive. A further 50 per cent increase has been forecast for the next few years.

BBC holdings are used for research purposes, repeat transmission, sales, repurposing and extract reuse. Our enquiries team of fifteen people offers a wide range of research, from simple enquiries for transmission history – 'What was the first transmission date of . . .?' or 'How many programmes has the BBC made on AIDS' to 'We're making a trilogy on the history of sitcom, can you help?' or 'The poet Laureate has died – we need footage for the *Six o'Clock*!'

Customers have online access to our databases or can visit the archive and do their own research. This is sometimes more appropriate as a considerable part of the catalogue is available only on cards and strip-indexes. Customers can also view the selected material on the library site – VHS; film or 2-inch Quad, 1-inch D3, etc. Otherwise, the material is sent on our vans to the main BBC buildings. Anything needed urgently goes on a taxi or despatch rider.

Copyright

Many view on VHS cassette first in order to narrow down their selection and then borrow the broadcast standard tapes to copy the sequences required. It is the responsibility of customers to ensure that any copyright or third party contribution rights have been cleared before they re-use the material. Through another part of Information and Archives, the Document Archives, the supportive production documentation is offered which is vital for this purpose. Increasingly, knowledge and understanding of contributors' rights is an essential part of using television material.

The expansionist plans of broadcasters mean that the increase in demand for the use of Archive holdings is growing to meet the needs of the BBC for five commercial channels – Gold, Arena, Horizons, Style and Play and for two public service channels – Choice and Learning. All of these rely heavily on repeat or reversioned programmes from the Archive. Commercial access to our services is provided in partnership by Information and Archives and BBC Worldwide Library Sales. A research service is also offered on a commercial basis and licenses worldwide the usage of BBC material in a range of new media – television and radio programmes, online, commercial, etc.

▶ CATALOGUING AND CLASSIFICATION

This climate of change and growth has a profound effect on library cataloguing systems. Films and tapes cannot just be lifted down from the shelf and flicked through to find out what they are about or where a specific extract appears; they need to be replayed on specialized (often expensive) equipment and possibly copied before they can be played. It is not conducive to the long-term conservation of film or tape to run them too frequently or to stop and start when viewing. Therefore, a detailed cataloguing system plays a vital role both in making the material accessible within an acceptable time-scale and in helping to protect the material. It is essential to understand how the properties of film and videotape have a significant effect on the cataloguing systems of libraries set up to look after them.

The systems of the BBC Television Library are constantly being developed by BBC computer services, together with librarians of Information and Archives, and are designed to form a fully integrated system documenting material held in both London and all the BBC regional libraries.

There are three main catalogues held on the BBC Information and Archives main database, INFAX. Library Programme Information (LIPI) includes the basic essential details of title, transmission date, medium of transmission, duration, regional origin and unique internal identification number which indicates production department. The film and videotape stock holdings and system control catalogue contains details of title, transmission and recording date, film gauge, videotape or cassettes held, duration and again the unique internal identification number. The Library Subject Index (LISI) to the notational classification scheme includes the classification number, alphabetical subject terms (including synonyms) and rules for the application of the classification. However, the catalogue may be consulted using natural language instead of the notation of the filing orders as the computer is able to translate the notation of the classification into natural language. Finally, the Subject Catalogue (LISC) is online text in the form of annotation with shotlist as applicable, describing in detail the subject content of the materials. Additional information regarding title, transmission date, medium, format contributors (some production credits), duration, copyright and once again the unique internal identification number is included.

There is so much material held in the BBC Library that detailed cataloguing is essential to identify sought sequences within a short space of time. As a result of such detail, the database is vast and therefore an equally detailed system of classification is needed. Approximately 100 000 messages are handled each day by all the library systems from 600 PCs sited in London and the BBC regions.

Cataloguing has been online for all programmes and news transmitted since 1983. The backlog has also been reduced and data transferred to the computer for some genres of programming, e.g. music and arts. Furthermore, news material from its earlier days in 1948 has been reviewed and re-catalogued. Nevertheless many news items are still only catalogued on a very old subject heading system.

These old catalogues in themselves are interesting as a source of information about the people of the time. Cars, televisions, radios, etc. were filed under inventions in the British Paramount catalogue. Vietnam is filed under Indochina in the BBC catalogue. It takes even experienced researchers a long time to try to think themselves into the minds of earlier cataloguers to find material to illustrate intangible concepts and ideas that are used in contemporary documentaries using archive/library material.

The BBC Television News database uses the Star free-text database which is run on Alpha Micro hardware. This is a multi-user database management and information retrieval system, designed expressly to handle descriptive information of all kinds. Key words and flexible text searching are used in conjunction with a thesaurus of controlled language. Natural language had been chosen by the BBC News Library in preference to a numeric classification scheme. Since July 1988, this system has been used to catalogue all BBC Televison News holdings – both edited stories and retained unedited originals or 'road cassettes'. This system has speeded up the answering of enquiries as the staff can now combine sought terms, and can make specific searches using text searching. Finally, the input of data into the system has been speeded up, as there is no more dreaded filing. As the database grows close attention will have to be paid to the control of language used and, as more key words and text need to be searched, the process of searching will be lengthened.

In general terms, media libraries have to face the conflict between 'archive' and 'production library'. The primary function of an archive is to preserve the material for the future, whereas the primary function of the production library is to make the material available. The demand for immediate access can often be at variance with the preservation needs as instant access may lead to damage to irreplaceable archive material. Equally, protection may reduce the availability of material. There is a difficult balance for the media librarian to maintain here. The Archive is being increasingly protected by making duplicate submasters of all the 2-inch tapes copied and of selected programmes at the first transmission.

▶ THE FUTURE

As part of the strategy to become a bi-media library, the BBC Library database has been developed to accommodate radio programme cataloguing data. The benefits to customers are numerous: only one system to search, easy to find radio output that would complement television and vice versa and common terminology and spellings. More efficiencies are created in the library, with only one system to maintain and support and, of course, training costs are reduced.

A further arm of this strategy was to store both our radio and television archives on one site. The Radio Sound Archive Collection was moved to the same location as Television in 1994. This enables us to gain economics of scale and staff to become familiar with both media.

In general BBC Information and Archives has made tremendous progress towards the goal of creating one whole broadcasting media information research service, whilst at the same time maintaining expertise in the particular media of television and radio.

Finally, recent times have seen a growing recognition of the value of this material both in cultural and financial terms. Organizations such as FOCAL and FIAT/IFTA (International Film and Television Archives) provide great support to the archives as professional bodies where staff can learn from the experience of others, and compare challenges and solutions to the many new and future issues. Both organizations also present annual awards for the best use of Archive material in new television programming. The BBC's *Death of Yugoslavia* won such an award in 1996.

However, it is important not to become complacent. Steve Bryant of the UK National Film and Television Archive fears that 'changes already underway or anticipated in the broadcasting ecology could easily reverse this trend. The view that TV programmes are not worth preserving can still be found and is in danger of making a comeback for both cultural and financial reasons' (Bryant, 1989). In this new era of burgeoning independent production companies, and satellite and cable broadcasting, it is perhaps possible that the archive potential of current and new production may not be fully appreciated and may therefore be undervalued once again. There will always be new and exciting challenges.

▶ REFERENCE

Bryant, Steve (1989) *The television heritage, television archiving now and in an uncertain future.* Series: The Broadcasting Debate 4. London: BFI Publishing

▶ FURTHER READING

Ballantyne, J. (1983) (ed.) *Researchers guide to British news reels* (Vol 1.). London: British Universities Film and Video Council

Ballantyne, J. (1988) (ed.) *Researchers guide to British news reels* (Vol 2.). London: British Universities Film and Video Council

Ballantyne, J. (1993) (ed.) *Researchers guide to British news reels* (Vol 3.). London: British Universities Film and Video Council

Federation of Commercial and Audio Visual Libraries (1998) *FOCAL international directory: 1998.*

Hanford, A. (1992) *Guidelines for establishing and maintaining television programme archives.* London: Royal Television Society

Oliver, E. (1989) (ed.) *Researchers guide to British film and television collections.* London: British Universities Film and Video Council

Rodgers, P. and Ross S. (1994) *Guidelines – television archiving: 1994.* Technical Department of Asia Pacific Broadcasting Union

13 The future of the BBC archives

Adam Lee

▶ INTRODUCTION

It is very appropriate to begin this summary of likely digital developments with a deliberate and direct link to the management of written records. In most companies, and broadcasting is no exception, the first experience of creating, distributing and storing digital material is gained from conventional office applications. This can range from the straightforward use of a word-processing package for creating a document, storing it on a local hard disc and distributing it through e-mail, to a highly complex electronic document management system which will provide twenty-four hour worldwide access to a company's internal records. Some companies still prefer to create electronically and then store on paper, but there has been a steady migration to electronic or digital storage for internal records, and the knowledge that has been gained can be applied to the management of digital material in general.

▶ ELECTRONIC DOCUMENT MANAGEMENT SYSTEMS

The functionality that has been developed for electronic document management systems provides the outline for almost any library or archive system which will be handling digital objects or files. Traditional library and archive cataloguing systems have contained cataloguing data which refers to an object (book, file, videotape etc.) which physically sits on a shelf. Much work is going on in Europe (e.g. The Electronic Library Programme, http://www.uklon.ac.uk/services/elib) and the USA (e.g. Digital Library Resources, http://www.lcweb.loc.gov/loc/ndlf/digital.html)

looking at the requirements for these new digital library systems which will hold the actual content as well as descriptions of it. In many respects, the document management industry has already been working on the same issues for the past ten years.

An electronic document management system has a series of attributes for holding digital files. The level and complexity of functionality within these main areas depends on the business requirement of each individual company, but are summarized by CIMTECH (1998) as follows:

- document capture. This is a method by which new material is placed on the system. It can be done automatically at the moment of creation;
- document indexing. This is usually done in two ways. Firstly, an indexing or profile form for each document is mandatory, and secondly, indexing data can be derived from the document itself. Full text indexing is the most obvious example;
- document storage. The systems provide the storage management capability. For the larger systems this will include automatic hierarchical storage management (HSM) where digital files are moved from online to near-line storage;
- document tracking. The purpose is to identify how material is being used and how it is being changed. The two most common examples are version control and audit trails. Version control gives control of the editing process for a document or digital file and can keep a detailed record of the different versions that have been created. An audit trail will trace the whole history of a document or file. It will show who has created it, who has edited it, where it has been distributed etc;
- index searching. These are the methods by which documents can be retrieved from the system. The assigned indexing information and/or derived indexes can be used;
- document retrieval and distribution. This is the actual method of retrieving and distributing the documents and digital files inside and outside of a company. Some systems are fully integrated with e-mail and others will also allow the creation of Web documents as an automatic process for the retrieval of documents from a digital store. This is only a very high level description of the available functionality. Electronic document management systems will also allow the viewing, editing and annotation of documents. Companies which have a highly structured business process also use such systems as part of their workflow and BPR (business process re-engineering) projects).

Systems such as this require a significant investment. The benefits need to be seen as being corporate-wide. An insurance company or a bank may view investment in such a system as one of the costs of conducting business, although the benefits may be less clear in other business environments. However, the conventional list of benefits includes:

- corporate standards. If there is a clear and enforceable policy on electronic document management, the records manager's nightmare of unrecorded and unstructured records can be avoided;
- reduced paper handling. People will continue to print documents for reading and for their portability but these will be working and ephemeral copies. The masters are held centrally;
- reduced duplication. As above, a trusted document management system reduces the need for 'extra copies';
- increased access to information. Common use of a common system will facilitate the flow of knowledge and information through a company;
- information security and legal requirements. These can be more easily enforced through a common electronic document system. The information is also more secure against physical deterioration and loss.

There are many other benefits associated with different products in the marketplace and the particular business applications to which such systems can be applied. However, the document management industry realized that standards were the key to the long-term success of such products. The purpose of the standards is to provide interoperability. Two *de facto* industries have come into existence:

1   Open Document Management API (ODMA: http://www.whatis.com/odma.htm). This ensures that individual applications (e.g. spreadsheet, WP package etc) work under the control of a document management system. It delivers a standard syntax for twelve basic document related operations including 'new', 'save', 'open' and 'close' a document;
2   Document Management Alliance (DMA: http://www.aiim.org/dma). This is designed to allow interoperability between different document management software from different vendors. The first DMA compliant products were launched in February 1998. The standards include the capability of searching across multiple libraries simultaneously and merging the results.

These standards were identified as vital to prevent the creation of isolated 'islands of information' within companies.

It is instructive to make a comparison between the relative maturity of the electronic document management systems available in the market place with the lack of standards and agreement for those of us working in the libraries and archives of the broadcast media. For example, in broadcasting many of the individual parts of the production chain have been digitized. Digital cameras are used to capture material; digital post-production and editing techniques are in common use; digital playout systems from servers are in daily operation; and digital formats, both digital videotape and optical disk are used for storage. However, the processes and new equipment have tended to be developed and implemented in isolation. There is no real commonality between much of the equipment in use. This means that currently as a digital file moves from one part of the production process to another, the re-keying of data is required as a minimum and there may be serious problems of incompatibility.

These problems are now starting to be recognized across the broadcasting industry. The ability to solve them will provide greater efficiency in the programme making process and will deliver savings which can in turn be reinvested in programmes. For example, the BBC has created a Media Data Project specifically designed to look at these issues and to propose a framework to eliminate duplication and improve efficiency (Owens, 1999). In particular, the project is looking at the metadata (http://www.ukoln.ac.uk/metadata) which is common throughout the production process, from idea and capture through to playout and archive.

While many of the principles of managing digital material have been established through the development of electronic document management systems, the broadcasting industry presents challenges which lie outside of the capability of a conventional document management system. For example, the management of work in progress is vital to the effective delivery of a service. In a news organization like the BBC there are multiple deadlines every day and new material is being received at the rate of 250 hours of broadcast standard video every day. This has to be turned into broadcast stories every day. The sheer scale of such operations and the complexity of creating new products every day in a digital environment are currently beyond the capability of conventional document management systems.

▶ THE DIGITAL FUTURE

Any attempt to predict the future is of course doomed to failure. In this section, a personal view of possible future developments is described, based on the experience of implementing change projects within the BBC's libraries and archives.

The main drivers for change are the service requirements of the users and customers of the BBC's libraries and archives. This can be summarized in one phrase: 'Desk Top Access'. This requirement can range from a modest desire to have traditional catalogues networked across the organization to a distant dream of full broadcast standard archive material available at every desk top for editing and then playout. The underlying theme is the changing role of the librarian/archivist/records manager. Our role is now to provide direct access to the catalogues, and where possible, to the content itself. The role as 'intermediary' between the customer and the content will and is changing. There is a real process of 'disintermediation' underway. Library staff are valued for their specialist skills, knowledge and experience in particular areas but for routine enquiries, customers expect and are expected to do the work themselves using user-friendly systems. These changes are not unique to broadcasting companies and have been much discussed in the professional library literature (e.g. http://www.unn.ac.uk/1~xcu2/hylife). However, those librarians and archivists working in a broadcast company can also establish a vital role for themselves though the use of their cataloguing and indexing skills. They are working with unique material which is not catalogued elsewhere (unlike the conventional publishing industry). These skills can also be applied at the start of the production process enabling the accurate tracking and retrieval of material all through the production process.

Establishing the customer and user requirements is the first stage in preparing the plan for a multimedia digital archive. The second is to establish a stable technical architecture for the project as a whole. This is the type of work for which highly skilled software experts are required. The creation of a digital archive requires substantial investment and no broadcasting organization can afford to invest in a closed, proprietary software application. The technical standards need to be open and manageable to reduce the risk of inappropriate development. In figure 13.1 below shows a high level diagram of a proposed technical architecture.

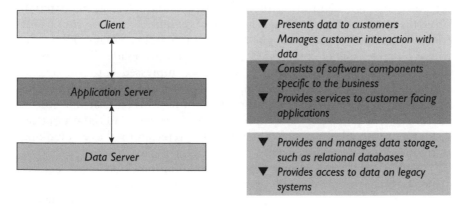

Figure 13.1 **Proposed technical architecture**

The third element in the foundations of the digital archive is preservation. This is of particular importance in organizations with large audio visual collections. All formats, whether film or videotape, are susceptible to physical decay. For example, acetate based film stock suffers from a chemical degradation commonly know as 'the vinegar syndrome' where acetic acid is released as the film stock decays. Videotape also has problems of physical vulnerability as the oxide coating gradually becomes separated from the tape backing. Videotape has further problems with obsolescent machinery required to replay the tapes. Spare parts are becoming increasingly difficult to source, and the skills required to operate the early videotape formats are becoming increasingly scarce. In the BBC, this is recognized as an important issue with the expansion of new outlets such as digital television and the Internet, all of which require content. The BBC archive holds 1.5 million items of film and videotape equivalent to 600 000 hours of content. It also hold 750 000 audio (radio) recordings equivalent to 300 000 hours of content. The choice of format for preservation is driven by the physical deterioration of the medium, the obsolescence of the equipment required to replay it and by the need of customers to re-use it. The problem of preservation is facing all owners of audio-visual collections around the world.

The main areas of work for the BBC are the moment are:

- Quad (two inch videotape), in use from c.1959 to c.1980;
- C format (one inch videotape), in use from c.1980 to c.1993;
- Acetate-based film soundtrack, in use from 1950's to mid 1970's;
- Umatic (¾-inch cassette format), in use from c.1982 to c.1990.

The BBC is also constructing a pilot project to evaluate the methods for preserving and digitizing audio material.

The preservation work is designed to transfer the material to the most appropriate and cost-effective format. Financial constraints do not yet allow the full digitization of broadcast standard television material. Until the cost of digital storage has fallen significantly, it is more cost effective to transfer from analogue formats to digital videotape. However, where possible, highly compressed digital copies are made. For example, the C Format transfer produces a MPEG1 compressed copy on optical disk which can be used for viewing and research purposes. It will also be possible in the near future to store these in networked near-line stores. For audio, it is possible to store transmission standard material on optical disk at a reasonable cost, and the audio pilot referred to above is looking at the practical issues involved.

Figure 13.2 below shows the three building blocks of user requirements, technical architecture and preservation, which form the foundations for a digital archive. The rest of the diagram shows the stages needed to achieve desk-top access.

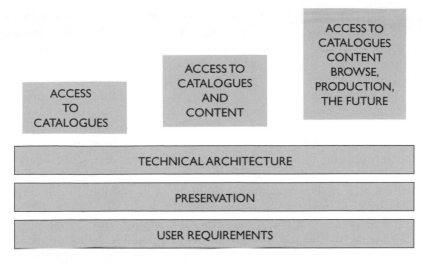

Figure 13.2 **BBC archive: digital initiative**

Universal access to the catalogues of the holdings is the first step. This is consistent with the move away from using library staff in their traditional role as interpreters of requests for information and content. The growing demand for instant access to the catalogues from customers will result in the development of user-friendly interfaces. New systems are now designed for both the requirements of the naïve or casual user and the professional librarian. The widespread use of the Internet has raised expectations, and easily searchable in-house catalogues have become a minimum requirement.

The second step is to provide desk top access to catalogues and a range of the content. The content that can be provided is largely limited by the available technology. It is now possible to deliver documents, broadcast standard still photographs and text based content directly to customers. It is not yet possible to deliver broadcast quality television programmes across a wide area network to a large customer base. At the BBC, for example, the digital stills system delivers both the catalogue and the transmission quality photographs direct to users. The digital images can then be used directly in the editing process or for transmission.

The third step is to provide more and higher quality content. The delivery of browse quality video is currently being planned. It is already possible to view video on the Web, for example. However in a broadcasting environment, the aim is to provide a practical tool which can enable some of the initial editing decisions to be made and implemented. For example, it will be possible to select sequences of shots with their timecode and to compile edit decision lists. Proven software technology exists to do this now. The long term aim of this third step is to allow production staff full access to the archive at broadcast quality with the ability to manipulate and edit material at their own PC before sending the finished material directly to playout. It will be many years before it will be possible to afford or achieve this aim.

Digitally stored content also provides new opportunities for deriving indexing data from the digital files themselves. Derived indexing from text based content is now a standard feature of most retrieval systems holding documents. When still, video and audio files are also stored digitally the opportunities for introducing new methods of searching increase. With video, it is possible to automatically select key frames (e.g. scene changes), it is possible to search by colour, shape and texture; it may be possible soon to search by face recognition. In audio, it is possible to convert the spoken word to text which can then be searched. All of these methods of indexing could, at a cost, be incorporated in an online digital archive.

Of necessity this is a high level view of a possible digital future. The rapidly changing production and broadcasting environment is challenging the traditional role and purpose of libraries and archive. It is still too early to predict what the future effects of the new digital production techniques that are currently being introduced will be. The role of an archive in the end to end production process is still under discussion. Are 'library' and 'archive' valid descriptions of future activity? The term 'media asset management' is being increasingly used to describe the activities of managing material in digital formats. Posts are already being created in some broadcasting organizations for 'media managers' who are responsible for the accurate identification and retrieval of digital material. The only thing we can be sure of is that the rate of change both of the technology and of the role of the librarian and archivist will continue to increase.

▶ ACKNOWLEDGEMENTS

Thanks to Francis Galliano and Mike Wood of the BBC Digital Archive Initiative for their help in preparing this chapter.

▶ REFERENCES

CIMTECH (1998) *Document management directory.* Centre for Information Management and Technology

Owens, C. (1999) The BBC data model for identifying and describing programme material. Paper given at the EBU Seminar in Programme Archives, Geneva, January 28

14 Ethical and legal issues for media librarians

Barrie MacDonald

▶ **INTRODUCTION**

Amongst the many challenges that now face librarians within the media are myriads of ethical and legal issues affecting information gathering, storage, communication and usage. New telecommunications and communications technologies now allow almost instant access to news and accompanying analysis, information and background material from around the world. The broadcast and print media industries are themselves an important part of this production of news and information, though they no longer have the monopoly in an increasingly competitive market. These twin forces of new technology and increased competition have heightened awareness of some of the ethical issues, and have certainly confused many others. So, is there a difference in the ethical issues of information handling between the pre-information age and now? Essentially the fundamental issues are the same, and we still draw on traditional values, but we have had to re-evaluate our ethical principles. However, any present day confusion within the information profession only reflects that of society in general on moral and ethical issues. This chapter will cover both the ethical principles for information handling in the media, as well broadly survey some legal aspects of information work.

▶ **GENERAL ETHICAL PRINCIPLES**

What do we mean by ethics or ethical principles? How are they relevant to this discussion? It is perhaps useful to examine briefly the theoretical and philosophical foundations of ethics in the information age. A useful definition of ethics, in the *Penguin dictionary of philosophy* (Mautner,

1997), is a 'rational enquiry into, or a theory of, the standards of right and wrong, good and bad, in respect of character and conduct, which ought to be accepted by a class of individuals', and (of particular relevance to our discussion) 'a body of standards that the professionals in question ought to accept and observe'.

So, ethics is about how people ought to act. The keywords are *ought*, *obligation*, *duty*, *right*, and *wrong*. It not only defines what we mean by moral terms, such as right and wrong, but also suggests a logical process for deciding what is the right thing to do in particular circumstances and a rational basis for action.

Ethical principles are the basis of many of the basic freedoms and rights that underpin democratic society – freedom of speech, freedom of the press, the right to know, and the right to privacy. The *Universal Declaration of Human Rights*, proclaimed at the United Nations General Assembly on 10 December 1948 has thirty articles establishing principles of freedom, justice and peace. Of particular importance to the media are: Article 12, a right to privacy; Article 19, a right to freedom of opinion and expression, including a right to seek, receive and impart information and ideas through any medium; and Article 27, the right to the protection of the moral and material interests resulting from authorship of any scientific, literary or artistic works. The *European Convention on Human Rights* guarantees similar rights to private and family life, and to freedom of expression.

Freedom of speech and the press has long been a part of the written constitution of the United States as the First Amendment, which states that 'Congress shall make no law ... abridging the freedom of speech, or of the press'. President Roosevelt called it one of the 'four essential freedoms'. The United Kingdom does not have a written constitution, but relies on legislation and common law. However, the *Human Rights Act 1998* does now give effect to the rights and freedoms guaranteed by the *European Convention on Human Rights*.

There is no absolute right to information. Freedom of information in the UK, though a long established 'moral right', has been limited by various legislative and legal instruments, particularly the *Official Secrets Act*, and the laws of libel. However, as a response to public expectation of greater openness and accountability, a Government policy document (*Your right to know*, 1997) has pledged the introduction of a *Freedom of Information Act* giving a general statutory right of access to official records and information. So, it is not yet a legal right, though to be informed has often been a legal requirement, and ignorance of the law has not been a defence.

▶ LIBRARY AND INFORMATION ETHICS

The application of general ethical principles to the conduct of professional or occupational groups, such as doctors, lawyers or librarians, is a branch of applied ethics. Librarians, no less than other professions, have developed standards of ethical behaviour, and promoted ethical conduct through professional bodies and codes. But they also work within organizations that have their own ethical stance and code of conduct for their employees.

Professional ethics

The professional ethics of the library and information world are distinguished by a strong commitment to intellectual freedom and freedom of access to information. There has always been a moral dimension to the provision of information in terms of deciding the people who should receive it, how much they should have, whether or not to charge, questions of copyright infringement, issues of confidentiality and commercial secrecy, and so on. Librarians have always had to take a position on a professional matters which are 'ethical' in essence.

Professionalism is all about doing a good job. Professional work according to Hannabuss (1998) should be characterized by knowledge, training, honesty and competance. Awareness of basic ethical and legal principles should be an essential part of training for information work, both through academic studies, professional accreditation and as part of in-house and on the job training. The failure to do a good job is a breach of our professional principles, and our commitment of care to our clients. It may also lead to accusations of negligence, or the possibility of a malpractice case.

So can professional philosophy merely interfere with efficiency, and is it any longer relevant? Foskett (1962) believes it surely is still necessary, otherwise there would be no reason or conviction of the value of work, only day to day existence.

Organizational ethics

As well as abiding by professional ethics librarians and information workers also have to work within the ethical rules and constraints of their parent organization. The information sector is made up of various organizational cultural ethics, some of which are identified by Hannabuss (1998) as more entrepreneurial and competitively secretive than others. There can be conflict between professional ethics and organizational objectives. How far should the professional commitments to information sharing and the values of information be reflected or influenced by the way the organization works? Can you be moral in an amoral organization?

The impact of organizational structure and ethos on the ethical conduct of its employees can be problematic. Management structures and environment should facilitate and promote ethical behaviour. Ideally an organization should give staff full involvement in defining and discharging professional work, moving away from authority-based relationship and personal self-interest towards community interest. Staff empowerment will produce better accountability and quality of work, and a more ethical approach to service.

Codes of practice

Professions define the skills and knowledge required of members, who voluntarily submit themselves to agreed standards of ethical conduct. Librarians, like other professionals, articulate their values and standards in codes of conduct.

Three types of professional codes have been identified (Harris, 1996, pp. 5–6): *codes of ethics* consisting of a fairly short set of broad principles; *codes of conduct* with more detailed and more specific principles; and *codes of practice* combining ethical principles with rules governing the way professional duties are carried out. Codes benefit two groups: the member of the professional body, and the public they serve. Members, both individually and collectively, benefit from the status and reputation that a code confers on them. For the public, codes offer protection against unprofessional conduct through articulation of standards of service that can be expected and disciplinary procedures for any misconduct. Harris (1996, pp.14) also identifies a relatively new use for a code 'in assisting members of professions who are employees to resist pressure from their employers to act in an unethical manner'.

The Library Association in the United Kingdom and the American Library Association have broadly comparable codes of conduct. The Library Association *Code of Professional Conduct* (1983) sets out standards of professional conduct expected of members, and indicates matters that may be regarded as contrary to the aims, objects and interests of the Association, and subject to the Disciplinary Committee. It emphasises members' primary duty to their clients, irrespective of the librarian's personal interests and views of the content of the material and the clients requirements. It states a positive duty to 'facilitate the flow of information and ideas and to protect and promote the right of every individual to have free and equal access to sources of information without discrimination and within the limits of the law'. It stresses the obligation of privacy and confidentiality with clients, and not to divulge any material, information or administrative record entrusted to them in confidence.

The American Library Association's *Code of Ethics* (1995) states the values to which its members are committed, and emphasizes the ethical responsibilities of the profession. Its list of broad principles includes: 'We are members of a profession explicitly committed to intellectual freedom and the freedom of access to information'. Unlike the UK Library Association code it states: 'We recognize and respect intellectual property rights'.

Another professional group whose ethical principles are similar to librarians and information scientists are journalists, who are also, of course, our clients in the media. *The Code of Professional Conduct* of the National Union of Journalists in the United Kingdom, articulates principles of particular relevance to us, ranging from the general defence of freedom of the press to specific issues of ensuring that information is fair and accurate, rectifying harmful inaccuracies, obtaining information and photographs by straightforward means, and without intrusion into private grief, and protection of confidential sources of information. More practical issues are also of concern in the British Computer Society's *Code of Conduct*, which is segmented into sections on: the public interest; duty to employers and clients; duty to the profession; and professional competence and integrity. In addition to the normal ethical requirements it provides for professional care and diligence, the code emphasizes the importance of not receiving inducements for the introduction of business, promising confidentiality to clients, and exercising independent judgement on behalf of clients in giving advice on products and services.

We may also, of course, have devised and published our own code or statement of service for our information unit embodying general professional principles. If we operate a commercial fee-based service, that 'code' may be part of a contract and binding service agreement with customers.

▶ MEDIA LIBRARIES AND INFORMATION UNITS

We have looked at ethical issues for the library profession as a whole, which will be met by librarians working in public service, education, business, or industry. Are libraries in the media different? Are there ethical issues unique to media libraries and information units?

The broadcast and print media are largely concerned with the dissemination of news, information and entertainment. Libraries support this work through provision of information, research and the materials used in programmes or publications, such as photographs, film and videotape, sound recordings, and music. To a certain degree the ethical concerns of librarians in the media are the same as those faced by the clients they serve – the broadcasters, producers, editors and journalists. These issues are: freedom of speech; freedom of information; the right to know; access and accountability; truth; honesty; accuracy; fairness; objectivity;

confidentiality of sources; and privacy. News librarians regularly face legal and ethical issues, mostly the same as those the journalists face, though occasionally in conflict with journalists on such issues as copyright and confidentiality.

Some general information ethics may be less relevant in the media. Acting as a moral arbiter might still be appropriate in a public library, but not in a newspaper library providing a journalist with information to write a balanced or investigative news story. Awareness of the ethical and legal issues of supplying obscene, pornographic or blasphemous materials is advisable (Robertson and Nicol, 1992, pp. 105–167). Police and courts can demand access to library materials in obscenity, libel and official secrets cases, raising potential dilemmas of whether or not librarians hand over files to the police in such cases.

However, given the wide dissemination of newspapers and broadcast programmes, the legal and fair use of information, particularly clearance of rights and authorizations, must be a basic tenet of faith for librarians within the media.

► SPECIFIC AREAS OF ACTIVITY AND ISSUES

The nature of information services, and the relationship between them and their clients raise many ethical questions, but also legal issues as well. The laws of major concern in information work identified by Eisenschitz (1997) are: intellectual property monopoly rights (copyright, patents, trade marks, and designs); personal rights (data protection and privacy); and the laws protecting against breaches of confidence. Here we will look in greater depth at some areas of information management and practice, and specific ethical and legal issues.

Library policy and management

In the development of policy, and the practice of management, library managers face many moral and legal issues. Librarians should contribute to corporate policy decisions if possible, particularly on the use of library, but also on general information issues. The librarians' commitment to openness and sharing of information (though possibly at odds with the parent organization) is a positive asset and can be a beneficial influence on the corporate ethos. Ideally, the library or information unit should compile a written policy statement on access, acquisition policy, services, and facilities that can be made available to management and customers.

Library managers have a responsibility to their staff. Employment policies are, of course, normally set and handled by the organization, but line managers have a day-to-day and personal responsibility for staff – allocation of work and opportunities, recommendation for promotion, training and career development, and generally for their 'moral health'. In setting firm principles for methods of working, quality of service, attitude to clients, etc, line managers must lead the way and set an example. A code of practice for library staff laying out rules and standards of service, perhaps as part of staff manual, is also advisable. Staff poor performance or misconduct may be due to poor management, lack of example, poorly defined standards of conduct, or pressure (real or perceived) from managers. The library management structure and environment should provide opportunity for discussion of ethical issues and maximum staff involvement in deliberation of policy in the professional areas of work.

The economic management of our resources, staff and accommodation has become increasingly important, bringing with it many 'ethical' concerns over the allocating of resources, apportioning time for enquirers, deployment and career development of staff and relationships with the users. Many libraries these days have to 'pay their way' within their parent organization, by clearing the cost of overheads, such as accommodation, staff and materials, or in some cases even be fully commercial profit-making services. They will need to charge internal, and/or external customers, through devising a 'rate card' based on estimated costs, giving the scale of charges and a service agreement guaranteeing aspects of the service.

Acquisitions policy and practice

Developing an acquisitions policy and the evaluation of informational material are traditional tasks for the librarian, but are they relevant anymore? The information explosion of the late 20th century has meant that most libraries are no longer able to collect all materials available within their area of interest, and to satisfy their user's needs entirely from their own collections. They now supply information from many sources – loan, document delivery services, online, CD-ROM, and the Internet. As we move from managing collections of informational materials to acting as information brokers our knowledge and understanding of the legal and moral issues of accessing and disseminating information must increase. We need to exercise even more judgement on the quality, integrity and accuracy of information obtained. The librarians' expertise is now more valuable to the user than the collections they manage. We also need to police the use of the information and adherence to the differing conditions, rules and regulations governing its acquisition and use.

In becoming an information broker have librarians lost their traditional role of gatekeeper? We may not be exercising the role of moral guardian, but we still have a responsibility to evaluate the various information sources we provide and advise our clients on their accuracy, integrity, comprehensiveness and currency. Surely, if we have a role at all beyond being an information-technician, it must be that we still exercise discretion and judgement in making informed professional decisions about the service we provide, and play a substantive role in the production and validation of information. But, this is now more difficult given the complex authorship of information sources, particularly electronic sources, and the traditional criteria for such evaluation being harder to apply. The Internet, for example, unlike a library, is not the product of selection, and only minimal self-regulation controls the placing of illegal, inaccurate or offensive Web sites.

News librarians have a responsibility for inaccurate or libellous material acquired for their library as articles, press cuttings, or photographs. They should consider the nature and importance of the error or inaccuracy, whether a published correction was made, and its value or relevance to library stock and the files. Coggins (1993) recommends identifying inaccurate or libellous material for future users so the errors or libels are not perpetuated, at least unknowingly. Photographs known to be digitally manipulated should be clearly identified as such, if they are to held.

Taste and decency issues may not seem relevant in this context, but libraries in the UK and the USA have been investigated by the police for making available books or pamphlets or photographs considered obscene or blasphemous – most recently the Madonna book of erotica, *Sex*, and a book of homoerotic photographs by Robert Mapplethorpe. Prosecution in the UK would be under the *Obscene Publications Act* on grounds that the offending material tends 'to deprave and corrupt', with defence on the 'harm' principle – did they actually harm anyone.

Acquisition of data for compilation of internal databases must meet the requirements of the *Data Protection Act 1998* if it contains personal or biographical information about individuals. Informed consent must be obtained in data collection. It must be collected and stored for the purpose originally intended (and notified). Information gathered for one purpose should not be used for another without permission. Respect for the moral and civil rights of information suppliers or providers, as well as those of the data subjects, is essential. Data protection issues are dealt with later in this chapter.

Liability of Information Service Provision

Library and information managers have always been accountable for the quality, accuracy and relevance of the services they provide. However, these days many information services are commercial, contract based services, whether within the public or private sectors, which elevates simple accountability to legal liability. Information providers contract to provide specialized information and research services to clients on a fee-paying basis.

If the service is contract-based, and money is charged, courts expect a higher level of service and care. The law in Britain requires suppliers of goods or services to use reasonable care and skill in their provision (*Supply of Goods and Services Act 1982*, Clause 13) Contractual liability begins when you fail to fulfil your obligations. Contracts may specify a turnaround time for enquiries, guarantees of accuracy, clearance of other rights (copyright licence payments, etc.). The professional ethic of librarians has always been to provide accurate, relevant and timely information, however, if it is a contract-based service there is extra imperative to get it right! When drafting a service agreement one solution might be to have an exclusion clause stating that, for example, 'We accept no liability for losses arising from negligence on our part'. However, such a catch-all clause may be invalid in law, and is certainly not a good advertisement for a service's professionalism. Insurance can be taken out for information services to cover liability.

The law of negligence is based on the assumption that as a citizen one owes 'a duty of care' to fellow citizens, and any harm or loss by negligence caused must be repaid with compensation. Sykes (1997) has identified that liability in tort is wider than in contract because there is no requirement of a mutual exchange of promises, and duty of care may be owed to a wider range of persons. Malpractice action is possible in cases of librarians providing false information or failing to check facts, and for any losses incurred as a result.

Handling enquiries and research

Some aspects of providing an enquiry service have already been touched on – those of evaluating and advising on the information provided, and the liability for the accuracy and timeliness of the information provided. However, there are other ethical issues in the handling of enquiries, particularly in the reconciling of professional ideals with the compromises and constraints of actual practice. The UK Library Association's *Code of professional conduct* states: 'The essential principle which lies behind the code is that the professional librarian's prime duty is to facilitate access to materials and information in order to meet the requirement of the client, irrespective of the librarian's personal interest, and views of the content of the material and the client's requirements'. The American Library Association similarly encourages members to distinguish between personal convictions and professional duties.

The first constraint will be to whom should the service be available. The old library ethic of access for all cannot unfortunately hold true in most cases. In practice we do have to ration our service – to decide to whom to give information, or not. In the case of a commercial information service it will simply be according to who will pay the cost. In a private company or organization it might be a 'house rule' only to serve staff of that body, and no external enquirers. An 'authorized users only' rule may be a legal safeguard in, for example, restricting the use of the library of a news organization to employees only. If we are permitted to also help secondary customers, for example members of the public, it may only be as resources and time permit. Even if we are a fully public service, and we have wide discretion as to whom to serve, for reasons of limited time and staff resources we will have to decide whom to serve and how much time to allocate to their requests.

Another access ethical issue for librarians in news organizations is whether to allow full access by their journalists to commercial, subscription or cost-based external information systems, as well as the newspapers own electronic library. Do you continue to act as a gatekeeper or mediator in the case of expensive external sources? Is cost the issue, or control?

The provision of information, and in particular the content of an enquiry can present a conflict between personal and professional ethics. For example, should a reference librarian accede to or refuse an enquirer wanting information on illegal or anti-social activities – remain neutral and do his or her best to supply whatever is requested, or take a stand and refuse? Foskett wrote (1962), 'no politics, no religion, no morals' – value neutrality! The American Library Association code requires 'accurate, unbiased, and courteous response to all requests'. How far should ethical neutrality go? In an experiment in the USA (Hauptman, 1975) an information science student contacted thirteen libraries (six public and seven academic) asking for information on how to construct a bomb. All thirteen agreed to his request, though one then refused him because he was not a student at that school. In another similar experiment on ethical neutrality (Dowd, 1989), a request made to libraries for information on how to freebase cocaine met with no refusal of help from librarians on moral grounds. Do we have a right to judge intent? Surely making assumptions about intent is overstepping the bounds of our profession. Librarians have an obligation to provide access to information and a responsibility to oppose censorship. And any way, such considerations may now be academic, as end users can circumvent the library and go straight to the Internet.

Most enquiries involve information that is fully published and in the public domain, but if it is not then it can present an ethical problem. Giving data on competitors or rivals from private or semi-published material (eg company brochures, annual reports, etc) is problematic. When contacting organizations for annual reports, accounts, investor brochures or information always be honest and identify yourself and your company. However, you may be asked by your enquirer, perhaps a journalist or business analyst, to hide your identity. Griffin (1997) suggests that a solution to this problem may be to use a neutral third party information broker, though outsourcing can be expensive.

Liability of information provision, as we have discussed in the previous section is increasingly important. The likelihood of legal action against information professionals may be limited, but librarians should always take reasonable care to avoid acts of omission or inaccuracy through careful checking and verification of information supplied. Carelessness may harm or cause loss. Inaccurate, or libellous material, supplied to a journalist, and used by the newspaper can result in legal action, retraction and damages.

Breach of confidence and confidentiality

Confidentiality laws afford a protection against the disclosure or use of information that is not publicly known, and has been imparted in confidence. They are important considerations in journalism, publishing and broadcasting, and it is therefore essential for librarians in the media to understand. Journalists often use confidential sources for obtaining information, and the protection of their anonymity or secrecy is an essential requirement of their ethical code. Of course, other professions have similar vows of confidentiality – doctors, priests, lawyers, etc. As members of a profession, librarians also owe their clients an assurance of confidentiality not to communicate the nature or content of their enquiry to others, particularly competitors.

Most forms of duty of confidence are contractual – domestic, governmental or legal. Contracted employees often have 'secrecy' clauses in their contract, obliging them to keep secret information gained in their work. Government employees, through their contracts and under the *Official Secrets Act* have a duty of secrecy. In recent years several cases of disclosure of 'official secrets' have hit the headlines, most notably those of British secret service agent Peter Wright and the revelations in his book *Spycatcher*, and former Security Officer David Shayler arrested in Paris in 1998 on a UK request for his extradition to face charges under the *Official Secrets Act* for his allegations of MI5 surveillance of prominent Labour politicians. Making public such information can only be justified if it is in the 'public interest', or if it can be proved that it is somehow already in the public domain. The *Public Interest Disclosure Act 1998* now provides protection for whistleblowers who make a disclosure of information that they consider is in the public interest (and they believe it to be substantially true). This is on the grounds that is shows a criminal offence has been committed, or failure to comply with the law, or a miscarriage of justice. The *Act* enables them to bring legal action against victimisation and for unfair dismissal provided the disclosure was made in good faith and no personal gain was derived from it. The *Act* will strengthen the position of investigative journalism and coverage of stories of malpractice.

A breach of confidence could exist if information obtained with agreed limitations as to use, perhaps for one purpose only, was reused without necessary consents and agreement. Such a case would be material derived through interviews, depending on the terms under which the interview was granted. If recordings or transcripts of such interviews are held in the library or records centre of newspapers or broadcasters, librarians and records managers must strictly adhere to those terms.

Privacy

In United Kingdom law there has been no general right to privacy, or substantive protection. Privacy legislation covering intrusion of privacy by the media has been rejected in favour of media self-regulation. Other countries, France for example, have had much stricter attitudes to and laws on privacy.

The Committee on Privacy and Related Matters, chaired by David Calcutt QC, was set up in 1990, following allegations of declining press standards and intrusion into privacy. It recommended making physical intrusion by the press a criminal offence, but preferred self-regulation by the Press Complaints Commission for publication of intrusive material. The Press Complaints Commission's *Code of Practice* was first drawn up in 1991, and revised in 1997 following concern over the death of the Princess of Wales and newspaper methods of gathering news. It obliges the press to maintain the highest ethical standards, to respect private and family life, home, health and correspondence, and not to obtain information or pictures through harassment, or intrusion into grief or shock. Violation of privacy by the media is often defended on the grounds that it is in the 'public interest', or because of its newsworthiness.

However, some UK legislation does impact on some aspects of privacy. The *Human Rights Act 1998*, enacts the *European Convention on Human Rights*, provision on the 'right to private and family life', though the Government has confirmed its support for the freedom of the media and its opposition to statutory privacy legislation. English law has always been more attuned to property than human rights, so privacy cases can often be processed under quasi-proprietary actions, such as trespass. Under the *Sexual Offences Act (Amendment) Act 1976*, the press and broadcasters do not report the names of victims in rape cases (unlike other crimes) because it is felt to place a stigma on the victim. Privacy in photographs commissioned for private and domestic purposes is protected by *The Copyright Designs and Patents Act 1988*, ensuring that unless the commissioner consents such photographs cannot be issued to or displayed in public, broadcast or included in cable programmes. As we will see later, the *Data Protection Act 1998* introduces some form of privacy legislation in requiring justification by organizations keeping personal information systems and greater rights to individuals to sue for damages caused by breach of privacy. *The Broadcasting Act 1990* empowers the Independent Television Commission to draw up a code on matters relating to the provision of programmes by its licensed television services. The *ITC Programme Code* section on privacy and gathering of information outlines a number of limitations to broadcasters arising from individual citizens right to privacy. These include: filming or recording of members of the public; filming in institutions or police operations; fairness to innocent parties; recorded telephone interviews; hidden microphones and cameras; scenes of suffering and distress; interviewing of children; and door-stepping interviews. Under the 1990 *Act* the Radio Authority has drawn up a comparable code for its licensed commercial radio stations. The *Broadcasting Act 1996* (Section 107) enables the Broadcasting Standards Commission to draw up and review codes on, amongst other things, 'unwarranted infringement of privacy in, or in connection with the obtaining of material included in (radio or television) programmes'. The BSC issued its *Code of Practice on Fairness and Privacy*, effective from 1 January 1998.

Media librarians should make themselves aware of the general privacy issues, and be wary of obtaining and handling information or photographs that may infringe privacy. The use of intrusive photographs is a problem in the media, particularly photographs that are taken without consent and of people in private situations where they could reasonably have expected privacy. Newspapers or broadcasters, and therefore librarians, should avoid using them. The moral rights of subjects of photographs of private events, or showing distress in war or violent situations are now clear from the legislation and codes, and are subject to strict guidelines as to authorization and consent. Oppenheim (1998) suggests a solution to this problem of intrusive photographs whereby automatic economic copyright protection for photographs is abolished (while retaining moral rights), and to attain economic rights and benefits a photographer could publish a copy of the photograph (on the Internet) to register it with a declaration that it is genuine, taken fairly and legally, and without intrusion.

There is a widespread concern about electronic gathering of personal information, and the sharing and possible abuse of it. The selling of individual's names, addresses and personal details for marketing purposes is a commonplace, but widespread abuse of privacy. Coggins (1993) concludes that to ensure personal data privacy rights society must restrict reuse by unauthorized individuals.

Defamation and libel

Defamation is of two kinds: libel – a false statement of fact printed or broadcast about a person which tends to injure that person's reputation;

and slander – a defamatory statement made by word of mouth or gesture. Spoken defamatory statements made in theatres and in broadcasts on radio and television are deemed to be libel and not slander. Defamation on the Internet is also libel, and early cases have involved academics arguing in email based discussion groups.

The essential elements in defamation actions are that the statement must be false, and the plaintiff must be able to prove that it has damaged his reputation by lowering the esteem, respect, goodwill or confidence in which he is viewed by right-thinking people generally, and produces adverse opinion of him. But, as Robertson and Nicol (1992, pp. 41) point out, truth, however tawdry or trivial, may be told without let or hindrance from libel laws. The law has to reconcile the right to communicate with the right to reputation.

The current law in the United Kingdom is the *Defamation Act 1996*, which amends earlier laws on defamation, and the limitations with respect to actions taken for defamation or malicious falsehood. It defines carefully who is, and most importantly for librarians, who is not responsible for publication of libel, replacing the earlier, rather uncertain, common law defence of innocent dissemination. Before this *Act* librarians (like distributors, booksellers or newsagents) had to use the innocent dissemination defence, unless it could be proved they were negligent or at least ought to have known the publication was likely to contain libellous matter. The author, editor or publisher of the statement is responsible for defamation, but not the printer or distributor of printed materials, the producer of a film or sound recording, the broadcaster of a live programme (where he can have no effective control over the maker of the statement), or the operator or provider of access to a communication system transmitting the statement.

It is important that news organizations are not hampered by the threat of libel and slander actions. They have a responsibility to the public to provide unrestricted access to the spoken and printed word. It is important that news librarians know the definition of libel law and be aware of what is filed within the library. With possible libel action in mind, should librarians only file published material (cuttings, etc), but not reporters', journalists' or researchers' notes, reports, and memos containing possible false material, in case future journalists use the material without checking or verifying the statements? Material held within a library, certainly a news library, could perpetuate libel, and be used as evidence in libel actions.

Copyright and Rights Issues

The term 'copyright' is generally used to designate the rights secured by law to authors of literary, dramatic, musical and artistic works, and to protect authors against unauthorized copying of their works. Copyright issues have become more prominent and complex in recent years, and affect information work quite considerably. Electronic dissemination of information has, in particular, heightened awareness of copyright issues.

Broadly speaking there are two rights: *moral* rights to be identified as the author, and to control the use of your work; and *economic* rights for the author, publisher or commissioner to enjoy economic benefit from work in royalties, sales and licences. The *World Intellectual Property Organization Copyright Treaty* (1996) recognizes the need 'to maintain a balance between the rights of authors, and the larger public interest particularly education, research and access to information'.

Libraries and librarians are the custodians of copyright material, and their duties are to maintain that balance between protecting origination rights and safeguarding those of users, but not ignore abuse of copyright. Cornish (1997) warns that librarians must know what the law is as ignorance of the law is no defence!

Copyright laws in the United Kingdom have existed since the 18th Century when the *Copyright Act 1709*, 'an act for the Encouragement of Learning', provided statutory rights to authors or their assignees (publishers, printers or booksellers) for the printing and reprinting of their work. Information products have been treated as personal property, according to Eisenschitz (1997), and are considered tradeable property rights of important benefit to authors and publishers. The *Copyright, Designs and Patents Act 1988* establishes the framework for copyright in the United Kingdom. It consolidated provisions from the previous *Copyright Act 1956*, but faced the enormous changes in intellectual property ownership and offered better protection to moral rights. The Act states that copyright is a property right that subsists in literary, dramatic, musical and artistic works, sound recordings, films, broadcasts, cable programmes, and, importantly, typographical arrangements of published editions, and affirms the right to enjoy the economic and moral rights of that ownership.

Duration of copyright provisions in the 1988 Act have been amended as a result of European regulations – *Council Directive 93/98/EEC of 29 October 1993 harmonizing the term of protection of copyright and certain related rights* – which has extended the copyright period from 50 years from the death of the author to 70 years. Enacted for the UK in *The Duration of Copyright and Rights in Performances Regulations 1995* (S.I. 1995/3297), the new rules now give protection to literary, dramatic, musical and artistic works for 70 years, to films for 70 years from the death of the principal director or screenwriter, and to sound recordings, broadcasts or cable programmes for 50 years from the date originally made. Inevitable problems were created for publishers and users by the revival of copyright, with such authors as Virginia Woolf coming back into copyright. Further amendments from that Directive, together with

Council Directive 92/100/EEC of 19 November 1992 on rental right and lending right and on certain rights related to copyright in the field of intellectual property, and *Council Directive 93/83/EEC of 27 September 1993 on the co-ordination of certain rules concerning copyright and rights related to copyright applicable to satellite broadcasting and cable retransmission*, are enacted for the UK by *The Copyright and Related Rights Regulations 1996* (S.I. 1996/2967). It harmonises the application of national copyright laws to satellite cross-border broadcasts, and affirms authors' and performers' rights in sound recordings and films, introducing new property rights for performers requiring their consent to rental and lending copies of recordings of their performances with provision for appropriate licensing schemes and bodies.

In 1998 the United States, spurred on by the need to implement the WIPO copyright treaties and be compatible with the European Union, passed laws through Congress also extending the post-mortem copyright term to 70 years, although they did not revive copyright for public domain works as Europe had done. Other measures include provisions limiting liability of online service and Internet providers. Grantham (1999) describes the legislation as a balancing act between the rights of the copyright industries, who will now enjoy a substantial copyright extension windfall of 20 more years of rights exploitation, and the burgeoning Internet industry which is anxious to limit its exposure to liability arising from the acts of others.

Copying of works without an appropriate licence is a restricted act infringing copyright. However, there are two exceptions that allow unlicensed copying, 'Fair dealing' (Sections 29–30) allows copying by individuals for their own purposes of research and private study or for criticism or news reporting. The 'fair use' rules of American copyright are more simple and flexible, with legislation providing for a statutory defence against charges of copyright infringement, depending on the purpose and character of the use, the nature of the work, amount and substantiality of portion used and effect on market values. 'Library privilege' (Sections 38–43) allows limited copying by a librarian at the request of an enquirer for their research and private study. Copying can also be done for preservation of an item that can no longer be purchased through being out of print. So no proactive or anticipative copying can done, or multiple copies to produce a selected dissemination of information service.

Copying which cannot be done within the 'fair dealing' or 'library privilege' provisions in the UK must be licensed, and 1988 *Act* sets the framework for licensing schemes and agencies to act on behalf of copyright owners in the granting of licences and collection of revenues. The Authors' Licensing and Collecting Society (ACLS) ensures copyright revenues due to authors are collected efficiently, and distributed speedily. It also covers cable retransmission, off-air recording, electronic rights and public reception of broadcasts. In association with the Publishers'

Licensing Society, it established the Copyright Licensing Agency (CLA) to administer licences for photocopying from books, journals and periodicals. It has a scale of charges according to the category of organizations undertaking copying, ranging from commercial to public bodies, recognizing a difference between commercial and non-commercial copying. There are other licensing schemes operating under the 1988 *Act*. Educational off-air recording by universities, colleges and schools is licensed by the Educational Recording Agency (ERA). Licensing of copying from newspapers is handled by the Newspaper Licensing Agency (NLA). Administering the rights due to performers in broadcasts, recordings and film is undertaken by the Performing Rights Society (PRS), and to composers and publishers of music for use of copyright material by sound, film, radio and television recordings by the Mechanical Copyright Protection Society (MCPS). These two bodies merged in 1997 to form the Music Alliance. Copyright management is becoming increasingly commercial and competitive, with the leading music, leisure and entertainment industries acquiring large libraries of copyright material. Libraries and academic publishers are small players by comparison.

Electronic storage, retrieval and dissemination of information and other rights materials have raised certain copyright problems. It is often difficult to establish precise authorship, and therefore moral rights, as electronic storage and distribution can change an author's work. Actions normal in paper environment are becoming illegal in an electronic environment. Most electronic publications are supplied with contractual limitations (restricting downloading, re-transmitting, networking, etc.) for CD-ROMs or online services – read the terms of reference. The European Union ruling that viewing information on screen is 'transient copying' and a restricted act, represents the destruction of 'fair dealing' in the electronic environment.

Problems posed for information and library services by electronic publishing have increased through the *Directive 96/9/EC of the European Parliament and of the Council of 11 March 1996 on the legal protection of databases. The Copyright and Rights in Databases Regulations 1997* (S.I. 1997/3032), which implements the database Directive came into force on 1 January 1998. In its acknowledgement that 'the making of databases requires the investment of considerable human, technical and financial resources while such databases can be copied or accessed at a fraction of the cost', it swings the balance from users to publishers or database providers, giving them greater control over use of their material. The regulations bring in a new property right in a database where there has been substantial investment in obtaining, verifying or presenting the contents of the database. A database is not required to be original in content or compilation, but can by publicly available data, have this new database right, only to have received substantial investment. The duration of copyright is 15 years from the year it was first made available, with further 15-year periods if any database is revised significantly during the first periods. This will give almost a perpetual monopoly in non-copyright data which could impede smaller publishers, such as educational or research establishments, who produce research databases, either in-house or for wider availability, and which need to extract from available electronic sources without too great a cost or a bar on commercial use. Books and journals can now be considered as databases if they are a collection of independent works, data or other materials, which are arranged in a systematic or methodical way, and are individually accessible by electronic or other means.

So, well-arranged and compiled printed reference books – directories, yearbooks, etc. – are now, like their electronic counterparts, subject to the new database right. Publishers can also declare a 'serious' periodical as a database in its own right as it will meet the specification in the new regulations. There are fair-dealing exceptions only where they do not damage the economic rights or undermine the investment of a database owner. These allow 'lawful users' of a database to extract and re-utilize insubstantial parts of a database contents, or substantial parts only for purpose of illustration, teaching or research, but not for any 'commercial' purpose. Raymond Wall (1998), commenting on the new database regulations, fears that libraries, in their use of printed databases 'can expect to suffer greater administrative costs, loss of funds which should go to services and stock, and tighter control of their activities in ways which can only be detrimental to education, research and authorship'. The new copyright legislation in the United States stopped short of any additional protection for databases despite heavy lobbying from the American information industry. The Internet and World Wide Web, though mounted on a publicly accessible platform, still has full copyright protection status. Making news library material available externally (and at a price) brings ethical questions of copyright ownership and republishing.

The 1997 proposal for a European *Directive on Copyright and Related Rights in the Information Society* will, if eventually adopted in its original form, mark a further shift towards producers of intellectual property products and services, and the concept of licensing, and away from the culture of limitation characterised by specific exemptions, such as special privileges for libraries in the UK. Currently the only exceptions for digital reproduction for libraries are ill-defined and with no room for discretion. It largely ignores such legitimate 'fair-dealing' users of copyright material as researchers, libraries and educational bodies, though some flexibility at national level on copying by libraries, museums and other establishments accessible to the public, is allowed so long as there is no direct or indirect, economic or commercial advantage.

Adherence to copyright rules, and the clearance of rights for the use of information, photographs, film and sound recordings is increasingly an important part of the work of librarians in broadcasting and the press.

Data protection

Awareness of data protection issues is important, as information profes-sionals can be users of personal data, data controllers of personal infor-mation systems or even data subjects of such systems. Increasingly sophisticated and widespread information technology applications pose a threat to individual privacy. Broadly, Davies (1997) defines the issue as respect for a person's privacy and affording confidentiality to personal infor-mation. Data protection measures are an attempt to enable fair and legiti-mate use of personal information, while respecting that right to privacy.

In the UK the *Data Protection Act 1998* (repealing the *Data Protection Act 1984*), governs 'the regulation of the processing of infor-mation relating to individuals, including the obtaining, holding, use or disclosure of such information'. It was intended to meet the requirements of the EU Directive 95/46/EC 1995, which aimed at harmonizing data protection across Europe, and, according to Walden (1988), will exert an on-going influence on the develpment of UK data protection law. This *Act* was designed to protect the interests of individuals, in respect of data held about them by others, by limiting the possibility of their being harmed by wrongful use of the data, but allowing its legitimate and proper use. It encompasses manual as well as electronically-held data if it can be described as any set of information relating to individuals and structured in such a way as to be readily accessible. It provides for acceptable (ethical) standards concerning the holding of personal data with eight principles ensuring that the data is:

- processed fairly and lawfully, with consent from the data subject;
- obtained only for the specified (and lawful) purpose, and not used for any other purpose;
- adequate, relevant and not excessive for the purpose alone and no more;
- accurate, and kept up to date;
- not kept longer than is necessary for the specified purpose;
- processed in accordance with the rights of the data subjects, and the individual is entitled to be informed of data and access to their entry;
- not processed in an unauthorized or unlawful way, or accidentally destroyed or damaged;
- not transferred from one country to another outside the European Economic Area without protection for the rights and freedoms of data subjects.

There are the inevitable exemptions for national security, crime and taxa-tion, health, education and social work, and regulatory activity. But most relevant to information professionals are the exemptions for journalism, literature and arts, and for research, history and statistical purposes, with safeguards for the use of data as an archive for long-term research and scholarship.

Those managing personal data systems, 'data controllers', can inform the Data Protection Commissioner, who maintains a register of notifications. Library records and files, such as membership records, circulation records, specialized information files, SDI profiles, and OPACs, can also come under the data protection regulations. Care must be taken in creating and managing a personal information system, particularly in establishing provenance and integrity of externally acquired information, and in awareness of breach of confidence and libel. The implication for users of personal data is that care must be taken to obtain any necessary consents or clearance before supplying it for use in publication or broadcasting.

► NEW TECHNOLOGY ETHICS AND EFFECTS

Leading American media ethicist Thomas W. Cooper (1998) commented that: 'Because new communication and information technologies are being introduced more rapidly into society than ever before, and into some societies for the first time, it is especially important to study the effects and ethical issues accompanying new communications media'. He expresses the concern of most of us about the rapidity of change and our inability to digest the social effects and ethical issues involved.

New definitions of library and information work and its scope are needed as the new technologies have altered the whole basis of the profession. They have not just changed the way we work, they have changed *what* our work is. Some would argue that electronic systems have freed librarians to do their real work. But, as Alfino and Pierce (1997, pp.19) have questioned: 'What is this *real* work of the librarian?' The traditional activities and values of library work remain – selection, acquisition, documentation, exploitation, dissemination and access – but redefined, or entirely new functions have augmented them.

New technologies have in particular introduced so many new means of communicating and disseminating information. In his ethical inventory of new technologies, Cooper (1998) identified many issues and effects. He argues that each new communications technology retrieves, amplifies, transforms, obsolesces or mixes ethical concerns from the past, or creates news issues for the future. Electronic access makes the manipulation of data easier, but it carries with it an obligation to use the services effectively and ethically. Electronic transmission of information can be impersonal, thereby eroding the commitments of person-to-person contact, and often anonymous, with no identity of sender or source, both giving opportunity for deception, insensitivity, invasion of privacy, libel or obscenity. Deceptions through digital manipulation, data massaging, propaganda, false information, concealed product promotion and consumerism are rife, and not always easy to identify. Confidentiality is prone to abuse as information can often be illegally obtained and easily redistributed. Defamation, too, is easily achieved by non-accountable, anonymous or falsely identified sources putting libellous statements about other persons or organizations on the Web. Security of data held electronically cannot be guaranteed, with piracy, theft and counterfeiting frequent problems. Illegal copying of other people's software, programs and data is too easy with the new technologies. Electronic developments have distorted property and privacy rights, with commercial exploitation given precedence over public interest. Traditional standards or ethical mores regarding ownership, intellectual property rights and privacy no longer hold, and copyright and patent abuse is widespread. If there are guidelines or codes governing the provision or use of electronically-held information they are difficult to implement or police.

The Internet, according to Eisenschitz (1998), is the most pure representation of the information society we seem to be evolving into – transnational, meritocratic, and open to any opportunity. But, once the self-regulating preserve of academic research institutions based on a code of honour – 'netiquette', it has now become a commercial tool. The basic right of freedom of expression is well served by the Internet, but it is sorely tested by the flood of poor quality, inaccurate, biased, obscene, racist, sexist, and often libellous material.

What is the solution for the problem? How do we as information professionals cope with it? For the information worker, the ethical concerns raised by these services demand a critical awareness of the issues, time to test and evaluate these new information products and time for reflection and good judgement. At a higher level governments and policy makers must keep pace with inventors and entrepreneurs to understand the effects of these emerging media, and legislate or regulate accordingly. Good research into the potential effects of new technologies and media products prior to marketing may help to identify the possible consequences.

Perhaps, before the information age, librarians had a greater moral clarity and certainty about their profession. The new technologies have put pressure on our values and ethical principles, and have forced us to rethink them.

▶ REFERENCES

Alfino, M. and Pierce, L. (1997) *Information ethics for librarians.* Jefferson, North Carolina: McFarland

Cabinet Office (1997) *Your right to know: the Government's proposals for a Freedom of Information Act* (Cm 3818). London: Stationery Office

Coggins, T. (1993) Legal and ethical issues for news librarians. In *News media libraries: a management handbook*, ed. B. P. Semonche, pp. 413–439. Westport, Connecticut: Greenwood Press

Cooper, T. W. (1998) New technology effects inventory: forty leading ethical issues In *Journal of Mass Media Ethics*, **13**(2), 71–92

Cornish, G. (1997) Copyright. In *Handbook of special librarianship and information work*, 7th edition, ed. A. Scammell, pp.303–318. London: Aslib

Davies, J. E. (1997) Data protection and the information manager In *Handbook of special librarianship and information work*, 7th edition, ed. A. Scammell, pp.319–342. London: Aslib.

Dowd, R. C. (1989) I want to find out how to freebase cocaine: or, yet another unobtrusive test of reference performance. *Reference Librarian* (25–26), 483–493

Eisenschitz, T. (1997) Information and the law. *Aslib Proceedings*, **49**(8), 201–205

Eisenschitz, T. (1998) Internet law and information policy. *Aslib Proceedings*, **50**(9), 267–273

Foskett, D. J. (1962) *A creed for librarians*. London: Library Association, 1962

Grantham, B. (1999) Legislative changes to the copyright law of the United States. *International Media Law*, **17**(1), 1–7.

Griffin, T. (1997) The enquiry service. In *Handbook of special librarianship and information work*, 7th edition, ed. A. Scammell, pp.223–241. London: Aslib

Hannabuss, S. (1998) Information ethics: a contemporary challenge for professionals and the community. *Library Review*, **47**(2), 91–98

Harris, N. G. E. (1996) *Professional codes of conduct in the United Kingdom: a directory*, 2nd edition. London: Mansell

Hauptman, R. (1976) Professionalism or culpability? An experiment in ethics. *Wilson Library Bulletin*, **50**, 626–627

Mautner, T. (ed) (1997) *Penguin dictionary of philosophy*. London: Penguin

Oppenheim, C. (1992) Legal aspects of information management In *Handbook of special librarianship and information work*, 6th edition, ed. P. Dossett, pp. 526–552. London: Aslib

Oppenheim, C. (1998) Dealing with paparazzi by copyright law. *Journal of Information Science*, **24**(1), 39–42

Robertson, G. and Nicol, A. G. L. (1992) *Media law*. 3rd edition. London: Penguin Books

Sykes, P. (1997) Liability for Information management. In *Handbook of special librarianship and information work*, 7th edition, ed. A. Scammell, pp. 343–351. London: Aslib

Walden, I. (1998) All change for Europe? The Data Protection Act 1998. *Communications Law*, **3**(6), 207–216

Wall, R. (1998) Comments on SI 1997/3032. *Managing Information*, **5**(2), 14–15

World Intellectual Property Organization (1996) *Diplomatic Conference on Certain Copyright and Neighboring Rights Questions, Geneva, December 2 to 20, 1996: WIPO Copyright Treaty*. Geneva: WIPO

Index